A History of Professional Economists and Policymaking in the United States

Over the course of the twentieth century, professional economists became a feature in the policymaking process and slowly changed the way we think about work, governance, and economic justice. However, they have also been a frustrating, paradoxical, and in recent years, controversial fixture in American public life.

This book focuses on the emergence and growth of professional economics in the U.S., examining the challenges early professional economists faced, which foreshadowed obstacles throughout the twentieth century. From the founding of the American Economic Association in 1885 to the depths of the Great Depression, this volume illustrates why some of the most optimistic and capable economic minds struggled to help smooth economic transitions and tame market fluctuations.

Drawing on archival research and secondary sources, the text explores the emergence of professional economics in the United States and explains how economists came to be 'irrelevant geniuses'. This book is well suited for those who study and are interested in American history, the history of economic thought and policy history.

Jonathan S. Franklin received his PhD in United States history, with a focus on business and economic history, from the University of Maryland. He has taught at Russell Sage College and Union College. His research interests include policymaking in the United States and professionalization.

Perspectives in Economic and Social History
Series Editors: Andrew August and Jari Eloranta

A History of Professional Economists and Policymaking in the United States

Irrelevant genius

Jonathan S. Franklin

Taylor & Francis Group

LONDON AND NEW YORK

First published 2016 by Routledge

2 Park Square, Milton Park, Abingdon, Oxfordshire OX14 4RN
52 Vanderbilt Avenue, New York, NY 10017

Routledge is an imprint of the Taylor & Francis Group, an informa business

First issued in paperback 2019

British Library Cataloguing in Publication Data
A catalogue record for this book is available from the British Library

Library of Congress Cataloging in Publication Data
Franklin, Jonathan S., author.
A history of professional economists and policymaking in the United States:
irrelevant genius / Jonathan S. Franklin.
pages cm
1. Economics—United States—History. 2. Economists—United States—
History. 3. United States—Economic policy. I. Title.
HB119.A2F69 2016
330.0973—dc23
2015034083

ISBN: 978-1-138-91375-2 (hbk)
ISBN: 978-0-367-87345-5 (pbk)

Typeset in Times New Roman
by Book Now Ltd, London

For Jesse and Irma Escue

Contents

Acknowledgments

This project was supported by an Alfred D. Chandler Jr. Travel Fellowship from the Harvard Business School; fellowships from the Institute for Humane Studies; an Oxford University Press fellowship from the Business History Conference; funding from the Duke History of Political Economy Center; and funding from the University of Maryland History Department. This support allowed me to work with the American Economic Association's papers at the Duke University archives, as well as the papers of numerous economists at the Wisconsin Historical Society and Harvard University. I am sincerely grateful for the opportunity provided by these fellowships.

I am also grateful for the assistance I received from numerous archivists and scholars; in particular, Harold Miller at the Wisconsin Historical Society, Elizabeth Dunn at the Duke Special Collections Library, and Lynda Leahy at the Schlesinger Library. I would also like to thank my advisor, David Sicilia, whose patience and generosity cannot be exaggerated. I own all of the errors in this project, naturally. I reserve special thanks for my wife, Patricia, whose love and support trumps all.

Introduction

Regardless of one's interpretation, it is clear that the 2008 Financial Crisis sparked questions to which millions sought answers. In a nation with a network of highly respected economics departments staffed by thousands of sharp minds – to say nothing of those economists employed by businesses and think tanks – no one seemed capable of building confidence around a solution to the problem. Unsurprisingly, Nobel Prize winners, Wall Street oracles, Fortune 500 executives, and Presidential candidates (to name a few) moved to convince the world that they best understood the mysteries of the markets as they sought to influence economic policy.

The ensuing race for the high ground was well-illustrated by the debate over the research of Harvard economists Carmen Reinhart and Kenneth Rogoff. Their work on the link between national debt and financial crises, *This Time Is Different: Eight Centuries of Financial Folly* and a follow-up working paper, fueled disagreement over government's response to the Crisis. Both sides of the political spectrum attempted to invoke Reinhart and Rogoff's work as evidence of their opponents' failure to grasp economic reality, although fiscal conservatives seemed to benefit most by virtue of the study's conclusion regarding a negative correlation between high national debt and economic growth. Yet any such advantage was overturned when a graduate student discovered errors in Rogoff and Reinhart's calculations, completely discrediting their conclusions for some, merely modifying conclusions for others, and laying bare for all the frustrations of applying economic expertise to public policy. The controversy no sooner faded from memory when the process repeated itself in 2014 – then in response to Thomas Piketty's *Capital in the Twenty-First Century*. This time around, it was fiscal conservatives' turn to reject the professional economist while their pro-interventionist counterparts lamented the lack of interest in economic expertise.

Such a contentious and politicized invocation of economists' expertise may strike some as evidence of a recent decline in the integrity and competence of both economists and politicians. In fact, the practice of choosing economists based on policies they prescribe, or selectively co-opting their ideas for political gain, is as old as the profession itself. Since their emergence in the late nineteenth century, professional economists have been a fixture in American public life. They have been a particularly frustrating and complicated fixture for policymakers and their constituents alike, however. Professional economists in the US have consistently been accused of being indecisive and unreliable, yet have continued to garner press coverage, prestigious awards, and advisory roles at the highest level of government.

This book explains the paradox by focusing on the roots of the dilemma, which can be traced back to the professionalization process. It was a process that began with the addition of economists to higher learning in the 1880s and culminated with the establishment of disciplinary norms and institutions by the late 1920s. In between, the challenges of defining economic expertise and bringing it to bear on the economic policymaking process in a democratic society were laid bare. Like their twenty-first century descendants, late nineteenth century professional economists struggled with an apparent paradox. They often made the *Who's Who* lists of the era, were routinely quoted by journalists, and advised powerful politicians. And yet, such social prestige rarely translated into the ability to fully settle debates within the discipline, to say nothing of successfully influencing the nation's leaders and their constituents.

I argue that the challenges early professional economists faced while establishing the discipline and attempting to translate their ideas into action sheds new light on the fundamental challenges faced by professional economists throughout the twentieth century. Rather than delivering clear and actionable research, as they had originally intended, the nation's first generations of professional economists found themselves hamstrung by doubt, criticism, and seemingly unshakeable social systems both within academia and public life.

The history of applied economics during these crucial years of development adds clarity to the policymaking process and offers an explanation as to why modern policymakers often fail to anticipate or properly respond to economic crises. My conclusions about the gap between economic theory and economic policy also call into question the stories we tell concerning the course of economic history in the US over the past century. Narratives that focus on the birth, life, and death of economic eras that revolve around the ideas of the academy are, I explain in the conclusion, built on the indefensible premise that professional economists have played a clear and pivotal role in shaping economic policy in the US.

Economists and historians have long debated the significance of changes in the field of economics around the turn of the twentieth century. The dramatic increase in the amount of resources committed to the study of political economy, combined with changes in methodology and theory, triggered a notable shift in attitudes toward the "dismal science."[1] Although there is little doubt that industrialization and the expansion of higher education precipitated the explosion in the study of economics, it remains unclear how the decisions about the role of economists during the professionalization process affected economic policy over subsequent generations.

In the succeeding chapters, I explain how economists in the US molded the discipline into a distinct profession, and examine the profession's influence on economic policymaking. Economists, not unlike doctors or psychologists, professionalized by creating institutions, professional networks, and terminology designed to distinguish themselves from amateur enthusiasts. In doing so, professional economists established themselves as social analysts whose value lay in their ability to wade through the complexities of the market and offer clear conclusions on which public policies could be built.

Historian Mary Furner has argued that the influence of intellectuals such as economists can be a subtle and indirect force. Intellectuals secure influence, Furner suggests, by "bringing policymakers to inhabit, in some sense, the same mental world that they do."[2] The public intellectual's influence is therefore rarely complete, but nevertheless omnipresent. Although appealing, such an assessment allows for the systematic dismissal of examples that suggest a distinct lack of influence. Using this understanding of influence to determine early twentieth century economists' influence can quickly lead to fuzzy math. How many examples of economists' general influence are necessary to outweigh examples of economists' lack of influence in the drafting of economic policies?

The frankness with which professional economists pursued policy reform at the turn of the twentieth century, the response of non-economists, and the juxtaposition of intradisciplinary debates with public policy debates make it possible for us to dissect policy histories in order to appraise economists' influence, or lack thereof, with reasonable precision. I have therefore attempted to bring clarity to the question of economists' influence by exploring the economic policymaking process at crucial stages in order to balance the tendency to assume general influence. This approach has left me critical of claims like Furner's about the nature and consistency of professional economists' influence in the early twentieth century and beyond. Despite the impressive growth of the discipline, American economists' influence was limited by obstacles inherent to a society with many competing interests. Economists quickly discovered that establishing economics as a vibrant facet of American higher education meant less than one might expect because the connection between knowledge and authority was tenuous at best.

Three recurring themes lead to this conclusion, the first being the persistence of what economist Paul Rubin calls "folk economics." Defined as "the intuitive economics of untrained people," the concept of folk economics offers a shorthand reference for non-professional economists whose ideas competed with those of professionally trained economists for the support of voters and lawmakers.[3] Folk economists' criticism of professional economists and their theories from 1880 to 1929 highlights economists' struggle to transform economics from moral philosophy based largely on tradition into a consistent and objective science. Cultural elites' efforts to reform economic theory took place alongside the efforts of the less well-credentialed, as the overlap between these two struggles often made clear. Many Americans harbored suspicions about the intent of professional economists. Socialism was taboo to most Americans outside the labor movement (and even to many within the movement), and the "European" ideas imported by young economists were readily exploited as evidence of malevolent intent. Concerns about the relationship between conservative academic economists and business leaders were just as ripe. In both cases, suspicions were exacerbated by the erection of barriers that helped distinguish between expert and amateur, which seemingly excluded dissenters on both sides of the political spectrum. Folk economists and their ideas survived and thrived because of their ability to exploit such fears and to offer economic policies that appealed to notions of common sense and egalitarianism.

A widespread suspicion among the public that economists, regardless of intent, lacked any special insight or claim to authority further exacerbated the rift between amateur and expert and undercut professional economists' relevance in the eyes of many. As economist David C. Colander has noted, economics is bound together by a "grand theory" that gives the discipline a greater sense of coherency than many other academic disciplines.[4] Yet within that "grand theory" fundamental disagreements persisted through a long past and continue to hold a promising future. The internal dissent that pitted economists against one another fed the notion that economists lacked meaningful insight and serves as the second notable theme in the professionalization process of economics. Tensions within the discipline were present from the formation of the American Economic Association through the 1920s and beyond. Economists disagreed about a host of issues including, but not limited to, methodology and the appropriate relationship between academia and politics. Although the discipline reached a general consensus on the broad outlines of economic policy at several key moments, such successes were undercut by internecine squabbling. The struggle between neoclassical economics and early American institutional economics (not to be confused with the institutional economics of the late twentieth century) established a pattern of conflict within the discipline and undercut any hope of professional cohesion. Despite heavy criticism, classical theory endured and remained central to American economic thought – not necessarily because it proved most accurate, but rather because it proved most reliable in a field perceived by outsiders as woefully unreliable.

Lastly, the conditions in which economists exercised notable influence over economic policy present a serious challenge to those who would argue (implicitly or explicitly) that the recent history of public policymaking has been distinguished by a consistent merging of theory and practice. Although networking or public prestige might secure an economist's access to the policymaking process in the early twentieth century, it rarely translated into direct influence. Lawmakers routinely dismissed economists' recommendations in favor of political expediency or their own opinion, thus underscoring the often tenuous connection between economic expertise and public policy. Furthermore, business leaders proved to be tough competition to those economists seeking the confidence of elected officials. In the public's eye, academic training and business success conferred the same degree of authority on economic issues. Private business groups, including farmers' associations, possessed additional persuasive powers thanks to their ability to fund media campaigns and lobby politicians. The most influential economists, I conclude, relied on a combination of personal networking, organizational skills, and the ability to engage with political battles that were tangential to their ideas about economics. Economists such as Richard T. Ely, Irving Fisher, and George F. Warren succeeded in influencing economic policy not because their ideas were universally acclaimed, but rather because they had a knack for maneuvering themselves into a position from which they would be consulted for advice.

These barriers limited economists' ability to effectively champion dramatic economic and social reform, but they did not stall efforts. Economists in the US, both those in academia and those who increasingly found positions in the public and private sectors, worked around such challenges in an effort to improve economic policy. In addition to noting setbacks and failures, I chronicle the substantial progress of professional economics in the early twentieth century, including the significance of long-running organizations and journals that continue to shape the discipline to this day.

These themes and their implications may leave the reader with the misapprehension that this study portrays economics as a failed discipline unworthy of continued investment or respect; quite the contrary. At the most basic level, the discipline's growth has ensured a steady supply of technicians armed with the necessary combination of training in critical thinking and research skills to give American businesses and government the capacity to improve efficiency. Such persons existed prior to the establishment of economics departments across the country, naturally, but it is impossible to envision the creation of agencies with a research capacity on par with that of the National Bureau of Economic Research or the Agricultural Research Service without trained economists.

Historians of economic thought may note that I am flying close to danger by beginning with the assumption that modern economics is "broken," with the intent of working backward through history in search of the root source of the breakdown. As E. Roy Weintraub notes, this would require the general rejection of modern economics, which seems overly rash and indefensible. Fortunately, my research has not led me to conclude that economics is broken, although there is always room for improvement. The discipline as a whole has consistently demonstrated a strong commitment to open discourse, rigorous peer review, and a deep-seated concern with ensuring the work done by professional economists will help improve everyday life. The connection between economic theory and public policy has proven frail, however. It has never been defined in a manner that is wholly coherent or acceptable to the many who depend on their government for sound, reasoned economic policy.

This study's key criticism is directed at the cultural and social institutions that have allowed so many Americans to largely ignore professional economists and their theories from the late nineteenth century onward. Even so, it is difficult to fault anyone for failing to more directly meld economic expertise to economic policy since that would so often require abrogating the democratic process. Such complaints can only be offered half-heartedly and with a catalogue of exceptions, as following an idea's trajectory from academia to the public sphere makes clear the important distinction between democracy and technocracy.

I hope readers share my more certain criticism of the discipline's long-running exclusion of women and non-professionals. The necessities of professionalizing understandably required the erection of barriers to entry, but it seems indefensible to claim that such necessity justified excluding large groups of Americans (a notable failure of virtually all the modern disciplines in the early twentieth century). One can only wonder what economic theory would look like if it better reflected the diversity of thought that characterizes American life.

This book drives toward its conclusions with assistance from the well-developed fields of policy history, the history of professionalization, and the history of economic thought. To date, scholarship that employs a similar approach has tended to downplay economists' significance prior to the Great Depression and the subsequent pursuit of managed growth in the post-World War II period. A glance at the number of economists in the US over the course of the century seemingly confirms this view, as the number of American Economic Association members per 100,000 Americans rose from 2.2 in 1920 to a high of 9.2 in 1970. Additionally, scholarship that recalls the efforts of economists on the Council of Economic Advisors (CEA) during the post-WW II years support the notion that while the Great Depression put economists and their craft on the map, it was the discipline's work during the Cold War that highlighted their influence in US society.

There are several flaws in this argument, beginning with the numbers. The number of economists in the US trained and engaged with the discipline certainly increased substantially from 1920 to 1970, but there was an equally dramatic rise in the number of economists from 1880 to 1900. From 1887 to 1930, the number of AEA members per 100,000 Americans rose from 0.48 to 3.1. Second, focusing on the CEA as evidence of economists' influence on economic policy, and therefore relevance to those interested in understanding the policymaking process, assumes that proximity yielded influence. But a casual reading of the literature on economists in Washington quickly leads to the conclusion that for much of their history, the CEA has not enjoyed a predominate voice in policy debates.

By dismissing this earlier expansion of the discipline and the influence of early twentieth century economists, we run the risk of discounting the past and romanticizing the present. When looking back at the policy miscues of generations past it is easy to assume naivety and, in some cases, irrationality. In fact, our predecessors grappled with many of the same questions that continue to paralyze policymakers, including the degree to which government should regulate the money supply and the level of aid necessary to maintain a healthy agricultural sector. Early economists also debated equally relevant philosophical issues, such as the proper role of expertise in a representative democracy and whether or not government should be adjusted in response to emerging social and economic trends. All these issues weighed heavily on the minds of early twentieth century Americans who welcomed the rise of the professional economist with wary enthusiasm.

Much of the scholarship on the history of economics at the turn of the twentieth century focuses on the methodological marginal revolution (or evolution, as some prefer) that changed the way the Western world thought of and spoke about the exchange of goods and services. A considerable amount of discussion has been devoted to the marginal revolution, particularly the source of the revolution and the reason for the methodology's apparent dominance. By the 1970s, most authorities acknowledged that the discipline's turn toward marginal utility theory – which focuses on maximizing utility in order to satisfy the greatest number of wants – constituted a fundamental shift away from the labor value theories that once preoccupied economists' attentions. Such a theory departed from the previous arguments that value derived from labor or similar factors of input and reflected the abundance that resulted from industrial production. The pressing questions therefore revolved around why W.S. Jevons, Carl Menger, and Léon Walras seized on this idea simultaneously in isolation of one another and why their ideas proceeded to redefine the study of economics in the Western world.

The debate was never truly resolved, although a reasonable consensus emerged that recognized the importance of industrial production and professionalization in codifying and spreading marginal utility theory. This consensus posited that the new problems associated with industrial production combined with a more sophisticated and coherent professional body of economists to provide marginal utility a place to grow. Once rooted, the theory proved resilient for reasons that continue to be debated. This study's focus on US economic thought precludes a thorough discussion of the birth of marginalism and its spread through Europe. Instead, the theory emerges in this study much as it did in late nineteenth century American colleges: in the final decades of the nineteenth century and in contention with the ideas of the German Historical School. At no point do I consciously advocate for the veracity of one theory or the other. Instead, I attempt to contribute to the discussion of marginal utility theory in the US by explaining why it proved so appealing and how it influenced the professionalization process. With a nod toward economic historian Geoffrey Hodgson, I conclude that it was a combination of marginalism's ability to present to the public the necessary airs and graces of scientific rigor, along with the heterodox economists' inability to deliver a similarly coherent alternative, that ultimately ensured neoclassicial economics' supremacy in the US. The intellectual "battle" between the two intellectual camps left a legacy of dissent that persists to this day, however.

Although it seemed for some time that the marginal revolution was swift and complete, a resurgence of interest in the work of heterodox economists in the US in the early twentieth century has reinvigorated the debate over the evolution of economics in America. Malcolm Rutherford and Hodgson's work stands out among the recent efforts to portray a more complicated and contentious state of economic theory at the turn of the twentieth century. Both Rutherford and Hodgson's championing of the heterodox American institutional school of economics (perhaps better thought of here as the "new economics" to avoid a confusing with the institutional economics of the last 30 years) suggests that the marginal revolution was not, in fact, as complete as once assumed. This study sympathizes with the turn toward understanding non-mainstream economic ideas, particularly the attempt to grasp why such dissenting voices failed to establish themselves within the mainstream of American economic thought. Still, because of American institutionalism's persistent inability to deliver on its grand promises to redefine how Americans viewed political economy, I disagree with the assertion that it was a powerful and viable alternative to neoclassical economics as late as the 1930s. Although relevant, the American heterodox thinkers never seriously challenged the standing of their neoclassical colleagues. Hodgson, Rutherford, and Mary S. Morgan are right to note the difficulty of characterizing early twentieth century American economics, but their insistence on emphasizing the unique value of individual economists' ideas exposes their analysis to the same pitfalls that eventually swallowed their subjects' influence.[5]

Focusing on the struggle between the German Historical School-inspired new economists and the more traditional neoclassical economists, I argue that marginalism was in fact dominant in early American economics and succeeded not because it was a perfect theory, but rather because it was the only theory that could strike a balance between the needs for efficacy, coherency, and marketability. This bifurcation is justified by the goal of this study, which is ultimately to explain economists' role in the economy policymaking process. However engaging analysis of the nuances of either neoclassical or institutional economics might be to some readers, it would ultimately detract from my central task and create a false understanding of how professional economists, policymakers, and those Americans engaged with public life viewed and understood economic theory. The vast majority of Americans were either uninterested or ill-equipped to quibble about the nuances of Veblenian psychology in relation to Alfred Marshall's *Principles*. They understood economic theory was a complex world, but strove for simplicity so as to obtain clarity in regards to which economic policies were worth pursuing.

This study also speaks to scholarship on the process of professionalization in the US, particularly in the social sciences. The work of those concerned with the genesis and evolution of the professional economist provided a thorough account of early struggles within the discipline from which I was able to ask questions regarding the relationship between folk and professional and the role of expertise in a democratic society. Although at times I delve deeper into the topics previously explored by scholars of professionalization, I ultimately seek to advance this line of inquiry by more directly connecting professional economists to the communities they sought to serve.

I have extracted my definitions of "professionalism" and "professionalization" from Thomas Kuhn by way of Thomas Haskell, whose explanation of the concept in the introduction of *The Emergence of Professional Social Science* struck me as reasonable and defensible. As Haskell notes, "professions are collective enterprises" and professionalization is marked by a three-part process in which the professionals distinguish themselves from the public at large, enhance communication and discipline within the group, and pursue heightened credibility in the eyes of the public.[6] Despite the clarity and crispness of this definition, professionalization was not a formulaic process. Questions abound, particularly in regards to the pursuit of heightened credibility in the eyes of the public. Evidence of such credibility must differ from profession to profession – a professional golfer cannot be subjected to the same standards of measurement as a professional doctor. In the case of professional economists, I argue that the standard of success was established in the closing decades of the nineteenth century when a combination of Americans' expectations and the enthusiasm of young economists led to assumptions regarding the discipline's ability to deliver clear-cut, actionable advice. Although tempered by the 1910s, these visions of a more technocratic society stuck and became the measure by which professional economists' success was judged. Professional economists' tendency to appear in the public sphere primarily as policy advocates from the late nineteenth century onward has served to deepen this misconception. As a result, professional economists' value to society has been consistently misconstrued by those outside the discipline (and even by some within).

A few works in this line of inquiry stand out as worthy of closer consideration, including Mary Furner's *Advocacy and Objectivity* and Dorothy Ross's *The Origins of American Social Science*. Furner's *Advocacy and Objectivity*, which is an account of the professionalization of the social sciences that largely focuses on economics, captures well the inner workings of the discipline through its early years. Furner's documentation of the tit-for-tat maneuvering that characterized the new economics provides insight about how professional economics was shaped by the personalities who held sway within academia at a crucial time. I engage with some of the same internal issues Furner analyzed while at the same time turning my focus outward to explain the crucial link between the growing discipline and the non-academic world they were so eager to influence.

I also challenge Furner's thesis regarding the loss of morality in American economics. Although I agree that much of the overt moralistic sentiment that drove new economists in the late nineteenth century gradually disappeared, I think one vital component remained – the privileging of intellectual freedom. A series of academic freedom cases clearly illustrated limitations as to what kind of theories their benefactors were willing to tolerate, and professional economists proved incapable of protecting their own as a result of reservations about overt propagandizing. The incidents, which labor historian Leon Fink has labeled an "intellectual Haymarket," have served to underline professional economists' coerced withdrawal from social action.[7] Yet it is clear that professional economists consistently placed a premium on intellectual freedom. They were sensitive to fact that the ostracizing of "outsiders" would irreversibly mark their profession as the brutish manifestation of vested interests. Early professional economists therefore worried about being labeled subjective intellectuals or written off as unduly influenced by their academic employers. To avoid such a fatal labeling, the American Economic Association supported academic freedom passively and from a distance, although the results were decidedly mixed. I also question the speed with which Furner suggests other aspects of morality were stripped from American economics. Whereas Furner argues that the discipline's internal fighting robbed US economics of its moralistic underpinnings by the 1890s, I argue that the new economists' inability to translate Christian ideals into practical economic policies are what gradually severed the more overt links between morality and economics by the 1910s. Beyond that point, questions of morality still permeated American economics, although the invocation of Christian values certainly did recede to the background of debate.

My argument about the general maintenance of academic freedom within professional economics leads me to disagree with Furner's conclusion, which is critical of the social sciences' failure to deliver on its early promises of expertise. Whereas Furner and Fink see the failure in large part a result of conservative pressure and individual economists' personal shortcomings, I identify overreach and cultural impediments that ultimately distribute the onus of failure to broad and necessarily nebulous forces. Professional economists did not fail to achieve morally sound and economically effective reforms because they wilted under the pressure of capitalist forces. They simply encountered the same questions of morality and the vagaries of the democratic process that had frustrated earlier generations and, faced with the choice of adaptation or complete irrelevance, chose marginal relevance through adaptation. As a result, some of the nation's most capable professional economists found themselves to be irrelevant geniuses who enjoyed notable respect, but little influence.

The arguments in succeeding chapters are more closely in line with those of Ross's *The Origins of American Science*, although I once again must note several distinctions that seem to arise from differences in methodology. Whereas Ross pursues a relatively straightforward intellectual history, I have attempted to balance my analysis of ideas with an analysis of policymaking through a series of case studies. As a result, our explanations of the failure of the new economists differ. Ross attributes the marginalist neoclassical economists' success to their compatibility with traditional American notions of exceptionalism. I, too, argue that American social and political institutions stymied heterodox economists' progress, but I also believe it crucial to understand how these traditional notions of individuality and democratic participation molded the professionalization process in the favor of advocates of neoclassical economics. Furthermore, drawing folk economists into the story of the professionalization of economics leaves me uncomfortable with Ross's general assertion that Americans rejected historicism in the social sciences because of seemingly irrational notions of American exceptionalism. Such a conclusion may apply to the intellectual elites who debated one another within academia, but such sophisticated distinctions were not visible in the debates between professional and folk economists. Instead, attention was focused on a combination of a proposed policy's origins (nefarious or not) and its potential material outcomes.

Similarly relevant is Michael Bernstein's *Perilous Progress*, an excellent account of the history of professional economics with which I also disagree throughout my study. Like Bernstein, I agree that the early decades of professionalization established a pattern of behavior and expectations that heavily influenced economic thought throughout the twentieth century. I similarly conclude with a fairly pessimistic portrayal of economists' influence over economic policymaking in the US. However, with some exceptions, I disagree with Bernstein's explanation of how and why professional economists in the US struggled to exert their will. My disagreement stems from two fundamental divergences in our methodology. First, whereas Bernstein consciously ignored "thought outside of debate among mainstream economists," I have attempted to give such discussions equal billing.[8] Second, I have dug deeper into select policy histories in an attempt to move past cursory observations and to more securely nail down the elusive concept of "influence." These two differences have led me to question Bernstein's portrayal of the relationship between professional economics and public policy in the United States. In particular, his claims in later chapters regarding the twilight of professional economists' influence with Washington policymakers from the Nixon administration onward strike me as peculiar and only defensible should we accept a relatively narrow definition of the professional economist as someone who subscribes to particular economic theories, as well as a timeline that emphasizes the preeminence of the 1950s and 1960s. Although this study focuses on the early twentieth century, the conclusions I draw directly challenge both premises.[9]

At its core, my book joins this rich historiography in considering the relationship between academic achievement and public welfare. Practitioners of most academic disciplines have visited this issue repeatedly since the modernization of higher education in the late nineteenth century, yet frustration persists regarding the perceived uselessness of academic pursuits or a lack of academic integrity. This pattern of introspection and skepticism suggests that reflection on the utility of academic achievement is not exceptional, but rather the norm. Each generation must consider the merits of academic pursuits in order to conceptualize their relevancy to public life. Exploring this issue, I believe, resonates not only with economic historians and those interested in understanding the development of economic policy in the twentieth century, but also with those curious about how knowledge has been generated and applied in the recent past.

As a whole, Americans embraced the concept of the economic expert at the turn of the century and heartily supported the growth of the profession despite reservations against allowing the discipline too much authority in the policymaking process. Attempts to document this story and analyze the meaning of this paradox led me to the economists themselves, most of whom possessed a keen awareness of the dilemma. Memoirs, obituaries, biographies, and manuscript collections pointed me toward the most significant people and events in the formative years of US professional economics that warranted closer study. Of particular interest were the papers of the Wisconsin School economists, housed at the Wisconsin Historical Society, and the personal papers of Charles Neill and Frank Taussig, which are held in the Harvard University Archives.

Such accounts are by nature relatively myopic, so I turned also to the records of the American Economic Association, held in the Rare Books and Manuscripts Library at Duke University. The AEA's secretaries proved to be fairly reliable record keepers, and their documentation of the organization's activities gave me a sense of the "big picture." As I note in Chapter 1, the AEA did not initially enjoy its current status as the preeminent economics organization in the US. I therefore turned to the leading journals for economists to fill in my understanding of the discipline's early years – namely the *Quarterly Journal of Economics*, the *Journal of Political Economy*, and the less specialized *Annals of American Social Science*.

Both the AEA's leadership and the work of individual economists proved sensitive to public criticism, shedding light on how public opinion shaped or was shaped by professional economists. My particular interest in precisely how professional economists fit into the broader world of public policymaking led me to take advantage of newspaper, magazine, and book databases, where advances in the digitization of primary sources has now made it possible for a single scholar to efficiently gather references to the discipline, individual economists, or particular economic issues. Combined with the secondary literature described above, these sources provide the evidentiary basis for the arguments I put forth.

This study begins shortly before the organization of the American Economic Association in order to capture the significance of US students' studies abroad to the rise of American economics. Although American graduate students did not return from Europe in intellectual lock-step with their foreign teachers, a critical mass of ideas did make the return trip and undoubtedly altered the US intellectual landscape. Furthermore, as Daniel Rodgers notes in his study of trans-Atlantic reform culture, European intellectualism carried a particular cachet in the US during this period. The connection between European intellectualism and American radicalism helps explain why professional economists had a hard time convincing their public audience to move past conclusions in order to understand the evidence. Those Americans who feared in particular socialist uprisings viewed the work of German-trained "new economists" with suspicion. Following World War I, prominent Yale economist Irving Fisher chastised American heterodox economists for subscribing to the ideas of intellectuals he judged to be in league with the imperialist German government. The origin of an idea (perceived or otherwise) weighed as much on the minds of turn-of-the-century Americans as it does today.

Alternating between an examination of the discipline's development and the specific policy battles with which economists engaged forces us to consider the relationship between theoretical and applied economics. Professional economists operated in two distinct worlds – the academic and non-academic – but rarely perceived the border between the two as insurmountable. Professional economists' activities outside academia are therefore just as important, if not more so, than the ideas they espoused in academic journals and lecture halls. Well-informed readers may note the absence of discussion about particular policies, such as the tariff or taxation. The decision to omit some key policy battles was based on time and space constraints and should not be construed as an implicit argument about the importance of one issue over the other.

After analyzing the struggle to "modernize" American economics in Chapter 1, I describe the role economists played in the lengthy struggle over monetary policy from the post-Civil War through the creation of the Federal Reserve. Professional economists' recommendation of a regulated, responsive money supply was largely obscured by the heated rhetoric of both "free silverites" and "gold bugs" leading up to the 1896 Presidential election. Although advocates on both sides of this hotly contested issue attempted to build the perception of unassailable expertise on monetary issues, neither seemed to grasp the nuanced argument presented by the overwhelming majority of economists at the time.

Chapter 3 returns to the institutional development of the discipline in order to explain how attempts to remake economics into a more practical science ran aground on interdisciplinary strife and on the limitations of economic theory. In what can best be described as a curious paradox, the study of economics and employment of professional economists expanded, while efforts to deliver on the promises made by the "new economists" failed to materialize. At fault was the combination of internal dissent and a reluctance to form disciplinary consensus. The continued rift between conservative economists, who tended to come from the classical cum neoclassical school of economic thought, and reform-minded economists, who largely embraced a mixed methodology that included heavy doses of historical and social inquiry, fueled lay suspicions that economics was merely politics disguised as scholarship. The AEA's sustained reluctance to push for and publicize a disciplinary consensus on issues relevant to the voting public encouraged the opportunistic invocation of economic expertise.

To illustrate this point, the fourth chapter analyzes how professional economists weighed in on the matter of labor reform in the early twentieth century, culminating with the missed opportunity of the US Industrial Commission (also known as the Walsh Commission). The Wisconsin School economists figure largely in this chapter, given their role as leaders within American economics at the time, particularly with regard to labor economics. Despite tremendous success in advising public policymakers at the state level, the period's leading labor economists were largely ignored by federal lawmakers and the voting public alike. The US Industrial Commission's descent into a politicized, unconstrained trial of John D. Rockefeller, Jr., and his fellow plutocrats alienated labor economist John D. Commons and stalled the momentum he and his pupils had built through research and action at the state level.

The fifth chapter, which is the last to deal with the profession's institutional and cultural development, examines what happened when the momentum the reform-minded New Economists enjoyed prior to the 1920s evaporated. Still, the new economics did not disappear. It was during the 1920s that serious attempts were made to bind the heterodox strands of American economic thought into a more coherent American Institutional School of economics. This chapter argues that the combination of pragmatism and the turn away from reformist impulses reinforced the neoclassical school's centrality in American economic thought. The discipline as a whole was elated by the fact that it had grown by such leaps and bounds; but this optimism must be balanced by the persistence of folk economics and the damage caused by ongoing dissent within the discipline.

A survey of farm relief efforts in Chapter 6 illustrates the cause-and-effect relationship between the struggle over economic ideas and their application to farm policy. Agricultural economists, unwilling to abandon the basic premises of supply and demand to endorse the McNary–Haugen Plan, engaged with farmers and lawmakers alike in an attempt to stabilize farm commodity prices and prevent the erosion of rural communities. The "farm question" raised an interesting dilemma for economists. Sure of the problem, but unable to reconfigure the political economy of the nation, the discipline was hard-pressed to offer an appealing solution. When the nation's leading agricultural economists did present a workable solution in the form of an allotment program, its adoption was delayed by want of political viability. The chapter concludes with a consideration of economists' role in the design of relief programs during the first half of the Great Depression, including the Agricultural Adjustment Act and gold purchasing program, to illustrate how the adoption of economic theories based on their political expediency likely prolonged unnecessary economic suffering. My study ends in the middle of the United States' struggle to rise up and out of the Great Depression in order to underscore that the "mold" of professional economics was set before that calamitous event, thereby challenging those who downplay the significance of early twentieth century economics by arguing that the Keynesian response to the Great Depression ushered in the era of modern economics.

The conclusion doubles as an epilogue in the hopes that it will help draw out the relevance of research on early twentieth century policymaking – a fitting end for a study of a discipline that so often inadvertently strays from high-minded purpose toward esotericism. In doing so, I risk breaching scholarly etiquette by using lessons from the early twentieth century to talk about problems in the twenty-first. It is a decision I defend twofold, first by noting that the vast majority of historians believe their research unlocks the secret of the present (regardless of whether they are foolhardy enough to admit so), and second by pointing out that the challenges surrounding the application of expertise in the twenty-first century are too great not to confront head-on. It has been a century since the first modern research universities were established in the US and still less than half of all citizens will receive a four-year college degree. Fewer still will earn the advance degree most deem necessary to engage with cutting-edge scholarly research. And yet the world still perceives of the West in general, and the US in particular, as a post-industrial democracy, blessed with a modern government that is informed by experts with the knowledge necessary to solve whatever problems the modern economy throws its way. It is a funny way of thinking given what we know about the past.

Notes

1 A term for economics coined in the mid nineteenth century by the Scottish historian Thomas Carlyle.
2 Mary O. Furner, "Social Scientists and the State: Constructing the Knowledge Base for Public Policy, 1880–1920," in *Intellectuals and Public Life: Between Radicalism and Reform*, ed. Leon Fink, Stephen T. Leonard, and Donald M. Reid (Ithaca, NY: Cornell University Press, 1996), 145.
3 Paul H. Rubin, "Folk Economics," *Southern Economic Journal* 70, no. 1 (July 2003): 157.
4 David C. Colander, "The Invisible Hand of Truth," in *The Spread of Economic Ideas*, ed. A.W. Coats and David C. Colander (New York: Cambridge University Press, 1989), 31–36.
5 It should be noted that this heterodox tradition has proven resilient and maintains a notable presence in the field despite criticism and confusion, however.
6 Thomas L. Haskell, *The Emergence of Professional Social Science: The American Social Science Association and the Nineteenth-century Crisis of Authority* (Urbana, IL: University of Illinois Press, 1977), 19.
7 Leon Fink, *Progressive Intellectuals and the Dilemmas of Democratic Commitment* (Cambridge, MA: Harvard University Press, 1997), 62.
8 Michael A. Bernstein, *A Perilous Progress: Economists and Public Purpose in Twentieth-Century America* (Princeton, NJ: Princeton University Press, 2001), 5.
9 This latter criticism regarding a relatively narrow depiction of professional economics and a privileging of the Kennedy and Johnson administrations can be extended to Norton's *Quest for Economic Stability* (1991), which places considerable emphasis on the transformative powers of the Employment Act of 1946. Unlike Bernstein's *Perilous*

Progress, Norton's *Quest* focuses exclusively on the intersection of economics and public policy post-World War II, however.

Although I readily acknowledge the significance of the Employment Act and subsequent progress within the discipline, my exploration of the early decades of the discipline have left me skeptical of Norton's claim that the creation of the Council of Economic Advisors had a truly transformative affect. The Act may have elevated the status of a few professional economists but it did little to answer long-standing questions regarding the discipline's social status and relationship to the communities they sought to serve, as I explain in the conclusion.

Bibliography

Aslund, Anders. "Reinhart-Rogoff Austerity Case Still Stands." *Financial Times*, April 19, 2013. http://www.ft.com/intl/cms/s/0/2df58ce0-a8ba-11e2-bcfb-00144feabdc0.html#axzz2R76xkyzq.

Barber, William J. *Breaking the Academic Mould: Economists and American Higher Learning in the Nineteenth Century*. Middletown, CT: Wesleyan University Press, 1988.

Bernstein, Michael A. *A Perilous Progress: Economists and Public Purpose in Twentieth-Century America*. Princeton, NJ: Princeton University Press, 2001.

Biddle, Jeff E., John B. Davis, and Steven G. Medema, eds. *Economics Broadly Considered: Essays in Honor of Warren J. Samuels*. New York: Routledge Press, 2001.

Black, R.D. Collison, A.W. Coats, and Craufurd D. Goodwin, eds. *The Marginal Revolution in Economics: Interpretation and Evaluation*. Durham, NC: Duke University Press, 1973.

Blaug, Mark. "Was There a Marginal Revolution?" *History of Political Economy* 4, no. 2 (Fall 1972): 269–80.

Coase, Ronald. "The New Institutional Economics." *American Economic Review* 88, no. 2 (1998): 72–74.

Colander, David C. "The Invisible Hand of Truth." In *The Spread of Economic Ideas*, edited by A.W. Coats and David C. Colander, 31–36. New York: Cambridge University Press, 1989.

Colander, David C., and A. W Coats, eds. *The Spread of Economic Ideas*. New York: Cambridge University Press, 1989.

Eagly, Robert V., ed. *Events, Ideology, and Economic Theory: The Determinants of Progress in the Development of Economic Analysis*. Detroit: Wayne State University Press, 1968.

Fink, Leon. *Progressive Intellectuals and the Dilemmas of Democratic Commitment*. Cambridge, MA: Harvard University Press, 1997.

Furner, Mary O. *Advocacy & Objectivity: A Crisis in the Professionalization of American Social Science, 1865–1905*. Lexington, KY: The University Press of Kentucky, 1975.

——. "Social Scientists and the State: Constructing the Knowledge Base for Public Policy, 1880–1920." In *Intellectuals and Public Life: Between Radicalism and Reform*, edited by Leon Fink, Stephen T. Leonard, and Donald M. Reid, 145–81. Ithaca, NY: Cornell University Press, 1996.

Hargrove, Erwin C., and Samuel A Morley, eds. *The President and the Council of Economic Advisers: Interviews with CEA Chairmen*. Boulder, CO: Westview Press, 1984.

Haskell, Thomas L. *The Emergence of Professional Social Science: The American Social Science Association and the Nineteenth-Century Crisis of Authority*. Urbana, IL: University of Illinois Press, 1977.

Herndon, Thomas, Michael Ash, and Robert Pollin. "Does High Public Debt Consistently Stifle Economic Growth? A Critique of Reinhart and Rogoff." Working Paper Series 322. Amherst, MA, April 2013.

Hodgson, Geoffrey Martin. *How Economics Forgot History: The Problem of Historical Specificity in Social Science*. London; New York: Routledge, 2002.

——., ed. *Recent Developments in Institutional Economics*. Cheltenham, UK; Northampton, MA: E. Elgar, 2003.

——. *The Evolution of Institutional Economics: Agency, Structure, and Darwinism in American Institutionalism*. London; New York: Routledge, 2004.

Howey, R.S. *The Rise of the Marginal Utility School, 1870–1889*. New York: Columbia University Press, 1989.

Krugman, Paul, and Robin Wells. "Our Giant Banking Crisis – What to Expect." *The New York Review of Books*, May 13, 2010. http://www.nybooks.com/articles/archives/2010/may/13/our-giant-banking-crisis/.

Marshall, Alfred. *Principles of Economics*. London, New York: Macmillan and Company, 1891.

Morgan, Mary S., and Malcolm Rutherford. "American Economics: The Charter of the Transformation." *History of Political Economy* 30, no. Supplement (1998): 1–26.

——., eds. "From Interwar Pluralism to Postwar Neoclassicism." *History of Political Economy* 30, no. Supplement (1998).

Norton, Hugh S. *The Quest for Economic Stability: Roosevelt to Bush*. Columbia: University of South Carolina Press, 1991.

Piketty, Thomas. *Capital in the Twenty-First Century*. Cambridge, MA: The Belknap Press, 2014.

Reinhart, Carmen M., and Kenneth S. Rogoff. "Growth in a Time of Debt." NBER Working Paper 15639. Cambridge, MA: National Bureau of Economic Research, January 2010.

——. *This Time Is Different: Eight Centuries of Financial Folly*. Princeton, NJ: Princeton University Press, 2009.

Rodgers, Daniel T. *Atlantic Crossings: Social Politics in a Progressive Age*. Cambridge, MA: Belknap Press of Harvard University Press, 1998.

Ross, Dorothy. *The Origins of American Social Science*. Cambridge; New York: Cambridge University Press, 1991.

Rubin, Paul H. "Folk Economics." *Southern Economic Journal* 70, no. 1 (July 2003): 157–71.

Rutherford, Malcolm. *The Institutionalist Movement in American Economics, 1918–1947: Science and Social Control*. New York: Cambridge University Press, 2011.

Samuels, Warren J. *Economics, Governance, and Law: Essays on Theory and Policy*. Northampton, MA: Edward Elgar, 2002.

Stein, Herbert. *Presidential Economics: The Making of Economic Policy from Roosevelt to Reagan and Beyond*. New York: Simon and Schuster, 1984.

Ward, Jon. "Bill Clinton Cites Economist Kenneth Rogoff To Argue Obama Needs Four More Years." *Huffington Post*, November 1, 2012. http://www.huffingtonpost.com/2012/11/01/bill-clinton-economist-kenneth-rogoff-obama_n_2061734.html.

Weintraub, E. Roy, ed. *The Future of the History of Economics*. Durham, NC: Duke University Press, 2002.

Williamson, Oliver E. "The Economics of Governance." *American Economic Review* 95, no. 2 (May 2005): 1–18.

1   The problems at hand

In his 1897 study of the history of American economic thought, economist Simon Sherwood suggested that Americans' preoccupation with practical matters for the first three-quarters of the nineteenth century – namely the building of its impressive economy – had left little time for the deep contemplation necessary to advance American economic thought beyond Adam Smith. He was, on one level, correct in commenting on the lack of economic thought. American intellectuals' interest in economic theory seemingly paled in comparison to that of their English or German counterparts, which was odd considering the nation's zeal for commerce and prosperity. The United States boasted a growing post-secondary education system that was certainly capable of supporting the type of exciting research that drove European debates of economic growth and national ambitions, yet very few thought of the academy as a guiding star for economic planners.

But what Sherwood and many of his colleagues failed to properly acknowledge was that Americans had been engaged in the study of economic theory. As early as 1897, the professionalization of economics had begun to obscure the fact that reformers had implicitly and explicitly challenged one another in debates over production and exchange throughout the nineteenth century. In doing so, they forged a brand of folk economics in the breech of social and political conflict that they then spread through the community and passed on to the next generation. The "modernization" of economic theory in the US would therefore depend not only on emulating the leading European economic theorists, but also supplanting the influence of the folk economists with that of academically trained professionals.

This push to modernize American economic thought followed the Civil War, when the economy expanded at a pace that delivered both incredible prosperity and instability. The search for ideas about how to manage a newly industrialized society led a cohort of young men to Europe, where they convinced themselves that the pursuit of scholarly economics in European universities held the key to improved quality of life back home. European scholars, they discovered, had already begun to address the unique challenges of industrial abundance through a formal system of study that appealed to those seeking order and control in an increasingly disorderly and uncontrollable society. These scholars' efforts following their return from Europe laid the groundwork for a dramatic expansion in the study of economics and modernized American economic thought. It also marked the beginning of an ongoing struggle to strike a balance between economic expertise and folk economics in a nation where democratic notions remained a powerful force.

The study of economics held a place in American higher education long before the economic upheaval of the late nineteenth century, but it was a fairly static field and far removed from the modern incarnation of the discipline. Academics and laymen alike referred to the study of exchange as "political economy," which conveyed the commonly held notion that public policy and economic behavior were naturally intertwined. Adam Smith's *Wealth of Nations*, and its caution against over-regulation of the market, was familiar to those few who attended America's colleges and universities. Such was the ubiquity of Smith's work that Johns Hopkins University's Simon Patten could, in an 1889 review of past scholarship, confidently assert that "every class of economic writer" had bestowed upon the Scotsman "all the laurels of victory" in the century since his death.[1] Smith's work, and subsequent contributions to classical economics by David Ricardo, James Mill, and Thomas Malthus, provided a common grounding for American economic thought and ensured a space for political economy among the varied topics pursued in America's colleges and universities.

But Smith's ideas were by no means the only ones in circulation. Political economy was a wide-open field in the US, as exemplified by Henry C. Carey. A successful businessman and self-taught economist, Carey managed to build a reputation as a leading political economist. He provided the intellectual heft necessary to justify protective tariffs and similar protectionist schemes throughout the mid-nineteenth century and advised Lincoln during the Civil War, albeit with mixed success (as Harvard's Frank Taussig later noted, Carey was "guilty of many curious versions of economic history").[2] Carey's work was largely ephemeral, but illustrative. Most Americans lacked significant exposure to rigorous academic economic theory and Smith's reach was likely rather limited. College was a rare experience for the overwhelming majority of Americans, as was access to advanced lectures on political economy. Like the frontier, American economic thought presented ample opportunity to build.

This is not to say that a lack of a formal canon meant a total lack of economic thought, however. As economist Paul H. Rubin notes, a lack of formal training or specialization does not prevent people from developing their own understanding of how the economy works. But it does influence the way they understand how markets and their participants interact. Lacking access to formal training, most Americans turned to personal experiences and preferences to build their assumptions about foreign trade, capital investment, the relationship between prices and production, and similar economic issues that impacted their everyday lives. Such an approach was eminently reasonable in a democratic republic that was largely committed to federalist policies and agrarian ideals (a commitment that had often been absent in debates about slavery, it must be noted). The economic turmoil of the post-Civil War decades altered these underlying conditions, however, and marked the beginning of a separation between professional and folk economics. The succeeding decades witnessed dramatic changes in the way economic thought was produced, packaged, and distributed, with the most striking developments taking shape in colleges and universities. From 1876 to 1892, instructional hours in political economy courses nearly sextupled from 2,250 to 13,116.[3] Part of this increase can be attributed to the growth of higher education in general. More people pursued opportunity through the academy, which led to an increase in the number of course hours offered in all subjects. Yet the general expansion of higher education accounts for only a fraction of the rapid increase in courses offered on political economy. Of the 66 post-secondary institutions surveyed by the *Journal of Political Economy* in 1892, 26 did not offer a single course in political economy for the 1876 academic year. By 1892 the same 26 schools offered a combined 1,337 course hours in introductory or elementary political economy, which accounted for 12 percent of the total increase in courses offered. The addition of course hours in introductory or elementary political economy at institutions that already offered similar courses in 1876 accounted for only 3.6 percent of the total increase in political economy course hours offered.

The upturn in instructional hours dedicated to political economy derived primarily from the addition of advanced courses. In just a 16-year span, leading institutions like Yale and Columbia had progressed from offering introductory political economy courses to advanced seminars on topics such as "Taxation and Distribution," "Public Finance and Economy," and "Corporate Finance." The University of Wisconsin, a prominent hub of economic thought in the early twentieth century and one of the 26 schools surveyed that did not offer any courses in political economy in 1876, added 612 course hours on advanced subjects including "Distribution of Wealth," "Public Finance," and "Recent Economic Theories."

More courses in political economy, naturally, meant more instructors, and as colleges expanded course offerings they created institutional support for those interested in pursuing the study of political economy on a full-time basis. This often meant recruiting those who had recently spent time studying in the centers of modern economic thought, primarily Germany, Austria, and England. Despite the growing supremacy of the American economy, US economic thought continued to follow Europe's lead prior to the twentieth century. Germany was a common destination for those who would go on to shake-up American economic thought – in particular the Universities of Berlin, Halle, and Heidelberg, where students were exposed to the Historical School methodology as practiced by Karl Knies and Gustav von Schmoller. In England, Alfred Marshall's pioneering work on the relationship between productivity and wages carried on the tradition of classical economic theory. Vienna stood as an equally respected destination for budding political economists, as it boasted Austrian school luminaries Carl Menger and Eugen von Böhm-Bawerk, whose work established the foundation for modern libertarian thought.

American students who encountered European political economy throughout the late nineteenth century shared a common enthusiasm for the discipline, and it was their eagerness to replicate the formality of European higher education that would establish the gulf between folk and professional economists. American economics at the time, Wisconsin's Henry C. Taylor noted, was perceived to lack the independent thought that made European schools so attractive. Americans continued to debate the appropriate manipulation of the tariff, assuming classical economic theory was "perfectly complete," while the new European masters opened debate on crucial matters, such as the proper role of the state.[4]

German economic thought, in particular, encouraged such enthusiasm. An 1880 article written by a young Richard T. Ely in Berlin, and published in *Harper's Magazine*, explained the allure. Higher education in the US, Ely declared, was in a "sad state" and failed to properly prepare young men and women for productive careers.[5] American students attended college to receive a general worldly knowledge, but left ill-prepared to make a living. Their German counterparts, on the other hand, focused on a narrow course of study that culminated in a set of examinations designed to ensure competency in a chosen profession. Unlike American students, German pupils specialized. German faculty, accordingly, offered advanced discipline-specific courses on a variety of topics, including political economy. The depth of training provided for German students prepared them to apply their knowledge to their chosen career in a manner that eluded American graduates. Europe offered, it seemed, not only knowledge of the complexities of economic policy, but also the training necessary to apply that knowledge in a manner that could alleviate the unintended consequences of rapid industrial growth in the US.

Not all notable late nineteenth and early twentieth century American economists studied abroad, but enough did to justify prevailing arguments that emphasized the influence late nineteenth century European ideas had on the modernization of American economic thought. Ely, Simon N. Patten, Edmund J. James, and Joseph French Johnson all enjoyed lengthy careers in economics following their studies abroad. Irving Fisher, Jeremiah Jenks, Frank Taussig, and Edwin Seligman each spent time at German universities as well. Together, these men taught nearly 250 years combined at Columbia, Cornell, Harvard, Johns Hopkins University, the University of Michigan, the University of Wisconsin, and Yale. All contributed greatly to the vibrancy of American economics and were mainstays in the professional economics community at the turn of the century.

The infusion of new ideas, combined with a lack of strong leadership in American economic thought, led to clashes among American economists. Historians of economic thought have long noted the tension that stemmed from the European importation of diverse approaches to understanding political economy. The consequences were far reaching, although disagreements were rarely dramatic or definitive. Nevertheless, the disagreements are revealing because they highlight the challenges of uprooting one intellectual heritage and replacing it with another.

The most oft-observed rift was between the advocates of the German-inspired historical school and the American adherents to the English-rooted classical school. The historical approach emphasized inductive logic, which required adherents to reach conclusions based on careful analysis of institutions and accumulated data. For historicists, it seemed foolish to attempt to understand and solve a particular economic problem without first gathering all the relevant data, since economic issues possessed peculiarities that could only be revealed by the facts.

Classical economists disagreed. They believed that human behavior was predictable enough to allow conclusions based on carefully constructed logic. Classical economists were not opposed to the collection of data. The difference lay in the amount of data necessary. Whereas historicists sought data for each particular economic question to account for regional, cultural, and historical differences, classical economists believed that a minimal amount of statistical evidence could be used to answer a host of economic questions through deductive reasoning. If man was a rational agent in the marketplace, classical theorists reasoned, then a simple baseline of rational behavior could be considered ample evidence from which to draw a broad theoretical conclusion.

Divisions on the ground were blurry and often tough to observe. As a matter of principle, most economists maintained an open mind and abstained from dismissing their intellectual rivals outright. Departments of political economy in the late nineteenth century lacked the ideological identities they came to embody over the course of the twentieth century. The University of Chicago, considered a stronghold for neoclassical thought in the mid-twentieth century, boasted a diverse faculty chaired by the orthodox J. Laughlin Laurence and staffed with heterodox economists such as Thorstein Veblen and Robert Franklin Hoxie. Columbia demonstrated a similar openness with the addition of John Bates Clark who, fresh from his studies at the University of Heidelberg, was far more radical than later in his career. Even faculty at the University of Wisconsin, which most aggressively pursued an institutional identity as a center of radical thought, maintained an open dialogue with their orthodox colleagues.

It is also difficult to draw sharp distinctions between schools of thought because the profession was only beginning to establish itself as a distinct discipline. Many economists saw their work as more appropriately described as sociological in nature and pulled double-duty as sociology instructors.[6] Indeed, W.W. Folwell's assertion at the third annual meeting of the American Economic Association that economics was in practice a sub-discipline of sociology met no resistance.[7] The distinction was so thin that sociology and political economy could often be discussed interchangeably; and some argued that the two fields had to be intertwined if reasonable conclusions were to be drawn. As sociologist Edward Ross cautioned his colleagues in 1889, ignorance of custom, tradition, and authority – the stuff of sociology – left economists ill-equipped to carry out their analysis of trade. The American Economic Association maintained ties with the *American Journal of Sociology* and published several articles that explored the relationship between the two disciplines, including Albion Small's "Relation of Sociology to Economics," which echoed Folwell's claim of interdependency. As Small's analysis reveals, economists were as busy defending their discipline as a free-standing field as they were their respective methodologies. Political economy in the US professionalized throughout the late nineteenth century, but it was a slow process.

More concrete and revealing than the methodological "rift" was the dispute over the role of political economy in American society – specifically the question of how to use political economists' work. The economic upheaval of the period was enough to encourage the study of economic behavior, but it did not offer clear-cut guidance as to what political economists should do with their newly acquired knowledge. The established orthodoxy in American political economics promoted a free-trade, hands-off approach.[8] The "new economists," as the "young Turks" fresh from study in Europe came to call themselves, argued for action.

The divergence in opinion was most pronounced during the early years of the American Economic Association (AEA). The young economists who returned from their European studies in the 1870s and '80s lacked a professional organization through which they could translate newfound knowledge into action. Members of the American Political Economy Club (PEC), which was formed in 1883, demonstrated a clear affinity for the orthodoxy of free trade and *laissez-faire* public policy against which the new economists conscientiously aligned themselves. The PEC had grown from the exchange of letters between orthodox economist J. Laurence Laughlin, then at Harvard, and Edward Atkinson, a prominent businessmen and amateur economist from Boston. The PEC ostensibly attempted to adopt a scientific and unbiased organizing principle, but in practice the group was quite conservative in terms of politics and economics. Its members and leaders leaned strongly toward the classical orthodoxy, and by its second year the PEC had acquired the same reputation for conservatism as the London Political Economy Club that had inspired its formation.

Founded just two years later in 1885, the American Economic Association soon became the preeminent organization for professional and amateur economists in the US. Although the PEC and AEA initially shared several characteristics, namely an ideological slant and academic leadership, the AEA proved more resilient. This stemmed largely from the stated goals of each organization. Whereas members of the PEC restricted the organization's activities to informal meetings, often at the home of a member, the founders of the AEA expressly sought to expand and widely disseminate information on political economy. Of the AEA's four founding articles, three addressed the expansion of the profession through encouragement of economic research, the publication of economic monographs, and the establishment of an information bureau to support members' research. The AEA also quickly surpassed the PEC in terms of membership and significance thanks to its willingness to admit any new member (including women, although, as we will see, their numbers were few) provided he or she could afford the annual membership fee of $3.00. This broad acceptance not only fostered lay support in the form of dues and peer advertising (the AEA attracted a number of reformers and clergymen in its early years), but also allowed orthodox economists to quietly join the organization without the drama that might have accompanied an exclusive application process.

Despite the AEA's comparatively rapid success, its early years were marked by uncertainty as disputes over the organization's leading principles alienated classical economists and discouraged a few prominent figures within the discipline from entering the group's ranks. The AEA's constitution proved to be a significant sticking point. This is not surprising considering its authors' reputations as "rebels."[9] All six founding members – Henry C. Adams, John Bates Clark, Simon N. Patten, Edmund J. James, Edwin Seligman, and Richard Ely – had spent time in Germany and expressed enthusiasm for the politically active arch-type economist. The six founders began with the assumption that economics was "a science of human relationships," the study of which should conclude with a plan of action.[10] If this was not enough to alienate the orthodox establishment in American economics, the group's overt mission statement was. With striking irony, the founding members of the AEA proposed to establish an organization dedicated to freedom of discussion, yet at the same time committed to uprooting orthodox doctrine (i.e. classical thought) from American economics. The AEA's original constitution made plain its founders' desire to meld political economy and social reform, not surprising given chief architect Richard T. Ely's endorse-ment of the controversial Knights of Labor in a book on labor drafted around the same time as the constitution.

Moderation gradually prevailed by means of an ongoing debate within the pages of *Science*, a periodical of the American Association for the Advance of Science.[11] Even Ely, the most ardent new economist, conceded that in order to ensure unbiased scientific inquiry and attract enough members to make the organization a legitimate voice for American economics, the founding members had to "tone down" the organization's constitution. The AEA settled on an innoc-uous charter that called for members to "promote independent economic inquiry" and "disseminate economic knowledge."[12] Despite these concessions to their orthodox colleagues, the authors of the AEA's organizational platform retained obvious signs of their philosophical and political leanings. The AEA's prospectus included references to the state as an "educational and ethical agency" that was responsible for "positive aid."[13] The charter expressly rejected the "final word" of previous *laissez-faire* economists and called attention to the ongoing conflict between capital and labor.

The AEA's founders and early supporters clearly envisioned an activist disci-pline that would engage with the hot-button economic issues of the day. Feedback on the prospectus illustrates the degree to which the early AEA tied itself to con-temporary reform movements that sought to change America's economic order. Dr. Albert Shaw, editor of the *Minneapolis Tribune* and a student of Ely's, met the prospectus with enthusiasm, declaring "the time is ripe for the movement …. It seems to me the society will be a success from the start."[14] President White of Cornell University applauded the group's rejection of *laissez-faire* orthodoxy, noting that it was "entirely inadequate to the needs of the modern state."[15] The prospectus garnered additional support from the Commission of Labor Carroll D. Wright as well as a promising student of Ely's, Woodrow Wilson. Although the AEA's founders scaled back the rhetoric, their intent was clear.

The AEA served as a common association to help facilitate research and legiti-mize the efforts of academic economists, a contribution to American intellectual life that cannot be underestimated. In order to follow through on its commitment to being an unbiased promoter of the field, the AEA undertook the publishing of monographs deemed relevant to the field at large. In its first 15 years, the AEA published titles by Jeremiah J. Jenks, Edmund J. James, and Frank Taussig – important milestones for scholars who would go on to contribute greatly to

American economics.[16] The AEA also attempted to establish a strong sense of direction through the work of its committees.

Committees were organized around topics of interest to both the application and the study of political economics. The work of committees was fairly straightforward; committee members collaborated to produce a committee report on their assigned topic, which was then presented at the annual meeting and published in the organization's quarterly journal. The influence of these early reports on the general public was likely minimal. They did not inspire widespread press coverage, nor were they granted special status at the annual meetings. Committee reports on the discipline's internal matters likely had a more significant influence. The Committee on Economic Theory, for example, developed into a clearinghouse for economic terms. The Committee's 1888 report highlighted its unintended influence on the discipline and pushed the AEA to embrace its role as a regulator of economic thought, although the organization would consistently move away from such responsibility. The goal, for the committee, was to "eliminate from economic discussion the most serious misunderstandings" that resulted from diversity in terminology.[17] It was a simple function, but significant in that it represented a concerted effort to transform economics into a coherent, professional discipline with a codified terminology.

Progress was slow and uneven during the Association's early years. Annual meetings were small, a fact that reflects the difficulties in organizing even the most enthusiastic of the professionalizing economists. The second annual meeting, held in Cambridge, Massachusetts, in 1888, attracted only 37 participants. The fourth annual meeting, held two years later in Washington DC, yielded 36. Geographic constraints were, in part, to blame. Both meetings drew exclusively from the Northeast and Mid-Atlantic, apart from one 1888 attendee from Milwaukee.[18] Despite drastically reduced transportation times, cross-country travel was still a financial and physical challenge. Early AEA leadership was sensitive to the matter and attempted to hold meetings further west to attract broader participation, but progress on that front was slow going. By 1894, the number of attendees had reached 64, but the origins of attendees still revealed a strong East coast bias.

The AEA also found it difficult to promote and publish economics on a large scale owing to the fragmented nature of the emerging profession. By the early 1890s the AEA was the most prominent national organization for economics, yet it still competed with a host of similar organizations. The AEA's monograph series editors searched for articles and circulation alongside several university-housed publications. Columbia, Harvard, the University of Pennsylvania, and Yale all published scholarly journals that accepted economics papers and required faculty members to contribute to in-house publications. The competition for quality papers was such that as late as 1900, Seligman expressed concern regarding the AEA's plan to publish conference papers because doing so might discourage faculty who were obligated to publish in their home institution's journal.

The discipline was still in the process of establishing the institutional and intellectual paradigms necessary to establish a sense of order in American economic thought. This is not to suggest that there were no "rules" to govern late nineteenth century American economists, however. There was a loosely defined boundary within which reputable intellectuals, academic or otherwise, were expected to remain. Disagreement over responses to the five most significant economic issues of the day (tariff, money, monopolies, labor, and agriculture) was expected, but not necessarily tolerated. In some cases, disagreement elevated to controversy and revealed the restrictions placed on public debate of economic issues. Such was the case in Madison, Wisconsin where Richard T. Ely was accused of promoting socialism in the classroom.

Policing the boundaries

The significance of late nineteenth century academic freedom cases lies in their ability to highlight intellectual boundaries in a society that ostensibly prided itself on a lack of such restrictions. As historian Mary Furner has noted, academic freedom incidents proved a crucial stepping stone in the development of the discipline because they placed limitations on what many middle-of-the-road and conservative Americans feared were unlimited social and intellectual movements.[19] What is particularly revealing about the academic freedom cases in relation to the professionalization of economics is the degree to which hearsay skewed peoples' perceptions of what was being said in the ongoing debate over economic issues.

In some cases, such as the dismissal of Edward A. Ross, hearsay proved reasonably accurate and the outcome not surprising given the social and political mores of the period. Ross, a professor of sociology and economics at Stanford University, was summarily dismissed by Mrs. Leland Stanford, widow of the school's founder in 1900. By Ross' own admission he had courted controversy. The Johns Hopkins-trained professor understood the risks he took when promoting ideas on the fringe of accepted discourse. Nevertheless, Ross was undeterred by the increasing regularity with which economists were "bulldozed into acquiescence" by those he labeled ruthless capitalists, and he vocally challenged the conservative political and ideological assumptions of his intellectual rivals.[20]

Ross' views were full of contradictions. He harbored a strong distrust of large corporations and business interests in general, yet also railed against the threat posed by the laborers he felt were being exploited by those very same business interests. Ross was also an early promoter of "race suicide" theories that proved popular during the late nineteenth and early twentieth centuries and made clear his particular disdain for Asian immigrants. Despite recognizing that his faculty appointment was at risk throughout his tenure at Stanford, Ross continued to promote his most controversial views in public. Matters came to a head following two lectures in the summer of 1900. In a statement distributed to the press, Ross explained that an address he had given to an organized labor group regarding the threat of Asian laborers and a later public lecture on municipal ownership of utilities and transportation were what sealed his fate. Both opinions had offended the widowed Mrs. Stanford, whose fortune had been acquired through the use of Asian immigrant labor to build the controversial and privately owned Central Pacific railway.[21]

Ross technically resigned amid the fallout, but by all accounts his resignation preceded Mrs. Stanford's dismissal by the slimmest of margins, although Stanford President Jordan refuted allegations the decision was made under pressure of "capital or other sinister influence."[22] Little came of the minor backlash over Ross' departure. Ross' recently appointed departmental colleague, Morton Arnold Aldrich, resigned in protest. No further resignations materialized, despite rumors of simmering discontent among Californian scholars.

Unlike Ross's dismissal, the Ely academic freedom case was marked by unsubstantiated claims and innuendo, thereby establishing the uncomfortable reality that economists would not always be evaluated according to their own words and actions. The Ely incident played out in the summer of 1894, shortly following his move from Johns Hopkins University to the newly formed History, Political Science and Economics department at the University of Wisconsin. By that summer, Ely had acquired a reputation as a leader of the new economics and a "happy warrior" who openly promoted his research among church leaders in an attempt to evoke action. He had also made clear that no subject was beyond interest; a point he drove home by attending socialist meetings and writing a noted monograph on the subject, *Socialism: An Examination of Its Nature, Its Strength, and Its Weaknesses, with Suggestions for Social Reform.*

The controversy began in July 1894 with a letter from Wisconsin school superintendent Oliver E. Wells to the editor of the *Nation*, the contents of which accused Ely of threatening to take away university business from a non-union printer following the economist's consultation with a labor "agitator" from Kansas City. The conservative *Nation* had been critical of Ely since the 1880s, and Wells' accusations that the economist had used his status in the community to bully a small business owner supported long-standing fears about the radical doctrines he was alleged to have espoused. Wells' position as state school superintendent seemingly imbued the charges with credibility, and the letter's weight rested in the assertion that the incident in question was merely an illustration of what Wells feared was a more serious issue. In addition to bullying local businesses, he warned that Ely also engaged in the deliberate and clever manipulation of students' minds. Ely, he claimed, promoted a dangerous doctrine of socialistic utopianism through the publication of books full of "glittering generalities and mystical and metaphysical statements," all promoted with University (i.e. public) resources.[23]

The University of Wisconsin's Board of Regents proved sensitive to the accusation that one of the state's more prominent minds was spreading socialist thought. Economics was a touchy subject, given that its study often led to criticisms of the status quo. It was easy to cross the line from acceptable discourse into unacceptable evangelizing. The Board's Executive Committee launched an investigation, and a public hearing was held one month after the *Nation's* publication of Wells' accusations. The Regents were supportive of Ely from the outset and declared his writings, the materials he used in class, and comments made prior to his employment at Wisconsin inadmissible.[24] Ely, with the support of his students, mustered a strong defense that included reference to the works of Smith and Ricardo, letters of support from notable figures such as US Commissioner of Labor Carroll

Wright, and testimony from past students. In addition, the investigative committee heard from Walking Delegate Klauk, the agitator Ely was alleged to have consulted with prior to threatening the local print shop. Klauk denied knowing Ely, let alone conspiring with the professor during a labor action.[25]

Nine days after the trial began it ended with humiliation for Wells. Frustrated by what he felt was a committee "destitute of power," Wells declined further participation in the trial, thereby ensuring Ely's acquittal. The investigative committee censured Wells for the rashness of his accusations, and the incident effectively ended his political career. The committee members took the opportunity of their final report to openly endorse academic freedom in higher education, concluding that "In all lines of academic investigation it is of the utmost importance that the investigator should be absolutely free to follow the indications of truth wherever they may lead."[26]

The conclusion of the trial was seemingly a moment of triumph for freedom of expression in American higher education, yet appearances are deceiving. In fact, the incident highlighted the tension surrounding higher education in general and economics in particular. Once the trial had commenced, it was clear that Wells lacked any compelling evidence. His accusations were the result of hearsay, as he had never stepped foot inside Ely's classroom. His invocation of Ely's written work was selective and ignored entire sections that explicitly denounced radical socialism and preached reform within the existing system. However, despite the obvious hollowness of Wells' charges, the Board of Regents still held a trial, which advertently or not placed the burden of proof upon Ely rather than his accuser.

The Ely incident also highlighted the relatively narrow band of thought within which economists were free to exercise their freedom of speech. Ely survived the ordeal and emerged stronger than ever, but only because he successfully proved that his work was not only non-socialist, but in fact acted as a bulwark against truly insidious socialist thought. Indeed, the basis of Commissioner Wright's support for Ely was the Professor's ability to draw laborers away from the more radical ideology espoused by less desirable intellectuals. Wright supported Ely because he was a trusted ally against what Wright perceived to be the "seductive" creep of state socialism in the US. Academic freedom, as with freedom of speech in general, had its limits. Ely was careful to preempt his critics in his written work and quick to refute his accuser with a pile of evidence when the time came. His persistent refutations of socialist leanings later led to criticism from more liberal peers and future historians. Less cautious economists who challenged mainstream ideas, and indeed collegiate faculty in general whose work evoked controversy, risked dismissal.

The new economists, along with the shifting economy, successfully challenged the "final word" of the old orthodoxy. Political economy was no longer a completed science, but rather an open debate with numerous lines of inquiry and conclusions. However, despite the chaos of economic debate and claims of academic freedom, public discourse over the pursuit of those numerous conclusions did have implicitly defined boundaries. In Ross's case, he boldly challenged them and paid for the transgression with his job.[27] Ely's case proves more compelling because the demonstrated willingness by some to act on hearsay raised troubling questions. If second-hand accusations were enough to imperil the career of an established scholar such as Ely then junior faculty were at even greater risk. Perhaps more troubling was the obvious conclusion that economists' ideas could seemingly be manipulated at will. Professional economists staked their social prestige on their ability to demonstrate conclusions through scientific inquiry. There was little the discipline could do to stop the public from ignoring the inquiry and skipping to the conclusions.

Unlike the overt pursuit of accused radicals, or those assumed to be in league with radical agitators, the intellectual censorship of women took place in less confrontational, everyday ways. Women were not excluded by law from engaging in economic thought in the 1880s and 1890s and in fact participated in the vibrant economics debates period to some degree. But just as the social and political climate pushed serious consideration of socialist solutions to the edges of most debate it also minimized the participation of women.

It is, of course, no surprise that women were underrepresented in debates over economics considering the political and social norms of the era. Women could not vote in national elections and were discouraged from working outside the home, barring those in working-class families that needed the additional income to survive. Increasing numbers of middle- and upper-class women had begun attending colleges and universities, but often struggled to find fulfilling employment upon graduation. These norms were changing, to be sure, and in time female pioneers successfully translated gendered assumptions into rewarding career paths. In the meantime, women straddled an awkward middle ground in American society. They were legally barred from voting in most states, but not excluded from the political process. They were allowed to pursue higher education, but discouraged from applying their education to a career outside the home. In a similar vein, women engaged with the contemporary debate over economics, but were largely confined to the margins of the professional community.

Such a claim would have likely drawn howls of objection from some economists of the day, particularly the new economists who prided themselves on their socially progressive prerogatives. Women published works on economic subjects and lectured to the public. One of the more successful economic texts of the time, *Political Economy for Beginners*, which went through ten editions from 1870 to 1924, was written by British suffragette Millicent Fawcett. Similarly, Beatrice Webb, the famed British socialist, enjoyed widespread recognition through her study of trade unionism and co-founded the London School of Economics in 1899. Less celebrated female faculty members taught political economy at a handful of colleges in the US – Katherine Coman most notably served as Chair of the Economics Department at Wellesley from 1883 to 1900. The AEA recognized the contributions of Amelie Rives Chandler and Claire de Graffenried for their work on child labor and women wage-earners, respectively, with an award and cash prize. Anecdotal evidence seemingly suggests a strong female voice in economic debate at the close of the century. The numbers, however, demonstrate otherwise.

Women were not represented during the founding of either the AEA or the PEC, the two preeminent professional economics organizations in the US at the time. The PEC never acquired female members, a fact that might be more a result of its short lifespan than organizational policy. The AEA did attract female members, but the numbers were small. The first meetings of the organization drew only a handful of female participants; two out of 37 attendees in 1888 and three out of 36 in 1890.[28] Time did little to address the disparity. The AEA only counted 17 women among its nearly 600 members at the close of the century.[29]

Furthermore, the anecdotal evidence that suggested a strong female voice in early American professional economics is problematic. Both Fawcett and Webb lived and worked in England and although they were certainly important figures, their reputations were tied in part to those of their husbands, economists Henry Fawcett and Sidney Webb. Additionally, the nature of their work likely minimized their significance by the 1890s. Fawcett's widely circulated textbook was a success, but by no means considered cutting-edge research. *Political Economy for Beginners* was never mentioned as anything more than an introductory level resource. Fawcett's contributions to husband Henry's 1872 *Essays and Lectures on Social and Political Subjects* proved more adventurous, but failed to establish her reputation as a leading economist in the US. Alfred Marshall hinted at the second-class status of female economists in an article published in Harvard's *Quarterly Journal of Economics*, where he suggested that the elementary role of the female economist was vanishing as the discipline professionalized: "Never again will a Mrs. Trimmer, a Mrs. Marcet, or a Miss Martineau earn a goodly reputation by throwing them [old economic principles] into the form of a catechism or of simple tales ..."[30]

Beatrice Webb's work enjoyed a stronger following, owing perhaps in part to her pursuit of labor issues that appealed so strongly to new economists in the US. Yet Webb's commitment to socialism ultimately limited her influence in American colleges. Socialism was a tainted philosophy, regardless of the advocate's gender, and undeniably colored US scholars' reception of the English economist.

Awards aside, women also faced resistance within the AEA despite the organization's open membership policy. Businessman and AEA member Stuart Wood expressed surprise when he learned the AEA allowed women to participate in the annual meetings. In his experience, the presence of women lessened the "seriousness" of proceedings. Wood's opinion on the matter was not the AEA's – that much he acknowledged. Yet, taken with the lack of female members and the limited number of female authors published by the AEA in the first 15 years of its existence, it is clear that women held a lower status than men in the community of American professional economics.

It was not much different outside academia. Women's participation in economics often took place outside the classroom and in the same spaces occupied by reformers and club members. Political economy was a mainstay of the women's club circuits, and lectures on the subject were quite common by the 1890s. The General Federation of Women's Clubs placed political economy alongside English literature, botany, and art work as topics of highest interest.[31] An estimated 213 clubs organized expressly to discuss the growing field of study. Women also joined in on discussions at Chautauqua meetings – the summer adult education camps that included lessons on political economy and enjoyed the support of consummate promoter Richard T. Ely.

As with academic economics, women were awkwardly integrated into the public debate over economic issues, however. An article run in the *New York Post*, and carried by the *Chicago Tribune*, snidely criticized aspiring female economists, noting that they now understand the intricacies of the modern economy, yet fail to comprehend a subject closer to their established role as a homemaker – plumbing.[32] Perhaps if they studied plumbing with the same enthusiasm they displayed during their reform efforts, the editorialist concluded, they may actually improve their lives.

Detractors aside, women continued to pursue their study of economics. The study of political economy coincided with the general increase in the number of women engaged in social reform at the end of the century. Economics spoke to the main causes of the day, such as temperance and urban reform, which attracted a large number of female reformers. A thorough knowledge of political economy also bolstered women's push for suffrage. As suffragette Ida McIntosh-Dempoy noted in an editorial letter to the *Chicago Tribune*, the study of political economy would provide women with the surest preparation for exercising their voice through the ballot.[33] The vote and the study of political economy were intertwined. And as Helen H. Gardener argued in an article published by the progressive *Arena* magazine, the study of political economy without an outlet for political expression was a societal liability.[34] Educated women understood the flaws in late nineteenth century society, yet lacked a political voice on par with that of their male counterparts. It was no wonder, according to Gardener, that women might smash up saloons in the name of reform out of frustration over knowing the problem, but being prevented from pursuing a solution.

Folk economists

Professional economists generally do not control the agenda for public debate of economic issues, and the early years of professionalization were no exception. The lack of focus on agricultural issues best reflects the disconnect between the academy and the public. The US was, after all, still a predominantly rural nation. There was little doubt that the future of the American economy lay in industrial centers, but not all Americans sought such a rapid transformation of American life. The Populist movement – a largely rural, agriculturally oriented political movement to preserve rural autonomy and integrity – sought to slow the change. Populists talked political economy, but did so outside of the academy. Not surprisingly, those who supported the goals of the reformist movement often looked for ideas outside academia and its institutions. The divergence between the focus of the Populist movement and the nascent field of professional economics foreshadowed the ever-present challenges economists faced in translating their economic theories into economic policy.

Populists believed they did not need academic economists, particularly those who focused on industrial issues. To be fair, many economists engaged in the sort of research that resulted in a better understanding of the economy as a whole. The immediate application to the plight of the farmer and rural merchant was unclear, however. In instances where the application was apparent, such as the nature of the money supply, the professional economist appeared antagonistic toward the farmer's interest. The conservative economists of the old economy exerted a strong influence on the national debate over the nature of the money supply and the desirability of the gold standard. J. Laurence Laughlin, most notably, campaigned vigorously for "tight" money, and as a result higher interest rates harmed perennial borrowers in rural America.

Furthermore, many economists engaged with the professionalization of economics fixed their attention on problems specific to the industrial economy. Whereas conservative, orthodox economists' sympathies appeared to lie with the institutions that funded industrial expansion, new economists preoccupied themselves with the relationships between industrial labor, consumers, and capital. The farmer, it seemed, was of secondary concern. It was not necessarily that professional economists ignored agricultural issues. Scholarly publications featured articles that specifically considered the farmer's situation in the American economy, and the AEA made the "Future of the Farmer" the theme of its ninth annual meeting in 1896. But the results of such discussion were hardly appealing to Populists. The reformers had some obvious allies within the AEA and academia in general, such as C.W. Walker of the Massachusetts Agricultural College, who warned of peasant-like conditions and encouraged cooperation and education to reverse the backslide. Such assessments were weighed against comments that may have given populists the impression that the majority of economists were antagonistic to their agrarian interests, however. Wisconsin economist William Scott disagreed with Walker's optimism and foresaw the declining fortunes of farmers as a natural decline from an unsustainable bonanza. It was an opinion shared by Edwin Seligman of Columbia, who argued that those who believe American farms could remain profitable and independent were living in a "fool's paradise."[35]

It is easy to see how such opinions could alienate populists who sought sustained prosperity for the small farmer in America's fields. They certainly clashed with those of populist icon and champion of the small farmer, Henry George. No stranger to poverty, George stood in sharp contrast to those academics whose opinions, terminology, and personal lives differed from those hard-pressed by a changing economy. Although George had run several newspapers, he was self-educated and unfamiliar with the academic world that provided the recently expanded support and structure for the study of economics. Nevertheless, in 1879 George published one of the most popular books on economics in US history, *Poverty and Progress*.[36]

Its success was such that by the late 1890s George was mentioned alongside Karl Marx as a paragon of intellectual influence.[37] *Poverty and Progress* spoke directly to the farmers and laborers who composed the Populist movement and many others who were sympathetic to anti-elitist rhetoric. The book was the fruit of George's thinking on the dilemma posed by industrialization. There was no doubting that rapid economic transformation had generated massive wealth, George conceded, but industrialization ultimately failed to improve the economic stability of the common citizen. Worse still, George argued, industrialization had robbed the average American of independence. The problem stemmed from increases in rent, or the amount of money spent on land from which goods could be produced. The increased productivity of an industrial economy, George reasoned, had raised the value of land. This increase in the cost of land (rent) left little for wages and profits.

In addition to articulating what George saw as the problem of the late nineteenth century economy, *Poverty and Progress* also provided a solution. The answer was seductively simple: tax land to lower its value. A single-tax on unimproved land, so-called because the revenues it generated would be enough to meet all of the government's expenses, would render land-speculation unprofitable. As a result, the value of land held by speculators would plummet, thus making land available to small farmers and workers. These average citizens could put the land to work, producing goods and services that would stimulate economic growth rather than extracting rents from the economy as unproductive land speculators had long done.

The popularity of his single-tax solution made George a celebrity and highlighted the growing distinction between amateur and professional economists. George enjoyed a large following among the public, but failed to win a following among those who made economics their life's pursuit. His misfortune stemmed in part, as historian Robert V. Andelson has noted, from the fact that he came to prominence as an intellectual at the same time that doing so without first obtaining the requisite degrees was increasingly frowned upon by the educated class. The discord was exacerbated by George's avowed contempt for academic economists and the merits of their professional process. In 1877, prior to the publication of his most famous work, George had been invited to the University of California at Berkeley to present on the subject of political economy. According to George's son and biographer, a strong showing likely would have resulted in George's appointment as the University's first chaired professor in political economics. However, George spurned the opportunity and denounced academics for their loyalty to the capitalist class that paid their salaries. Regardless of whether George consciously sabotaged a shot at academia or his son fashioned the tale to highlight his father's attitude toward intellectuals, the lesson remains the same. George maintained a difficult relationship with academic economists for the rest of his life.

George's theory was met with intense and sustained criticism from professional economists.[38] Yale's Francis Walker took George to task for a host of errors in several venues, including *The North American Review* and a series of lectures at Harvard throughout the 1880s. Arthur Hadley had similarly criticized George's plan as simplistic and ill-conceived. Arguments regarding the "land monopoly," Hadley countered, had grossly overstated the role of real estate, which led to the false impression that breaking the alleged land monopoly through taxation would resolve economic inequality.

Arguably the most famous economic thinker of his day never joined the AEA, or its short-lived rival the PEC. George held a deep-seated skepticism of professional economists that showed no sign of diminishment at his participation in the 1890 annual meeting of the American Academy of Social Sciences, where he again asserted that as members of the property-owning class all professors were opposed to reform. Rebuttal at the meeting came from Seligman, recently returned from Germany and at the beginning stages of his long career as a top tax economist. Seligman's response laid the matter bare: "[T]he reason why college professors are not counted among his followers is not because they are afraid of consequences, but because they utterly repudiate the adequacy of his solution."[39] It was the first in a long line of devastating critiques Seligman levied against George and his theory over the course of his career. *Poverty and Progress* – in particular its promotion of the single-tax as a panacea to the problems caused by the modern economy – failed to meet the developing standards of professional economists.

What was hailed by "Georgists" as the brilliance of George's policy recommendation, in particular its simplicity and easy-to-follow logic, was criticized in academia as ill-conceived. Seligman elaborated on his dislike for the single-tax plan at an AEA conference three years later during a discussion of taxation and the farmer, where he argued that the theory "fail[ed] of equality and uniformity."[40] George's single-tax may have addressed those who amassed fortunes through real estate speculation, but would likely fail to appease the populists who similarly lamented fortunes made elsewhere, Seligman noted. In his discussion of public versus private ownership, Joseph Lee, in an article published by the *Quarterly Journal of Economics*, dug deeper for his criticism and attacked George's inconsistent stance on natural rights.

Whatever their response to the single-tax plan, professional economists could do little to persuade George and his supporters of its shortcomings. The former newspaper editor's commercial success, as well as the popularity of the actions he proposed, was a formidable match for the expertise carved out by professional economists in those last decades of the century. The frustration expressed by J. Laurence Laughlin in the first issue of his department's economic journal captured the situation well:

> Certain it is that expositions by men of high abilities and scholarship have had little or no influence on thinking in general. No one in the United States should indulge the hope of attempting to reach the great masses of men, or of such classes as the working-men, through the usual channels of economic writing. Scientific ideas can be disseminated through books and magazines only to a limited circle of intelligent readers. The great working classes can be reached only by the literature which comes from within their own ranks.[41]

Moving forward, the burden was on professional economists to establish an influential place in American society. George was not the only prominent folk economist capable of challenging the nascent discipline, as explained through the analysis of economic policy histories in subsequent chapters. Professional economists' social role, newly defined and invigorated through strong institutional support in American colleges, left them poised before a skeptical yet eager public audience desperate for solutions to several pressing issues. Additionally, the AEA may have begun to integrate "old" and "new" economists into a single professional organization, but it had done little to brook arguments over methodology and policy proposals. Nevertheless, the commitment of colleges and universities to the advanced study of economics assured progress in the comprehension of the economic challenges that accompanied industrialization. Convincing the public and, more importantly, politicians of the value of expertise was another matter.

Notes

1 Simon N. Patten, "Malthus and Ricardo," *Publications of the American Economic Association* 4, no. 5 (September 1889): 9–34.
2 F.W. Taussig, *The Tariff History of the United States* (New York: G.P. Putnam's Sons, 1888), 116.
3 The *Journal of Political Economy*'s survey covered a sizeable fraction of colleges that offered political economy courses in the US, although it is difficult to determine the size of that fraction. Anecdotal evidence suggests the study omitted dozens of schools that offered additional courses. Of the 66 respondents to the *JPE*'s survey, only six were located west of the Mississippi river, omitting institutions with at least one instructor of political economy such as California – Berkeley, Leland Stanford University, and the University of Oregon. Combined with the curious exclusion of eastern institutions like Johns Hopkins University and Amherst, it is clear that impressive as the above figures are, they underestimate the expansion of instruction in political economy from 1876 to 1893.
4 Henry C. Taylor, "Class Notes for The History of Economic Thought," 1987–1898, Henry C. Taylor Papers, 1896–1968 Box 1, Folder 7, Wisconsin Historical Society.
5 Richard T. Ely, "American Colleges and German Universities," *Harper's New Monthly Magazine*, July 1880, 253–60.
6 Economists who taught sociology or conducted sociological research in the 1880s and 1890s includes, but is not limited to, F.A. Wyckoff, Richard T. Ely, John R. Commons, Edward A. Ross, and Guy Callender.
7 Richard T. Ely, "Secretary's Report," *Publications of the American Economic Association* 4, no. 4 (July 1889): 64.
8 Interestingly, iconoclast historian Charles Beard attempted to dismiss the fact that classical economics, with its preference for *laissez-faire* policies, dominated American economic thought by arguing William Graham Sumner and J. Laurence Laughlin imported the notion in the post-Civil War period. His argument contradicted the recollections of every early twentieth century economist and was built on scant evidence.
9 Richard T. Ely, *Ground Under Our Feet: An Autobiography* (New York: The Macmillan Company, 1938), 132.
10 Ibid., 121.
11 Mary O. Furner, *Advocacy & Objectivity: A Crisis in the Professionalization of American Social Science, 1865–1905* (Lexington, KY: The University Press of Kentucky, 1975), 91–102.
12 Richard T. Ely, "Report of the Organization of the American Economic Association," *Publications of the American Economic Association* 1, no. 1 (March 1886): 5.
13 Ibid., 6–7.
14 Ibid., 8.
15 Ibid., 9.
16 The monographs referenced here were hybrids, of sort. They were often shorter than what would be considered a monograph-length study by later generations, yet longer

than a journal article. The AEA referred to the publications as monographs and marketed them as such. See Jenks (1889); James (1886); Taussig (1892).

17 Ely, "Secretary's Report," 62.

18 Additional information on the lone Mid-Westerner in attendance, Jarrett Droppers, has been elusive.

19 Furner, *Advocacy & Objectivity*, 125–42.

20 Edward A. Ross, *Seventy Years of It: An Autobiography* (New York; London: D. Appleton-Century Co., 1936), 64.

21 Mrs. Stanford's fortune stemmed from the success of her late husband and railroad magnate Leland Stanford, whose controversial business practices have been well-documented in Richard White's account of the late nineteenth century railroad empires.

22 "Row at Stanford University," *New York Times*, November 16, 1900, 5.

23 Oliver E. Wells, "The College Anarchist," *The Nation*, July 5, 1894, 27.

24 The Board initially declared all of Ely's written work would be barred from consideration. However, Wells' attorney, Col. George W. Bird, successfully petitioned to include Ely's written work that was assigned to his students on the grounds that such material was necessary to gain an accurate understanding of what Ely taught his students.

25 The People's Party account of Klauk's participation in the trial corresponds with Ely's recollection of a Kansas City Walking Delegate in *Ground Under My Feet*, however, Ely never names Klauk directly.

26 "Prof. Ely Exonerated," *The Weekly Wisconsin*, September 22, 1894, 6.

27 Furner's account of Henry C. Adams' censure at Cornell University offers a similar conclusion. Adams promoted pro-labor arguments fully knowing the conservative bent of the school's benefactors and subsequently came under scrutiny. Unlike Ross, Adams fought to placate the administration and was able to preserve his career, albeit as a much more conservative scholar.

28 There is some uncertainty surrounding these numbers, as some of the entries in the attendance books are illegible. However, assuming all of the illegible names in the attendance books were those of female attendees the numbers would still be striking – only seven female attendees in 1888 and five in 1890. "American Economic Association Annual Meetings Attendance Book," 1905 1886, American Economic Association Records, 1886 – Box 2, Duke University Rare Book, Manuscript and Special Collections Library.

29 According to the AEAs 1900 membership list, the organization had a total of 706 members, 111 of which were colleges or libraries. Gender was determined by looking at first names, which is reliable but not infallible. In some instances, only an initial appears in place of a full first name, which creates further uncertainty. However, even accounting for these issues it is clear female membership was strikingly low.

30 Alfred Marshall, "The Old Generation of Economists and the New," *The Quarterly Journal of Economics* 11, no. 2 (January 1897): 117.

31 This article indicates that the confederation of women's clubs is the source of information, which is likely the title the paper gave to the GFWC in its early days before official founding in 1890. "For the Ladies," *San Francisco Chronicle*, April 21, 1889.

32 "New Field for Women," *Chicago Daily Tribune*, June 6, 1891.

33 Ida McIntosh-Dempoy, "Twenty Thousand Women Voters," *Chicago Daily Tribune*, November 11, 1894.

34 Helen H. Gardener, "The Danger of an Irresponsible Educated Class in a Republic," *The Arena*, August 1892.

35 "Future of the Farmer," *The Sun*, December 30, 1896, 6.

36 Exact publication figures are difficult to come by, but all of George's biographers and contemporary observers agree that *Poverty and Progress* was the most successful book on political economy ever published in the US in terms of sales.

37 More specifically, Stuart Wood paired Marx and George together in that their writings were so powerful they had large "currency" in contemporary social movements (Wood 1889).

38 See Andelson's *Critics of Henry George* for greater detail on George's American critics outside of professional economics, as well as professional economists in Europe.
39 "Remarks of Professor Seligman (Friday Evening, September 5)," *Journal of Social Science Containing the Transactions of the American Association* no. 27 (October 1890): 89.
40 S.M. Dick, "The Taxation of Personal Property and the Farmer," *Publications of the American Economic Association* 8, no. 1 (January 1893): 45–46.
41 J. Laurence Laughlin, "The Study of Political Economy in the United States," *The Journal of Political Economy* 1, no. 1 (December 1892): 3.

Bibliography

"American Economic Association List of Members." *Publications of the American Economic Association, 3rd Series* 1, no. 1 (February 1900): 7–36.

Andelson, Robert V., ed. *Critics of Henry George: A Centenary Appraisal of Their Strictures on Progress and Poverty*. Rutherford, NJ: Fairleigh Dickinson University Press, 1979.

"Appendix I: Courses of Study in Political Economy in the United States in 1876 and in 1892–93." *Journal of Political Economy* 1, no. 1 (December 1892): 143–51.

Beard, Charles A. "The Idea of Let Us Alone." *The Virginia Quarterly Review* 115, no. 4 (Autumn 1939): 500–514.

Bemis, Edward W. "The Discontent of the Farmers." *Publications of the American Economic Association* 8, no. 1 (January 1893): 74–76.

Bernstein, Michael A. *A Perilous Progress: Economists and Public Purpose in Twentieth-Century America*. Princeton, NJ: Princeton University Press, 2001.

Blaug, Mark. *Great Economists before Keynes: An Introduction to the Lives & Works of One Hundred Great Economists of the Past*. Atlantic Highlands, N.J.: Humanities Press International, 1986.

——. "Was There a Marginal Revolution?" *History of Political Economy* 4, no. 2 (Fall 1972): 269–80.

Brumberg, Joan Jacobs, and Nancy Tomes. "Women in the Professions: A Research Agenda for Americans Historians." *Reviews in American History* 10, no. 2 (June 1982): 275–96.

Bryson, Phillip. *The Economics of Henry George : History's Rehabilitation of America's Greatest Early Economist*. New York: Palgrave Macmillan, 2011.

Coats, A.W. "The Economic and Social Context of the Marginal Revolution of the 1870's." *History of Political Economy* 4, no. 2 (1972): 303–24.

——. "The Educational Revolution and the Professionalization of American Economics." In *Breaking the Academic Mold: Economists and American Higher Learning in the Nineteenth Century*, edited by William J. Barber, 340–75. Middletown, CT: Wesleyan University Press, 1988.

——. "The First Two Decades of the American Economic Association." *The American Economic Review* 50, no. 4 (1960): 556–74.

——. "The Political Economy Club: A Neglected Episode in American Economic Thought." *The American Economic Review* 51, no. 4 (1961): 624–37.

Cord, Steven. *Henry George: Dreamer or Realist?* Philadelphia: University of Pennsylvania Press, 1965.

Dick, S. M. "The Taxation of Personal Property and the Farmer." *Publications of the American Economic Association* 8, no. 1 (January 1893): 43–48.

Ely, Richard T. "American Colleges and German Universities." *Harper's New Monthly Magazine*, July 1880.

——. "Constitution By-Laws and Resolutions of the American Economic Association." *Publications of the American Economic Association* 1, no. 1 (March 1886): 35–46.

——. "Report of the Organization of the American Economic Association." *Publications of the American Economic Association* 1, no. 1 (March 1886): 5–32.

——. *The Labor Movement in America*. New York: T.Y. Crowell, 1886.

——. "Secretary's Report." *Publications of the American Economic Association* 4, no. 4 (July 1889): 43–95.

——. *Socialism: An Examination of Its Nature, Its Strength and Its Weakness, with Suggestions for Social Reform*. New York: Thomas Y. Crowell & Company, 1894.

——. *Ground Under Our Feet: An Autobiography*. New York: The Macmillan Company, 1938.

Fawcett, Millicent Garrett. *Political Economy for Beginners*. London: Macmillan & Company, 1876.

Fox, Daniel M. *The Discovery of Abundance: Simon N. Patten and the Transformation of Social Theory*. Ithaca, NY: Cornell University Press, 1967.

Furner, Mary O. *Advocacy & Objectivity: A Crisis in the Professionalization of American Social Science, 1865–1905*. Lexington, KY: The University Press of Kentucky, 1975.

Gardener, Helen H. "The Danger of an Irresponsible Educated Class in a Republic." *The Arena*, August 1892.

George, Henry. *Poverty and Progress: An Enquiry into the Cause of Industrial Depression and Increase of Want with Increase of Wealth*. New York: H. George & Co., 1879.

George Jr., Henry. *The Life of Henry George*. New York: Doubleday & McClure Company, 1900.

Hadley, Arthur T. "Private Monopolies and Public Rights." *The Quarterly Journal of Economics* 1, no. 1 (October 1886): 28–44.

Hansen, W. Lee. *Academic Freedom on Trial: 100 Years of Sifting and Winnowing at the University of Wisconsin-Madison*. Chicago: University of Chicago Press, 1998.

Hodgson, Geoffrey Martin. *Economics in the Shadows of Darwin and Marx: Essays on Institutional and Evolutionary Themes*. Cheltenham, UK; Northampton, MA: Edward Elgar, 2006.

James, Edmund J. "The Relation of the Modern Municipality to the Gas Supply." *Publications of the American Economic Association* 1, no. 2/3 (July 1886): 7–76.

Jenks, J.W. "Road Legislation for the American State." *Publications of the American Economic Association* 4, no. 3 (May 1889): 9–83.

Kinley, David. "Farm and Home Proprietorship and Real Estate Mortgage Indebtedness." *Publications of the American Economic Association, New Series*, no. 2 (March 1899): 219–45.

Lampman, Robert, ed. *Economists at Wisconsin 1892–1992*. Madison, WI: University of Wisconsin Press, 1993.

Laughlin, J. Laurence. "The Study of Political Economy in the United States." *The Journal of Political Economy* 1, no. 1 (December 1892): 1–19.

Lee, Joseph. "Ethics of the Single Tax." *The Quarterly Journal of Economics* 7, no. 4 (July 1893): 433–58.

Marshall, Alfred. "The Old Generation of Economists and the New." *The Quarterly Journal of Economics* 11, no. 2 (January 1897): 115–35.

Milonakis, Dimitris, and Ben Fine. *From Political Economy to Economics: Method, the Social and the Historical in the Evolution of Economic Theory*. London; New York: Routledge, 2009.

Morgan, Mary S., and Malcolm Rutherford. "American Economics: The Charter of the Transformation." *History of Political Economy* 30, no. Supplement (1998): 1–26.

Nasar, Sylvia. *Grand Pursuit: The Story of Economic Genius*. New York: Simon & Schuster, 2011.

Patten, Simon N. "Malthus and Ricardo." *Publications of the American Economic Association* 4, no. 5 (September 1889): 9–34.

"Remarks of Professor Seligman (Friday Evening, September 5)." *Journal of Social Science Containing the Transactions of the American Association*, no. 27 (October 1890): 87–98.

Rieser, Andrew Chamberlin. *The Chautauqua Moment: Protestants, Progressives, and the Culture of Modern Liberalism*. New York: Columbia University Press, 2003.

Rodgers, Daniel T. *Atlantic Crossings: Social Politics in a Progressive Age*. Cambridge, MA: Belknap Press of Harvard University Press, 1998.

Ross, Edward A. *Seventy Years of It: An Autobiography*. New York; London: D. Appleton-Century Co., 1936.

———. "The Sociological Frontier of Economics." *The Quarterly Journal of Economics* 13, no. 4 (July 1899): 386–95.

Rubin, Paul H. "Folk Economics." *Southern Economic Journal* 70, no. 1 (July 2003): 157–71.

Rubinstein, David. *A Different World for Women: The Life of Millicent Garrett Fawcett*. Columbus: Ohio State University Press, 1991.

Samuels, Warren J. *Essays in the History of Heterodox Political Economy*. New York: New York University Press, 1992.

Schlabach, Theron F. "An Aristocrat on Trial: The Case of Richard T. Ely." *The Wisconsin Magazine of History* 47, no. 2 (Winter 1963–64): 146–59.

Sherwood, Sidney. *Tendencies in American Economic Thought*. Johns Hopkins University Studies in Historical and Political Science. Baltimore: The Johns Hopkins Press, 1897.

Small, Albion W. "The Relation of Sociology to Economics." *Publications of the American Economic Association* 10, no. 3 (March 1895): 106–17.

Stone, N.I. "Agriculture." *Publications of the American Economic Association, New Series*, no. 2 (March 1899): 204–18.

Taussig, F.W. "The Silver Situation in the United States." *Publications of the American Economic Association* 7, no. 1 (January 1892): 7–118.

———. *The Tariff History of the United States*. New York: G.P. Putnam's Sons, 1888.

Walker, S.C. "The Movement in the Northern States." *Publications of the American Economic Association* 8, no. 1 (January 1893): 62–74.

Wells, Oliver E. "The College Anarchist." *The Nation*, July 5, 1894.

Whitaker, John K. "Enemies or Allies? Henry George and Francis Amasa Walker One Century Later." *Journal of Economic Literature* 35, no. 4 (December 1997): 1891–1915.

White, Richard. *Railroaded: The Transcontinentals and the Making of Modern America*. New York: W.W. Norton & Company, 2011.

Wood, Stuart. "The Theory of Wages." *Publications of the American Economic Association* 4, no. 1 (March 1889): 5–35.

2 The money question

In the late nineteenth century, the recently organized professional and folk economists in the United States got their first significant opportunity to translate theory into practice during the struggle over monetary reform. It was a contentious issue that came to a point in the 1896 "Battle of the Standards," but had roots that stretched back several decades. In what would become a common pattern, professional economists fought to redefine understanding of monetary policy while advising the public and policymakers on their options for reform. The affair foreshadowed the ambiguous role economists would play in debates about American political economy. Though professional economists' status imbued them with a degree of social prestige, it was largely offset by the all-powerful forces of electoral politics. Forced to accept a role as passive advisors, the discipline's leading experts largely observed as the nation moved toward a strict gold standard that they had warned would prove untenable; a prediction made true by the panic of 1907.

If ever there was an issue that seemingly required the calculating expertise of a professional economist, it was the money question. On the surface, the "problem" seemed rather straightforward – which monetary standard would ensure the appropriate level of growth and stability? The problem was not nearly so simple, however. Until the late nineteenth century, very few Americans, economist or otherwise, conceived of the money issue in purely scientific terms, which made the debate about more than just the money supply.

The money issue was as much a matter of morals and politics as it was statistics. As Cornell economist E. Benjamin Andrews illustrated in an 1889 survey of the issue, public discourse regarding the monetary supply often included reference to the "sacred moral rights" that accompanied ownership of money. Accordingly, debate revolved around the moral obligation of the state to protect and preserve private property. The United States was, after all, a nation deeply committed to the values that inspired its revolutionary birth, including political philosophies that emphasized the sanctity of private property.

Andrews and a growing number of economists, including the bulk of those who studied abroad and embraced the new economics, increasingly rejected this view of money policy. The money issue had less to do with property rights, they argued, and more to do with the changing nature of the US economy. As an avowed bimetallist,

Andrews posited that price fluctuations were an inescapable reality regardless of the monetary standard. Gold mines dried up, economic activity expanded, and the value of currency adjusted regardless of the established monetary standard.

The key to addressing the money question therefore lies in acknowledging the changing dynamics of the US economy. As Andrews noted, the very nature of economic exchange in the US had undergone a tremendous transformation, the net effect of which was to increase the demand for circulating currency. Specialization had disbursed the production process, increasing the number of accounts that producers had to maintain – as well as demand for coin in lieu of credit. Similarly, industrialization continued to supplant the barter system through which so many transactions had once been conducted, further increasing the demand for coin where credit had previously sufficed. Gold bugs and like-minded conservative money men were not wrong to demand a "steady" dollar, Andrews concluded, but the realities of the modern economy meant that steady value depended on careful government regulation. Andrews' overview of the money problem, published by the AEA's newly established monograph series, concluded with vague references to action that were characteristic of work published by the organization in its early years.

Andrews' study appears to have summed-up early AEA members' sentiments, loose though they were. The AEA's commitment to growing a diverse membership barred the possibility of an explicit policy position, but the articles and addresses published by the organization clearly demonstrated general support for some degree of monetary reform. Harvard economist Frank Taussig's "The Silver Situation in the United States," an exhaustive review of the nation's tentative move toward bimetallism, echoed Andrews' sentiments and encouraged the federal government's further manipulation of the money supply. Taussig's conclusions turned the conservative money men's arguments against bimetallism on their head, concluding that "The expansion of the silver currency has followed, and not preceded, the rise in prices, the speculative activity, and the other phenomena which are associated with an increase in the supply of money."[1] While the conclusion led Taussig to support the coinage of silver, he fell short of recommending the unrestricted or "free" coinage of the metal. Instead, he promoted active management of the money supply by freeing the Treasury from "mechanical limitation" while allowing it to monitor the nation's money supply and inject currency into the economy when necessary. It was precisely the type of recommendation one might expect from an expert, as it required specialized knowledge, objective analysis, and an eye for detail.

Relegating questions of morality to the background while bringing consideration of technical details to the foreground was no small task, however. The money question had featured in American politics in one form or another since the Declaration of Independence, and by 1890 its long legacy of sectional conflict evoked powerful emotions in the public. The National Banking Acts of 1863 and 1864, passed during the Civil War to finance the Northern war effort, firmly established the federal government's authority over the nation's banking system. Although no one seriously challenged Washington's authority over currency thereafter, many did question the execution of such authority.

Disagreement revolved around the volume of currency in circulation. "Loose" money advocates – predominantly farmers, laborers, and those in Western states where large silver deposits had recently been discovered – encouraged the federal government to print currency backed by both gold and silver deposits. Advocates of this policy argued that allowing the printing of silver-backed bank notes (i.e. paper money) in conjunction with the printing of gold-backed bank notes would increase the nation's money supply and ease the burden on debtors attempting to find the currency necessary to satisfy their creditors. Loose-money advocates viewed the tightening of the money supply as despotism and the antithesis of democracy.

Creditors and non-debtors – who largely came from the ranks of finance and industry – encouraged a "tight" money supply. They argued that a bimetallic system would increase inflation, which would in turn discourage savings, devalue the currency, and destabilize the economy. Large manufacturers and those engaged with foreign trade were particularly concerned. High inflation might drive consumption, but it could also lead to unpredictable credit markets and disrupt foreign exchange at a time when manufacturers were spending vast sums on large manufacturing facilities.[2] Tight money policy, in other words, would preserve the real value of profits that derived from loans and encourage future saving and lending.

A series of back-and-forth policies had stoked controversy in the decades prior to professional economists' entry into the debate. The 1873 Coinage Act, later referred to by free silver advocates as "The Crime of the Century" because it was passed with little public debate, effectively shrank the money supply through the demonetization of silver. In 1878, Congress authorized an international conference to discuss among representatives of the world's leading economies the relationship between silver and gold. Despite considerable enthusiasm from the American delegation, the conference ended with little to show for the effort, much less a consensus broad enough to resolve the issue.

The 1879 Bland-Allison and 1890 Sherman Silver Purchase Acts both required the Treasury to resume purchasing and circulating silver-backed currency in set amounts. Both acts stopped short of allowing the unlimited coinage of silver that many bimetallists sought, but they still upset tight money advocates who wanted the US treasury to maintain a strict gold standard. The Sherman Silver Purchase Act in particular intensified debate, as the partial coinage of silver seemingly situated the nation in between two possible monetary systems. Resting in between a strict gold standard and a bimetallic system lent ammunition to both sides of the debate – gold bugs blamed the creep of silver as the source of economic woe, while bimetallists claimed that the limited purchase of silver held back an economy starving for more currency. In 1893, investors challenged the viability of the Sherman Silver Purchase Act and began to exchange dollars issued through the purchase of silver for gold bullion. The Treasury, obligated to redeem the notes in either silver or gold at the request of the holder, struggled to maintain its gold reserves. This, combined with a financial panic caused by the overbuilding of the nation's railroad system, had created one of the worse depressions in US history.

Despite the apparent need for some sort of guidance, Andrews and Taussig's vision of managed bimetallism failed to gain traction. With the economy in freefall and the nation's gold reserves rapidly evaporating, President Cleveland had little choice but to repeal the Sherman Silver Purchase Act and call on powerful investment banker J.P. Morgan to restore confidence in the markets. The incident seemingly settled the matter: increased coinage of silver had produced financial instability. But bimetallists read events quite differently, asserting that repeal of the Silver Purchase Act was what had panicked investors.[3]

The nation's professional economists were ill-positioned to influence the course of events, but populist advocates for the free coinage of silver had little trouble attracting attention in the early 1890s. Throughout the 1890s, voters – not only in Central and Western mining states, but also those in the South and East – rallied around the push for free silver. The ensuing war of words between the populist movement's intellectuals and professional economists reveals how the power of publicity and showmanship proved as important as expertise in the fight over monetary policy.

Justifying free silver

Had the free silver movement gathered significant momentum just 20 years earlier it would have found a powerful champion among the ranks of American political economists – those "outdated" intellectuals who preceded professionalization. Henry C. Carey, one of more notable among Lincoln's advisors, had directly addressed the money question. In his 1868 book *The Finance Minister, the Currency, and the Public Debt*, Carey railed against the "financial despotism" of post-Civil War American financial system. Carey's criticism derived from his conclusion that, contrary to Secretary of the Treasury Hugh McCulloch's assertions, the nation's money supply was dangerously low. An over-reliance on credit in the absence of circulating currency, Carey explained, raised interest rates and depressed prices outside of the nation's financial centers in the Northeast and Chicago.

As it was, Carey's voice was virtually silent by the 1890s. His death in 1879 meant that one of the leading American political economists had no hand in the formation of the nation's leading economic associations and was unable to articulate his arguments through the letter and journal networks that increasingly defined "expert" economic thought. Intellectual justifications for free silver instead derived from a combination of politicians and self-taught folk economists who worked through pamphlets and rousing speeches. They employed scientific methodologies and tended to rely on narratives that contained moralistic arguments their audience found accessible and appealing. Conspiracy among the nation's elites was a particularly popular explanation, as were rumors of an international cabal's plan to control the nation's money supply so as to consolidate economic control.

Such arguments resonated with hard-scrabble farmers and respected politicians alike. William Jennings Bryan, the famed lawyer and orator who challenged McKinley for the White House in the dramatic Presidential election of 1896, secured his candidacy with the well-known "Cross of Gold" speech that compared the economic suffering of Americans to the suffering of Jesus on the cross. Senators Henry M. Teller (R-CO) and John H. Mitchell (R-OR), who broke with their party to protest Republicans' commitment to the gold standard, offered less widely known but equally public proclamations.[4] In an 1890 speech, delivered on the Senate floor, Mitchell decried the monetary situation and argued that it was clearly a case of one class (the rich) holding down another (the poor) through conspiratorial means. Teller voiced similar suspicions throughout the 1890s, and was unafraid to offer more direct accusations. During the push to repeal the Sherman Silver Purchase Act in response to the panic of 1893, Teller pointed his finger directly at President Cleveland and at alleged backroom machinations with Wall Street to ensure the future of the gold standard.[5] Both the Senators and populists were correct in their suspicions of Wall Street's influence on Congress, but to argue that the influence was total and benefited only Wall Street was an exaggeration that ignored the economic exigencies of the time.

The build-up and maintenance of popular support for the free and unlimited coinage of silver required a more clearly articulated vision than could be credibly and effectively espoused in such fiery rhetoric. The speeches, lobbying, and accusations were vitally important to the free silver movement, but their authority stemmed from popular appeal and their actions only carried weight as long as a significant fraction of the voting public rallied behind their cause. Securing votes required intellectual heft to counter professional economists' criticisms of free silver policy. Free silverites found this expertise in a variety of places – local newspapers, public meetings, bars, and similar venues in which late nineteenth century men and women openly discussed politics and ideas. These informal gatherings were informed by a cottage industry of pamphleteers, newspaper serialists, and amateur book authors that sprang up to meet the demand for expert analysis that fed free silverites' predispositions.

The popularity of such works was staggering. George Henry Shibley's self-financed *The Money Question* enjoyed multiple printings and was widely circulated among populist voters. A lawyer by training, Shibley was self-taught in the ways of money and finance. A bit unwieldy at 723 pages, *The Money Question* nevertheless attracted readers through its easy-to-follow logic and straightforward argument about the benefits of the free coinage of silver. *Ten Men of Money Island*, a more manageable 142-page treatise written by lawyer and journalist S.F. Norton, was distributed as a pamphlet and serialized in the *New York World* prior to publication in 1891. The book's publisher claimed to have distributed more than 500,000 copies of the promotional pamphlet prior to the book's publication, with still more copies to be translated into German, Norwegian, Swedish, French, Bohemian, and Hebrew.

William Hope Harvey's *Coin's Financial School* and *A Tale of Two Nations* were the central texts of the free silver movement, however. First published in 1894, both volumes enjoyed enough success to ensure multiple printings and to earn its author the nickname "Coin" Harvey. Exact figures are elusive, but the *Atlanta Constitution* placed sales at well over 500,000 copies, with widespread distribution on both sides of the Mississippi River by 1895. That figure likely was surpassed considering that the free silver issue did not peak in relevance until after the 1896 presidential election. The National Silver party alone sent out an additional 125,000 copies in 1896. *Coin's Financial School*'s popularity exceeded that of an earlier best seller that had proven influential in American politics – *Uncle Tom's Cabin*.

To many Americans, self-taught men such as Shibley and Harvey, rather than professionally trained economists, were the nation's authorities on economic policy. They wrote with a passion and urgency that echoed the populist movement's discontent and mistrust. Harvey's dedication in *Coin's Financial School*, "To those trying to locate the seat of the disease that threatens the life of the nation …," was only outdone by the plotline of his follow-up project, *A Tale of Two Nations*, also self-published in 1894.[6] Whereas *Coin's Financial School* used a fictitious lecture hall as the setting for a discussion of monetary issues, *Nations* conveyed a similar pro-free silver message through a story that was equal parts romance and international thriller, with an ending that predicted Western civilization's collapse at the hands of a British conspiracy. Harvey's antagonist, Victor Rognasner, declared in a dramatic speech that "Money is the protoplasm of society. Without it, civilization is impossible, crime increases, and barbarism is the result."[7]

Both *Coin's Financial School* and *The Money Question* contained the sort of conspiratorial accusations that were impossible to deny and therefore an insurmountable defense against professional economists' criticisms. Harvey used allegory to suggest that London financiers covertly demonetized silver in 1873 to increase profits from the repayment of Civil War debt. Shibley matter-of-factly asserted that an international cabal of 600 firms controlled $830,000,000 and actively fought to control the world's money supply. He further stated that the combined strength of the London and New York houses of the Rothschilds and Morgans was sufficient enough to overrun American interests.

President Cleveland's infamous open "silver letter" of 1895, in which he drew "the line of battle" and confronted the growing free silver movement head-on, seemingly resolved any lingering doubts about the power of the gold lobby. For Chicago Bimetallic League secretary George E. Bowen, the letter plainly revealed Cleveland's "harmony" with the nation's bankers. The Toledo-based *Commercial* editorial staff was similarly unsurprised by the declaration, considering Cleveland's allegedly well-known association with gold bugs. The militaristic language with which Cleveland declared his stance on the money question no doubt fed free silverites' deepest suspicions and concerns. With such a powerful policy foe established, the folk economists who promoted free silver policies could effectively challenge contradictory evidence as the product of a massive conspiracy.

Free silverites perceived that the grassroots nature of the movement legitimized their arguments in a manner that was fundamentally different from that of the gold standard lobby. Whereas the gold standard lobby derived considerable support, both logistically and ideologically, from financiers and their "bought" economists, the free silver movement's support emanated from a folkish wisdom and sense of justice. In an 1895 public debate with *New York Weekly Tribune* editor Roswell G. Horr, "Coin" Harvey went to great lengths to downplay the support of silver miners to the applause of the audience.[8] Such strenuous denials were commonplace and found in pro-silver editorials throughout the country.

Herein lays a peculiar aspect of the free silver movement: populists maintained that free silver advocates' expertise stemmed from a dual font of intense introspection and intellectual independence. Free silverites would benefit from the unlimited coinage of silver, but self-interest was not perceived to be a strong motivation for free silver intellectuals. Objectivity, or at least the illusion of objectivity, was crucial to establishing economic expertise and free silverites' use of conspiracy gave them a significant advantage over professional economists in this matter.

Of course, the free silver movement did enjoy support from the business community, particularly in the Central and Western states. Local organizations of businessmen supported the movement through the publication and promotion of pamphlets, books, and speeches similar to those produced by men like Harvey and Shibley. These organizations gradually expanded from local to national in scope. In 1895, three national bimetallic organizations merged into one, forming the American Bimetallic Union (ABU) with offices in Chicago, Washington, DC, and San Francisco. The ABU's tremendous success played a substantial role in the Democratic Party's adoption of free silver in the 1896 election.

The free silver movement's aversion to what could be described as "mainstream" analysis of the money question appears to have stemmed from this deep-seated mistrust of anyone or any group that challenged the conclusions of free silver intellectuals. Newspapers throughout the 1890s occasionally made reference to the "many economists" who supported the free silver movement, but there were very few professionally trained economists willing to promote the unlimited coinage of silver – Edward Ross being the exception that proves the rule. Ross was still employed by Leland Stanford University when he publicly agitated for free silver in the mid- to late-1890s. As biographer Sean H. McMahon notes, Ross' whole-hearted support of the free silver movement first alerted the administration to his fondness for agitation.[9]

Lacking professional economists of national repute, "Silver clubs" and bimetallic rallies occasionally drew upon local economists to provide keynote addresses. The Young Men's Silver Club of St. Louis had to settle for an address by Col. A. Ollei, an economist whose professional career failed to register far beyond the confines of Litchfield College in Southern Illinois. Still, it was arguably more impressive than the overwhelming majority of silver club meetings that turned to the self-taught for expert testimony.

Such was the force against which professional economists worked to satisfactorily resolve the money issue. The ideas and policy recommendations of university-employed economists were dismissed as controlled by the moneyed interests and therefore unreliable due to bias. Agitation from well-known industrialists like Andrew Carnegie, J.P. Morgan, and J.D. Rockefeller, all of whom had a strong interest in price stability, seemingly confirmed suspicions about collusion between academic economists and their wealthy benefactors.

Economists have their say

If the response to Henry George and his single-tax proposal is any indicator, then professional economists did not explicitly conspire to exclude particular groups or ideas in the early years of the professionalization process. Despite populist allegations of backroom scheming, the lack of free silver advocates among professionally trained economists was in reality the result of rapid changes in the study of economics. By the 1890s, professionally trained economists had established a peer review process that quickly expanded the chasm between layman and expert. The variety of academic journals and bulletins described in Chapter 1 had begun to insulate the two worlds. Both lay and professional economists pursued the same goal – accurate analysis of economic problems with an eye toward offering productive solutions. But while professionally trained economists increasingly offered their work to the peer review process in an attempt to validate research, folk economists rushed ahead and released their work. The results tended to expose a dogmatism that, although certainly not unknown to the professional community, seemed to characterize the work of the non-professional.

It is not surprising, therefore, that the exposés and grand explanations offered by folk economists frequently withered in the face of serious criticism. Such was the case with *Coin's Financial School*, a revised edition of which had continued to find a large audience when Wesleyan economist Willard Fisher reviewed the work in *The Quarterly Journal of Economics*. Impressive sales figures aside, the review concluded that the book was an intellectual failure. Fisher was not entirely hostile, although he delivered his greatest compliment with the back-handed observation that "This work is just about what ought to be expected from an untrained thinker of considerably more than average ability."[10]

Fisher's criticism stemmed not only from the numerous statistical errors ("in most cases these inaccuracies are due either to carelessness or to simple inability to select the proper data"), but also from the calculated distortion of facts that were central to Harvey's argument about the merits of free silver.[11] Harvey's claim that the world's silver supply was diminishing struck Fisher as particularly problematic, as it was unsubstantiated. Given the body of statistical knowledge of the US and world economy in the 1890s, Fisher noted, Harvey's claims regarding silver's knock-on effects could only be described as wild guesses, at best.

The gap between folk and professional was most clearly illustrated by Harvey's terminology and theory. Poor word selection marred Harvey's conclusions in key passages. By conflating "value" and "price," for example, he suggested that inflation increased value across the board. And the populist icon's fixation with the physical properties of gold bemused Fisher, as did his poor understanding of fractional reserve banking. In sum, one of the free silver movement's leading experts failed the peer review process. The verdict was striking coming from Fisher, a self-described "cautious radical" who was by no means averse to adopting policies designed to help the worker at the expense of Wall Street.[12]

As critical as it was, Fisher's review likely only circulated among the professional economics community. University of Chicago economist J. Laurence Laughlin's campaign to discredit the free silver movement had a much larger audience, however. Although his "attacks" were certainly less caustic than those found in titles like *Farmer Hayseed in Town or The Closing Days of Coin's Financial School* and *Coin's Financial Fraud*, Laughlin nevertheless fueled the free silverites' animosity toward professional economists through a public campaign against free silver. Like most of his peers, Laughlin opposed free silver, although unlike most professional economists he wholly embraced a monometallic gold standard. He had first articulated his stance while an assistant professor at Harvard, and maintained the position after his move to Chicago in 1892. Such was his zeal for a strict gold standard that many of his fellow economists felt Laughlin's refutation of the quantity theory of money represented a fine example of a scholar fashioning facts to fit a conclusion. As the debate over money intensified, Laughlin became more vocal and was soon in direct conflict with not just his colleagues, but the populist movement as well.

Laughlin had earned a reputation for being tolerant of dissenting opinions, although he remained outside the AEA throughout the 1890s in defiance of the Association's commitment to government intervention. But he was also known for the conviction with which he promoted his most cherished ideals and policy recommendations. According to one of his former students, Laughlin "could not forbear 'taking sides' and strongly supporting the 'side' to which he had given his conviction."[13] The conservative co-founder of the Political Economy Club clearly felt a bimetallic system, to say nothing of free silver, was untenable. As such, he chose his side and pursued the issue intently by engaging in a public campaign to discredit Harvey's work.

Laughlin's crusade gathered considerable steam in early 1895, starting with an article in *The Forum* that was likely his most hostile treatment of the free silverites. Unlike most of Laughlin's earlier work, "Coin's Food for the Gullible" targeted a lay audience. In addition to declaring *Coin's Financial School* "untrustworthy" and "childish," Laughlin characterized Harvey as a charlatan and opportunist. Furthermore, he argued that Harvey's populist audience, to use Laughlin's analogy, was the ignorant soil in which Harvey planted his fallacies.

A public debate with Harvey himself, arranged by the Illinois Club, followed just one month later. The debate was carefully orchestrated. After some haggling, both participants agreed to the debate's single question: "Is free coinage of silver at the ration of 16:1 by the United States, independently of other countries, desirable?" Harvey and Laughlin each was allowed one hour in which to make his case, including a 15 minute rejoinder. Personal criticisms were expressly forbidden. Accounts of the debate, which ran in newspapers from New York to Los Angeles, noted the charged atmosphere that prevailed throughout the contest. True to form, Harvey suggested an international conspiracy to manipulate the currency that involved President Cleveland and the Rothschilds, while Laughlin attacked Harvey's argument as rife with factual inaccuracies. Both men received strong support from the enthusiastic audience, although as an editorial from the *Chicago Tribune* noted, it was unlikely anyone changed their opinion as a result of the spirited contest.[14]

Laughlin later leveraged his public attack on Harvey with the publication of *Facts about Money*. The lengthy volume, also written for a lay audience, included a transcript of the May debate. In terms of original research, *Facts about Money* was unimpressive. Ironically, it garnered criticism from Fisher in the same article that picked apart *Coin's Financial School*.[15] Despite its deficiencies, as a piece of popular literature, *Facts about Money* successfully pressed Laughlin's attack on free silver and provided sound money advocates with a valuable arrow for their quiver. It was soon followed by a reprinting of the more scholarly *The History of Bimetallism*.

As the debate intensified, it became increasingly clear that the money question had to be answered. The 1873 Bland-Allison and 1890 Sherman Silver Purchase Acts had proven themselves stop-gap compromises and the push for a legislative resolution to the money question reached a crescendo in the final years of the nineteenth century. It was clear that professional economists rejected free silver as a legitimate policy option, but still had to offer policymakers an alternative. The discipline was split regarding the remaining options – a monometallic gold standard or a bimetallic standard. The two camps, crudely drawn, consisted of those AEA members who long supported bimetallism and their more conservative counterparts who remained at arm's length from the AEA and promoted a strict gold standard.

Andrews, the aforementioned President of Brown University, and Francis A. Walker, President of MIT, had spoken on the issue throughout their respective careers and come to represent the bimetallic movement among professional economists. Both endorsed a controlled move toward a bimetallic money supply and cautioned against the adoption of free silver. As noted above, a year before the free silver movement noticeably intensified, Andrews' 1889 "An Honest Dollar" had inveighed in favor of a controlled transition to a bimetallic system, provided it was done in conjunction with foreign nations to ensure the switch was sustainable. He remained in-tune with the ongoing debate, as evidenced by his support of the Bimetallist Committee of Boston and New England. Not to be confused with the numerous free silver advocacy organizations that often placed "bimetallic" in their name, the Bimetallist Committee of Boston and New England only supported the coinage of silver provided it was regulated in accordance with yet-to-be established international standards. The specifics of such an international agreement, as Andrews reported in *The Quarterly Journal of Economics*, were vague. Despite decades of discussion, no one seemed capable of explaining how to return to silver without allowing free coinage, and there was no precedent for drawing on professional economists to resolve the matter.

Walker, another expert voice in the silver debate, had also denounced the 1873 demonetization of silver as an enormous blunder that threatened the national economy and called for a move toward a bimetallic monetary system. For years he had elaborated on his concerns about the insufficient circulation of currency and doubts about the ability of credit to replace currency – most recently in papers directed toward an academic audience following the 1893 financial panic and repeal of the Sherman Purchase Act. In 1896, Walker published a series of lectures on the money question through Henry Holt Publishers, who no doubt hoped to cash in on one of the hottest talking points of the impending Presidential election.[16] The book, titled *International Bimetallism*, presumably secured a larger audience than Walker's academic journal articles that had circulated in the low thousands (at best), although estimates are not forthcoming. The more widely circulated book was nothing new to those familiar with Walker's earlier writings on the subject. Once more, he encouraged the remonetization of silver, but cautioned against free coinage. Indeed, he even quoted an emphatic line from his 1878 *Money, Trade, and Industry*:

For us to throw ourselves alone into the breach, simply because we think silver ought not to have been demonetized, and ought now to be restored, would be a piece of Quixotism unworthy the sound practical sense of our people.[17]

The book was followed by a series of articles in which Walker reiterated his stance on the money issue. Shortly after the release of *International Bimetallism*, Walker traveled to England to take part in a meeting of The Bimetallic League of Great Britain. The trip, as well as Walker's comments denouncing free silver and promoting bimetallism, was reported on the front page of the *San Francisco Chronicle* and the *Detroit Free Press* in July of 1896. The trip was also less prominently reported by the *New York Tribune* and *Chicago Tribune*, among others.

Both Andrews and Walker, therefore, were key figures in the public debate over the money question. There seems to have been a genuine opportunity for these professional economists to leverage their expertise into influence during the 1896 Presidential election, and in doing so, tip the debate in favor of a bimetallic standard. But two forces conspired to diminish their influence on the eve of the election.

First, the press and free silverites misled the public about the two economists' conclusions – whether by design or intent is unclear. As Logan C. McPherson, author of yet another opinion on the money question, noted, by 1896 the term "bimetallism" had been given so many different meanings that its use meant nothing without further explanation. Andrews certainly became aware of the potential confusion when the Brown Board of Trustees removed him from his post as president following false allegations that he was a free silver advocate. The sensational claim that Andrews' teachings were "out of harmony" with the vast majority of opinions at Brown University and the state of Rhode Island in general betrayed the political nature of the attack. Andrews certainly showed greater willingness to accept the coinage of silver than many of his colleagues, but he never supported free silver outright, as a quick consultation of either his written work or a discussion with one Brown's other economic professors would have confirmed.

The ambiguity of "bimetallism" was further underscored by Walker's experience with the press. Arguing for bimetallism while declining to elaborate on the mechanisms allowed activists and candidates to hedge their bets. Democratic nominee Bryan appeared to do just that on the campaign trail, according to the *San Francisco Chronicle*.[18] By voicing his support for bimetallism, but avoiding an in-depth discussion of the issue, the presidential hopeful could avoid directly challenging the position of professional economists who endorsed a particular brand of bimetallism. Similarly capitalizing on this tactic, free silverite George Fred Williams invoked Walker's support for free silver in a speech to a capacity crowd of 900.[19]

By the end of October 1896, Walker apparently had had enough. The oft-referenced economist refused to allow reporters to hear his views on currency as he addressed the Twentieth Century club – unless they agreed not to publish an account. A reporter for the *Boston Daily Globe* (ironically) reported, "It looked as if Gen. Walker intended that whatever he should say would not be used as ammunition in the present campaign by the orators of either of the political parties ...."[20] A later observer noted the liberal use of Walker's ideas in his obituary, writing,

> He [Walker] found himself … placed in an embarrassing position. Some of his views on bimetallism were published as campaign literature by the Populists and free silver Democrats, while other of his views were used in the cause of sound money.[21]

Confusion over professional economists' exact policy stance on the eve of the 1896 election (willful or otherwise), only served to color the debate between folk and professional economists. Professional economists, with the notable exception of Laughlin, generally stood outside either reform movement's propaganda machine. Only the free silver movement attracted significant criticism from the ostensibly objective academics. Professional economists' criticisms of the free silver movement had little effect on the devout, thanks to their belief that such experts were in the pockets of eastern bankers. Still, such uniform opposition to free coinage of silver surely influenced the undecided in the months leading up to the 1896 Presidential election. The journal articles, books, public lectures, and newspaper summaries of professional economists who urged monetary reform rather than revolution were undoubtedly a factor in the fight over monetary policy, but it was the political process that ultimately drove action.

Moving on reform

November 1896 marked a turning point. Presidential campaigning ended and McKinley emerged victorious. The forces of populism, which included the agrarian and the laborer, confronted the forces of industrial capitalism and lost. On a less dramatic but no less important level, the conclusion of the election enabled movement on the money question. Free silver was off the table and the key question moving forward was the issue of gold monometallism. McKinley quickly signaled his intent to settle the issue as soon as possible by dispatching Walker and bimetallist Colorado Senator Edward O. Walcott to Europe once again to feel out the British regarding a return to international bimetallism. Walker's unexpected death less than a week after the trip's announcement left Wolcott as the sole representative. The trip, like the 1878 conference, confirmed the difficulty of establishing an international agreement to mint both silver and gold. Wolcott returned empty handed, and it is unlikely Walker's presence would have made much of a difference.

Movement on the issue eventually was instigated by the Indianapolis Monetary Convention (IMC) – one of several private monetary reform organizations that had succeeded in attracting the people and resources necessary to make something happen. Several historians have described the IMC as either a minor stepping stone to meaningful reform or as evidence of a conspiratorial power grab.[22] James Livingston's assertion that the IMC should be considered part of a larger process "in which a corporate business elite began to work out a world view and a program appropriate to its control over and leadership of an emergent modern-industrial civilization" is closer to the mark. But such a view obscures the role of the professional economics community. There is no doubt that professional economists lacked the political and social capital necessary to dictate the IMC's activities. The profession was too young and unorganized to lead reform efforts, and it was only natural that private interests assumed the task. At this crucial juncture, professional economists embraced a role as passive advisers despite grand talk about a new era in economic management. That the IMC was in position to advance pro-gold standard reform was partly the result of economists' refutation of free silver. Likewise, the AEA's subsequent endorsement of the IMC's proposed legislation helped move monetary reform efforts forward. Still, it is clear that professional economists' influence was largely confined to the margins.

The work of the IMC began immediately after McKinley's victory in November 1896. Hugh H. Hanna, President of the Indianapolis-based Atlas Engine Works, beseeched the Indianapolis Board of Trade to hold a convention on the issue of monetary reform. The Board then invited representatives from twelve cities to attend the conference, the result of which was a plan for a larger convention the following January. The mid-January conference (and subsequent activities of the organization) attracted support and participation from a broad swath of the American business community, including soon-to-be secretary of the treasury, Lyman Gage.[23]

Over the next two years the growing organization engaged in a struggle to translate the prerogatives of its broad coalition of businessmen into legislative action. The January 1897 meeting resulted in the appointment of an Executive Committee, which in turn established headquarters in Washington, DC, in order to better lobby for Congressional action. In July 1897, pro-silver Democrats continued to block movement on the issue and denied McKinley's request for a Congressional Commission to study the money question. Undeterred, the IMC pushed forward and established an 11-man Commission tasked with drafting legislation for Congressional consideration. Congress' refusal to appoint a commission had left room for the IMC to create its own authoritative body, and it did so by forming a diverse body of more than just bankers and financiers.[24] The inclusion of J. Laurence Laughlin sent a clear message regarding the sort of expertise the IMC would solicit, however.

Interestingly, Laughlin dissented with the Commission on grounds that would have appealed to free silverites' populist sentiments. The Commission labored from July until December 1897, at which point it released its report calling for the legal establishment of the monometallic gold standard while avoiding an "injurious contraction" of the nation's money supply.[25] Foreshadowing what was to come, the report also expressed support for allowing the Secretary of the Treasury to effectively pump money into the economy through the purchase of US bonds. Laughlin objected to the suggestion on the grounds that it would create a dangerous linkage between the government and the banking community. The Chicago economist signed the report below a brief statement noting his objection.

The AEA held its 1897 annual meeting just weeks after the completion of the IMC's report and just over a year after McKinley's election. At the meeting, a committee was formed to investigate the possibility of arriving at a consensus regarding currency reform. Walker was deceased, and by late 1897 Andrews likely chose to avoid the issue in the wake of the free silver scandal at Brown, although archival records shed no light on his curious omission. Still, the AEA's Currency Committee consisted of an impressive list of economists that included Taussig (Harvard), F.M. Taylor (University of Michigan), J.W. Jenks (Cornell University), Sidney Sherwood (Johns Hopkins University), and David Kinley (University of Illinois).

Although none of these men played a role as public as Andrews or Walker had in the run-up to the Bryan–McKinley election, they were certainly engaged with the money question throughout the 1880s and 1890s. All five endorsed a gold standard, although each included in his assessment the need for appropriate "elasticity" to meet the demands of a seasonal industrial economy. Taussig, as noted above, had endorsed a sound but flexible monetary system in a series of writings geared for an academic audience. Of the men chosen for the Currency Committee, he probably commanded the most public reputation. But his writings were nowhere near as popular as those of Harvey or Walker.

F.M. Taylor, whose greatest fame derived from his work on market socialism, similarly endorsed an elastic gold standard. His March 1896 piece published in the *Political Science Quarterly* highlighted Taylor's conviction that gold elasticity could be derived from targeted bond-purchasing programs. Sherwood echoed a similar sentiment about the desirability of flexible bond purchases, but apparently did not reveal this conviction until after his participation on the Currency Committee. Sherwood's stance prior to his participation on the committee is not entirely clear, but his comments regarding longstanding elasticity issues throughout American history in a primer on economics strongly indicates that he too saw the wisdom in greater monetary elasticity. Kinley's analysis of the American Independent Treasury displayed a similar concern with elasticity.

Jenks rounded out the Committee. As with Sherwood and Kinley, his exact stance on the issue is less clear than that of Taussig or Taylor. The German-trained economist did not factor much in the build-up to the Bryan–McKinley election, and he focused much of his attention on the monopoly question throughout the 1890s. Jenks' commitment to the gold standard was confirmed instead by his participation in the IMC and his later foray as economic advisor to the Chinese government, where he encouraged the adoption of the gold standard. His attitude toward the necessity of greater monetary elasticity remains unclear.

That each member of the Currency Committee – with the possible exception of Jenks – promoted an elastic gold standard is crucial to note. Although their answers to the money question differed in specifics, each Committee member expressed the desirability of a monetary system actively backed and managed by a responsive US government.

Throughout 1898, therefore, two Commissions actively pursued monetary reform. The IMC, a coalition of private businessmen, and the AEA's Currency Commission, a commission of professional economists, pondered and debated for the next year. Despite their concomitant work, it is clear that one followed the other in terms of significance. The IMC had already issued its report by the time the AEA's Currency Committee was formed. Furthermore, the IMC's resources far outweighed those not only of its Currency Commission, but of the entire AEA.

Donations from supporters such as J.P. Morgan and William E. Dodge ensured the IMC had $50,000 with which it could cover members' transportation costs, acquire research materials, conduct a survey, and publicize its efforts. The AEA entered the year with $609.40 cash on hand. In order to have any sort of influence, the AEA Currency Commission would have to work through the IMC.

In mid-January, the IMC called a second convention so that delegates could consider the report of its Commission. Approximately 400 delegates attended the second meeting of the IMC – each a representative of a chamber of commerce, a business organization, or a manufacturers' association from around the country. Several members of the AEA's Currency Commission turned out as well, although they attended as representatives of local business organizations. Jenks represented the Ithaca Business Men's Association, Taussig the Cambridge Merchants' Association, and Taylor the Ann Arbor Business Men's Association.

The professional economists' specific contributions to the January 1898 convention have been obscured by time, but subsequent developments strongly suggest they walked away from the meeting satisfied with the role they had played, or at the very least convinced that the IMC was moving toward serious action. Jenks thought enough of the IMC Committee's report to pass along Laughlin's offer to mail a copy to every member of the AEA.

The AEA Committee's final report, which represented an attempt to "command the assent of economists generally," was presented at the 11th annual AEA meeting in December 1898. The 13-page report followed the lead of the IMC's reform efforts. It offered general support for monetary reform provided that it secured the gold standard ("the actual monetary standard is now, and for some time to come will be, gold") and ensured monetary flexibility ("to furnish the sort of elasticity which is needed in a panic").[26] The report garnered only a modicum of attention in newspapers throughout the country, and although it offered a broad analysis of the money question, it did not present a clear plan of action. The professional economics community had proven adept at blocking the reform efforts of the free silverites, but was largely incapable of offering a workable alternative. While the economists on the AEA's Currency Commission agreed on the merits of an elastic, gold-backed money supply, they could not settle on a specific policy proposal. This was in contrast, of course, to the IMC's expressed interest in directly sponsoring a legislative bill.

Whereas the AEA Currency Commission's report received only brief notices, newspapers and periodicals across the nation tracked the progress of the IMC as it presented its findings and lobbied for legislative action. The report of the IMC's Commission met with the support of delegates, professional economists included. The IMC convention ended with a resolution to mail a copy of the Convention's conclusions to members of Congress. Progress continued, and in May 1898 Hanna expressed enthusiasm for the House Banking Committee's decision to report the Walker Bill, which embodied most of the measures urged by the IMC. At that point the Spanish-American War consumed the nation's attention and made serious reform unlikely. Progress resumed in February 1899, when Republican House members formed a Committee on Monetary Legislation to rally support around IMC-backed McCleary Bill. After an additional year of negotiating, Congress finally passed the major currency reform sought by the IMC and endorsed by the overwhelming majority of professional economists. The Gold Standard Act, as it became known, achieved the legal maintenance of the gold standard. The final section of the Act left open the possibility that the US might someday embrace bimetallism in the unlikely scenario that the world's leading nation's agreed on an international bimetallic monetary regime.

Taussig's post-mortem, "The Currency Act of 1900," ran in the next edition of *The Quarterly Journal of Economics*. It predictably praised the general spirit of the Act, but cautioned that Senate floor compromises had left the US financial system unnecessarily unpredictable. In particular, Taussig pointed to the clause that allowed the Treasury to satisfy outstanding bonds with payment in either silver or gold, which essentially established two classes of debt. He further criticized the Act's redemption procedures, which required the Treasury to constantly shift gold on hand rather than maintaining it in a simple reserve fund in anticipation of future redemptions. Taussig attributed the flaws he perceived to "uninitiated" senators and temporary fiscal conditions that induced the Treasury accept such measures. He also questioned the long-term viability of the Act, and in doing so, foreshadowed the Panic of 1907.

A missed opportunity

The Gold Standard Act appeared to settle the long-running debate over the money question by establishing a monometallic gold standard. But as the events of 1907 revealed, it was ultimately the stop-gap measure Taussig predicted. In the fall of that year, panic once again seized the nation's finances and sent the federal government scrambling for a solution. The currency aspect of the money question had been answered, but deep flaws in the nation's banking system remained. When a failed attempt to corner the copper market coincided with the seasonal rush of money from eastern banks to farm communities throughout the nation, a collapse ensued.

The Aldrich–Vreeland Act, co-sponsored by one of the "uninitiated" senators Taussig referred to in his review of the Gold Standard Act seven years prior, temporarily restored confidence by granting banks the authority to issue emergency currency backed by numerous securities (not just government bonds) on a temporary basis. The emergency act also provided for the establishment of a government commission to explore the possibility of serious banking reform. The National Monetary Commission (NMC), established in 1910, consisted of nine Senators and nine Representatives. The group labored for two years before delivering its recommendation to Congress, the end result of which was the passage of the Federal Reserve Act in 1913.

The narrative of the Federal Reserve Act unfolded much like that of the Gold Standard Act. Professional economists – most of whom had pushed for Congress to affirm the gold standard provided that it was accompanied by a system designed to allow monetary elasticity – once more found themselves in a paradoxical position. On the one hand, the profession was called on to provide guidance and advice. In the course of its work, the NMC called on numerous economists – Joseph French Johnson, Davis R. Dewey, O.M.W. Sprague, David Kinley, and E.W. Kemmerer, among others – to provide a wealth of information regarding national banking systems from around the world.[27] The NMC's efforts were guided, in part, by expert assistant and Harvard economist A. Piatt Andrews. Andrews was also responsible for editing the 26 volumes generated by the NMC (which included the work of various economists, including those mentioned above). Professional economists surely had transcended the influence of the more popular folk economists of the late nineteenth century.

On the other hand, the expertise of professional economists was weighed against both the persuasive powers of the private business community and the prerogatives of Washington politicians. In the end, a small group of banking community representatives molded the NMC's recommendations. National City Bank of New York President Frank A. Vanderlip, Senior Partner of J.P. Morgan Company Henry P. Davison, President of First National Bank of New York Charles D. Norton, Kuhn, Loeb, and Company partner Paul M. Warburg, and Senator Nelson Aldrich gathered at a Georgia resort to draft legislation for the reform of the nation's banking system. The final product, the Aldrich Plan, proved impassable for political purposes. The NMC had been established under a Republican administration while Aldrich was at the peak of his political powers. But Democratic victories in 1912 shifted the tide in Washington and made the passage of a Republican-sponsored bill impossible. Just as politics had delayed efforts to act on the currency issue in the wake of the 1896 Presidential election, political maneuvering once more altered the final product. Upon taking office in March 1913, President Woodrow Wilson acted quickly to put an end to the nearly four years of banking reform debate. Enlisting the aid of Senator Carter Glass, Wilson made it clear that any proposed banking reform measures were to feature stronger government control than provided for in the Aldrich plan.

The money question had slowly evolved from a discussion regarding the moral merits of two competing monetary systems to a debate regarding the best way to ensure a healthy economy. As champions of a scientific approach to the problem, professional economists found themselves maligned by populist folk economists who traded on pseudo-science and moral struggle. The business community, on the other hand, successfully tapped the professional economics community for both guidance and credibility. It was a victory of sorts for advocates of professionalization, but the discipline still struggled to find its identity and professional economists remained an uncertain fit in American public life.

Notes

1 F.W. Tussig, "The Silver Situation in the United States," *Publications of the American Economic Association* 7, no. 1 (January 1892): 61.
2 The concerns of bankers, insurers, and large manufacturers were clearly articulated in Henry Varnam Poor's 1878 Memorial to Congress, which is explored in Chandler's biography. See Chandler (1981).
3 The Sherman Silver Purchase Act was suspended in October 1893, 8 months after the first signs of economic duress in February.
4 Although Mitchell returned to the Republican Party, Teller refused to do so and remained a Silver Republican. See Ellis (1932).

5 "Senator Teller Is Shocked," *New York Times*, July 9, 1893, 8.
6 W.H. Harvey, *Coin's Financial School* (Chicago: Coin Pub. Co., 1894), xi. W.H. Harvey, *A Tale of Two Nations* (Chicago: Coin Pub., 1894).
7 Harvey eventually furthered his dire predictions of societal collapse and attempted to construct a massive pyramid to hold artifacts of soon-to-be collapsed Western civilization in the 1920s. The project was eventually abandoned before completion. See Kennan (1947).
8 Roswell Horr, *The Great Debate on the Financial Question Between Hon. Roswell G. Horr, of New York, and William H. Harvey, of Illinois the Six Chapters of "Coin's Financial School" the Subject of the Debate*. (Chicago: Debate Pub. Co., 1895), 412.
9 McMahon also quotes Ross as stating he and E. Benjamin Andrews were the only two prominent academics who supported the free silver movement. However, it appears he used a loose definition of "free silver" that included those such as Andrews who simply supported a managed money supply. Brown's decision to censure Andrews may have understandably led McMahon to misread Andrews' position.
10 Willard Fisher, "'Coin' and His Critics," *The Quarterly Journal of Economics* 10, no. 2 (January 1896): 189.
11 Ibid., 190.
12 "Roosevelt An Egotist, Says Professor Fisher," *New York Times*, October 20, 1904, 6. Nor was Fisher averse to taking action. The outspoken economist also criticized Republicans as incapable of delivering economic justice and ran for mayor of Middleton, CT on the Democratic ticket. "Fisher Thinks He'll Be Mayor," *The Hartford Courant*, December 20, 1905, 16.
13 Alfred Bornemann, *J. Laurence Laughlin: Chapters in the Career of an Economist* (Washington: American Council on Public Affairs, 1940), 18.
14 "Honest Money or Free Silver," *Chicago Daily Tribune* (Chicago, May 19, 1895), 36.
15 Fisher's review led to a reply from Laughlin, who strongly objected to Fisher's criticisms, but both held their ground. The debate, like Fisher's original article, likely garnered much less attention than Laughlin's public campaign.
16 The book was released in the first week of July, four months before the contest was decided.
17 F.A. Walker, *International Bimetallism* (New York: H. Holt, 1896), iv.
18 "Bryan and Silver," *San Francisco Chronicle*, August 14, 1896, 6.
19 "Talk On Silver," *Boston Daily*, October 8, 1896, 7.
20 "Reporters Retired," *Boston Daily Globe*, October 29, 1896, 5.
21 "Gen. Francis Walker Dead," *New York Times*, January 6, 1897, 9.
22 Richard Timberlake hints at the influence of the IMC by noting the similarity between the IMC's proposed legislation and the Gold Standard Act, but ultimately focuses instead on the influence of then Secretary of the Treasury Lyman J. Gage. The conservative banker from Cleveland was certainly influential, but he was hardly the focal point of monetary reform efforts. Robert Wiebe only briefly references the organization as a stop-gap failure on the way to the creation of the Federal Reserve.

Gabrielle Kolko and Murray Rothbard have each appropriately granted the IMC greater influence in their narratives, but their concluding analysis proves problematic. Both scholars read conspiracy in the motives of the men who first assembled in Indianapolis to organize in support of monetary reform. For Kolko, the success of the IMC in influence legislative action confirms the business community's "capture" of a significant regulatory apparatus. For Rothbard, the success of the IMC highlights the dangers of government intervention because, he argues, the men of the IMC successfully undermined public good for personal gain through backroom politicking and underhanded lobbying.

These conspiratorial interpretations, although well-articulated and supported with a wealth of circumstantial evidence, ignore the reality of late nineteenth century political economy. The men of the IMC did not bulldoze their populist competitors. Serious movement on monetary reform was painstakingly slow and gathered serious momentum

only after the matter was aired in the public forum through numerous debates, editorials, and a Presidential election. See Timberlake (1978, 1993); Wiebe (1962); Kolko (1977); Rothbard (2009).
23 Gage's involvement with the IMC began early on, as evidenced by Hanna's December 1896 trip to Chicago where he spoke with the then Chicago-based banker.
24 The Commission's eleven members represented ten states. The states represented were Alabama, California, Illinois, Indiana, Minnesota, Missouri, New York (2), North Carolina, Pennsylvania, and Vermont. Both Republican and Democratic sound money men were represented. Commission members were George E. Leighton, president of the regional National Sound Money League; Charles S. Fairchild, former Secretary of Treasury under President Grover Cleveland and the President of the New York Security and Trust Company; Stuyvesant Fish, a prominent railroad director; Thomas G. Bush, who held interests in the iron industry; John W. Fried, textile manufacturer; and William B. Dean, hardware supply wholesaler. Laughlin also brought along a student, H. Parker Willis, as an assistant.
25 Newspapers referred to the group as the Indianapolis Monetary *Commission* post-July 1897.
26 American Economic Association, *Economic Studies*, vol. 4 (New York: MacMillan Company, 1899), 36, 40.
27 See Mitchell (1911) for a complete list and review of the works published and reviewed by the NMC.

Bibliography

American Economic Association. *Economic Studies*. Vol. 4. New York: MacMillan Company, 1899.

Andrews, E. Benjamin. "An Honest Dollar." *Publications of the American Economic Association* 4, no. 6 (November 1889): 7–50.

——. "The Bimetallist Committee of Boston and New England." *The Quarterly Journal of Economics*, 1894, 319–27.

Bliss, H.L. *Coin's Financial Fraud*. Chicago: Donohue, Henneberry & Co., 1895.

Bornemann, Alfred. *J. Laurence Laughlin: Chapters in the Career of an Economist*. Washington: American Council on Public Affairs, 1940.

Bruner, Robert. *The Panic of 1907: Lessons Learned from the Market's Perfect Storm*. Hoboken, NJ: John Wiley & Sons, 2007.

Carey, Henry. *The Finance Minister, the Currency, and the Public Debt*. Philadelphia: Collins Printer, 1868.

Carnegie, Andrew, and John Lubbock. "The Silver Problem." *The North American Review* 157, no. 442 (September 1893): 354–78.

Chandler, Alfred Dupont. *Henry Varnum Poor, Business Editor, Analyst, and Reformer*. Ayer Publishing, 1981.

Chernow, Ron. *The House of Morgan: An American Banking Dynasty and the Rise of Modern Finance*. New York: Atlantic Monthly Press, 1990.

Clements, Kendrick. *The Presidency of Woodrow Wilson*. Lawrence, KA: University Press of Kansas, 1992.

Edmunds, George. *Report of the Monetary Commission to the Executive Committee of the Indianapolis Monetary Convention*. Washington, DC: Secretary of the Monetary Commission, 1897.

Ellis, Elmer. "The Silver Republicans in the Election of 1896." *The Mississippi Valley Historical Review* 18, no. 4 (March 1932): 519–34.

Fisher, Willard. "'Coin' and His Critics." *The Quarterly Journal of Economics* 10, no. 2 (January 1896): 187–208.
——. "Facts About Money: A Rejoinder." *The Quarterly Journal of Economics* 10, no. 4 (July 1896): 467–73.
Friedman, Milton, and Anna Schwartz. *A Monetary History of the United States, 1867–1960.* Princeton: Princeton University Press, 1963.
Galambos, Louis. *The Rise of the Corporate Commonwealth: U.S. Business and Public Policy in the Twentieth Century.* New York: Basic Books, 1988.
Girton, Lance, and Don Roper. "J. Laurence Laughlin and the Quantity Theory of Money." *Journal of Political Economy* 86, no. 4 (August 1978): 599–625.
Glad, Paul. *McKinley, Bryan, and the People.* Philadelphia: Lippincott, 1964.
Harvey, W.H. *A Tale of Two Nations.* Chicago: Coin Pub., 1894.
——. *Coin's Financial School.* Chicago: Coin Pub. Co., 1894.
Horr, Roswell. *The Great Debate on the Financial Question Between Hon. Roswell G. Horr, of New York, and William H. Harvey, of Illinois the Six Chapters of "Coin's Financial School" the Subject of the Debate.* Chicago: Debate Pub. Co., 1895.
Johnson, Joseph French. "Popular Discussions of the Money Question." *The Annals of the American Academy of Political and Social Science*, 1895, 158–62.
Kennan, C.B. "Coin Harvey's Pyramid." *The Arkansas Historical Quarterly* 6, no. 2 (1947): 132–44.
Kinley, David. *The History, Organization and Influence of the Independent Treasury of the United States.* New York: T. Y. Crowell, 1893.
Kolko, Gabriel. *The Triumph of Conservatism: a Re-interpretation of American History, 1900–1916.* New York: Free Press, 1977.
Laughlin, James L. *Facts About Money.* Chicago: E.A. Weeks, 1895.
——. "Coin's Food for the Gullible." *The Forum* 19, no. 4 (July): 573–85.
——. "Facts About Money: A Reply." *The Quarterly Journal of Economics* 10, no. 3 (April 1896): 337–40.
——. *The History of Bimetallism in the United States.* New York: D. Appleton, 1896.
Livingston, James. *Origins of the Federal Reserve System: Money, Class, and Corporate Capitalism, 1890–1913.* Ithaca, NY: Cornell University Press, 1986.
McMahon, Sean H. *Social Control & Public Intellect: The Legacy of Edward A. Ross.* New Brunswick, NJ: Transaction, 1999.
McPherson, Logan. *The Monetary and Banking Problem.* New York: D. Appleton and Co., 1896.
Mehrling, Perry. "Economists and the Fed: Beginnings." *The Journal of Economic Perspectives* 16, no. 4 (Autumn 2002): 207–18.
Mitchell, Wesley C. "The Publications of the National Monetary Commission." *The Quarterly Journal of Economics* 25, no. 3 (May 1911): 563–93.
Morrison, Rodney J. "Henry C. Carey and American Economic Development." *Transactions of the American Philosophical Society, New Series* 76, no. 3 (1986): i–ix, 1–91.
Munroe, James. *A Life of Francis Amasa Walker.* New York: H. Holt and Co., 1923.
Norton, Seymour F. *Ten Men of Money Island, or, The Primer of Finance.* Chicago: Chicago Sentinel, 1891.
Postel, Charles. *The Populist Vision.* Oxford; New York: Oxford University Press, 2007.
Powers, Le Grand. *Farmer Hayseed in Town or The Closing Days of Coin's Financial School.* St. Paul, MN: Industrial Pub. Co., 1895.
Reti, Steven. *Silver and Gold: the Political Economy of International Monetary Conferences, 1867–1892.* Westport, CT: Greenwood Press, 1998.

Rothbard, Murray. *The Origins of the Federal Reserve*. Auburn, AL: Ludwig von Mises Institute, 2009.

Sherwood, Sidney. *Tendencies in American Economic Thought*. Baltimore: Johns Hopkins Press, 1897.

Shibley, George. *The Money Question The 50% Fall in General Prices, the Evil Effects the Remedy, Bimetallism at 16 to 1 and Governmental Control of Paper Money in Order to Secure a Stable Measure of Prices–stable*. Chicago: Stable Money Pub. Co., 1896.

Simon, Matthew. "The Morgan-Belmont Syndicate of 1895 and Intervention in the Foreign-Exchange Market." *The Business History Review*, Winter 1968, 385–417.

Steeples, Douglas, and David Whitten. *Democracy in Desperation: the Depression of 1893*. Westport, CT: Greenwood Press, 1998.

Stephenson, Nathaniel. *Nelson W. Aldrich, a Leader in American Politics*. Port Washington, NY: Kennikat Press, 1971.

Taussig, F.W. "The Currency Act of 1900." *The Quarterly Journal of Economics* 14, no. 3 (May 1900): 394–415.

——. "The Silver Situation in the United States." *Publications of the American Economic Association* 7, no. 1 (January 1892): 7–118.

Taylor, F.M. "Do We Want an Elastic Currency?" *Political Science Quarterly* 11, no. 1 (March 1896): 133–57.

The Annals of America. Chicago: Encyclopædia Britannica, 1976.

"The Twelfth Annual Meeting." *Publications of the American Economic Association, 3rd Series* 1, no. 1 (February 1900): 37–43.

Timberlake, Richard. *Monetary Policy in the United States: An Intellectual and Institutional History*. Chicago: University of Chicago Press, 1993.

——. *The Origins of Central Banking in the United States*. Cambridge, MA: Harvard University Press, 1978.

Trescott, Paul B. "Western Economic Advisers in China, 1900–1949." In *Research in the History of Economic Thought and Methodology*, edited by Jeff Biddle, Ross Emmett, and Warren J. Samuels. Bingley: Emerald JAI, 2009.

Walker, Francis A. "The Free Coinage of Silver." *The Journal of Political Economy* 1, no. 2 (March 1893): 163–78.

——. "The Value of Money." *Publications of the American Economic Association* 9, no. 1 (January 1894): 47–56.

——. "The Quantity-theory of Money." *The Quarterly Journal of Economics* 9, no. 4 (July 1895): 372–79.

——. *International Bimetallism*. New York: H. Holt, 1896.

Warburg, Paul. *The Federal Reserve System Its Origin and Growth*. Vol. I. New York: Macmillan, 1930.

Wells, Donald. *The Federal Reserve System : a History*. Jefferson, NC: McFarland & Co., 2004.

Wiebe, Robert. *Businessmen and Reform : A Study of the Progressive Movement*. Cambridge, MA: Harvard University Press, 1962.

3 On firm ground

The drawn-out battle over monetary reform demonstrated that the future of applied economics was uncertain, but the growth of the discipline was not. The complexities of a modern industrial economy and its consequent social issues continued to drive thinkers toward economics. The American Economic Association's loose membership requirements and recruitment drives continued to build institutional support, while universities across the country added or expanded economics departments (still called departments of political economy at many schools). In 1890, there were 20 chairs in economics. By 1900, the number grew to 51, as each new economics faculty member spawned additional economics majors and graduate students. Doctoral candidates alone numbered 94 by 1905 and rose to 151 just five years later.[1] The abandonment of "branch associations" of the AEA in 1894 resulted in a temporary dip in membership, but the subsequent direct communication with those who opted to join the main association proved worthwhile. AEA membership correspondingly grew from 706 to 2,301 from 1900 to 1920 and the ratio of economists per 100,000 Americans grew from 0.93 to 2.2.[2]

These two decades of substantial disciplinary growth and professionalization did little to resolve debates over methodology and application, however. Academic freedom, one source of the discipline's success in professionalizing, was also a source of continued turmoil. The AEA's commitment to academic freedom, albeit a selective and fragile freedom, made methodological and ideological consensus impossible. This was, of course, the case with most disciplines that professionalized, but would lead to a particularly acute credibility problem in economics. The rift between the "new economists" and the "old orthodoxy" continued, albeit in modified terms. The ideas of the old orthodoxy, especially their appreciation of classical theory and a general preference for unrestrained markets, lived on through the students and admirers of classical economists who had begun to update their theories in the face of criticism. The discipline's continued efforts to bridge theory and practice made clear the Herculean nature of the goals America's early professional economists had set for themselves, though enthusiasm remained high as the AEA marked its twenty-fifth anniversary.

Growth and expansion

With its existence secured, the AEA sought to shed its northeastern bias and develop geographic diversity. Annual meetings from the early 1900s onward reflected as much, as the Association increasingly drew members from outside the northeast corridor. This expansion was viewed as necessary if the AEA's claim as the nation's preeminent economics organization was to hold. As then-Secretary T.N. Carver noted in a 1909 letter soliciting membership over the more regional American Academy of Political and Social Sciences: "Our organization [AEA] is, as I have stated, first, the older organization, and second, it is a more strictly national organization."[3] Regional economics associations continued to meet – and indeed continue to do so to this day – but care was taken to avoid the geographic fragmentation that might undermine professional cohesion.

The growth of the AEA was accompanied by the increased employment of professional economists, which in turn led to increased institutional support for the discipline through membership dues and a larger audience for economics publications. Moving forward, economists turned toward discipline-specific publications, as opposed to general periodicals such as the *Yale Review* or the *North American Review*.[4] The number of institutions that subscribed to the AEA's monograph and periodical series expanded from 116 to 426 within the generation that spanned from 1900 to 1920. Changes in the composition of subscribing institutions reflect specialization, as the application of economic science further widened the gap that had already emerged between folk and professional economists in the late nineteenth century. The number of schools that subscribed to the AEA's publications, overwhelmingly colleges and universities, remained steady at 45 percent of subscribing institutions, while the percentage of public libraries dropped from 39 to 26 percent. The decline as a percentage was made up by public offices, such as state and federal research divisions, as well as private business, that accounted for 13 and 10 percent of total subscriptions in 1900 and 1919, respectively.[5]

A larger subscription base enabled scholarly publications to flourish – a crucial requisite for professionalization because economics-specific publications allowed for a more consistent and in-depth discussion of economists' theories. The Harvard-housed *Quarterly Journal of Economics* (*QJE*), which had begun publishing in 1886, continued to publish quarterly but ran an average of 21.5 articles per year from 1900 to 1919, up from the average of 16.2 articles per year in its first 14 years of existence.[6] The University of Chicago-housed *Journal of Political Economy (JPE)* proved more aggressive. From its founding in 1892 to 1906, the *JPE* published on a quarterly basis – each issue typically containing four academic articles, four sets of notes, and 10 book reviews. In 1906, the *JPE* moved to a monthly publication schedule (barring a two-month break in August and September). The amount of material per issue fluctuated, but output increased from an average of 17.4 to 33.2 articles per year following the shift to monthly publication.[7] The earliest figures available place circulation of the *JPE* at 700 in 1905.

The two university-run journals were eventually joined by what has since been the AEA's flagship journal, *The American Economic Review (AER)*.[8] The *AER* was the culmination of a decade-long effort to establish an American economics journal on par with that of the British Economic Association's *The Economic Journal* and the American Historical Association's *American Historical Magazine*. Despite the success of the *QJE* and *JPE*, a 1902 AEA report on the desirability of establishing a quarterly journal lamented the absence of an "accredited, representative serial in which the best and only the best economic thought – lay and academic – of the country as a whole may find expression."[9] The *AER* would differ from the previously established American economic journals in that it relied exclusively on the efforts and support of an organization, rather than on a university department. The assumption was that a journal backed by a professional organization would be less subject to outside interference than a journal managed by an academic department that reported to university officials and board members. It was an important distinction for a discipline concerned with intellectual neutrality.

Proponents of an AEA quarterly journal expressed equal concern over the ideological content of the journal, with unanimous agreement that any reputable publication ought not favor one school of thought over the other. Neither the *QJE* nor the *JPE* contained an overt political message, yet suspicions lingered owing to the journals' status as "private" publications, and economists were careful about where they pledged their allegiances.[10] Both journals published articles written by a diverse array of economists who supported competing ideologies and methodologies, yet this did not preclude the journals' reputations for being less than completely objective.

The report's two additional conclusions – that an explosion in the number of academic quarterlies threatened to dilute the discipline and that a representative journal would boost the discipline's image in Washington, suggests that the AEA's executive membership continued to envision an expanded role for economists in the policymaking process. Correspondence between Jacob Hollander (the report's author) and AEA members expressed enthusiasm for a scientific journal backed by a representative professional organization, although proponents were careful to note that it must strike an appropriate balance between economic theory and practical economic affairs to maximize the discipline's influence. No one noted the inherent difficulties in maintaining professional neutrality while influencing economic policy, nor did anyone suggest that a journal full of conflicting viewpoints would undoubtedly frustrate policymakers searching for clear and concise advice.

Financial and logistical considerations forced the AEA to put its publishing ambitions on hold until 1908, when the short-lived *Economic Bulletin* debuted. The *Bulletin* – a quarterly periodical featuring miscellaneous notes and reviews – was published alongside the *American Economic Association Quarterly* – a continuation of the monograph series that had run since 1886. The two quarterlies eventually merged in 1911 to form the highly successful *American Economic Review (AER)*. Hopes that the presence of a reputable, non-department-controlled journal might encourage the *QJE* and *JPE* to either cease publication outright or merge with the *AER* persisted through 1911, but proved unfounded. Together, these three journals formed a solid foundation on which economists could continue to build professional economics in the United States. They served as an outlet for new research and a reference base for scholars. The article format quickly challenged pamphlets and books as the preferred publication method for cutting-edge research in the early twentieth century. They also began to reflect the growing complexity and the development of ideas specific to economics.

The combination of increased institutional support and intellectual specialization allowed economists to gradually drift away from related disciplines. When asked to reflect on the discipline's development, one unnamed observer noted the departure of political scientists and sociologists in the opening years of the twentieth century.[11] The terrain between economists and their colleagues in related disciplines had certainly shifted since W.W. Folwell had argued that economics was a sub-discipline of sociology in 1889. By 1908, AEA Secretary Winthrop M. Daniels could confidently reject overtures for a joint meeting from both the American Sociological Association and the Association for the Advancement for Social Sciences, declaring "My notion is that the American Economic Association is the 'dog' and the others are another part of the canine anatomy; and I favor the orthodox initiative in the process of wagging."[12] Evidence of continued support for the interdisciplinary approach that helped economics flourish in its infancy suggests that the discipline's reputation for academic insularity was still some decades in the future, however. Famed sociologist Herbert Spencer remained a relevant figure in American economics. Furthermore, the AEA did still hold joint meetings with the ASA since such arrangements did have their logistical advantages.

Tellingly, the greatest opportunity for collaboration between the two disciplines largely came to naught. The late nineteenth and early twentieth century witnessed an explosion in research dedicated to identifying and characterizing different races. Not coincidentally, this explosion in research was accompanied by a wave of immigration as workers from predominantly Europe and Asia rushed to the US in search of economic opportunity. The study of eugenics was largely conducted by sociologists and biologists, though there were notable exceptions. Wisconsin's noted labor economist John R. Commons published a book on the subject in 1907 (although he dropped the issue thereafter and ignored it in his autobiography) and Irving Fisher, who never discussed eugenics in his academic research, but lent support to those who did.

Workers' aptitude and behavior could be easily linked to questions of economic efficiency. The eugenics movement was intimately intertwined with political and social issues, however. By evoking expertise and declaring a position on the validity of eugenics an economist risked impugning his or her credibility, and in doing so, the credibility of the discipline.

Unsurprisingly, questions regarding the relevancy of eugenics weighed on some within the professional economics community, including James A. Field, then at the University of Chicago. Field captured the ambiguity of the issue in a letter to then AEA Secretary Thomas Carver when he commented on a proposed symposium on immigration, stating "That 'Race or Mongrel?' book seemed to me, when I had occasion briefly to review it last year, to be extraordinary nonsense or fanaticism, but I confess that nobody knows what is the truth in such matters."[13] Carver concurred with Field's apprehension, but encouraged careful review of the book in question on the grounds that there was a "good deal of confusion and a great many conflicting opinions on this question [eugenics], and there are doubtless some people who think that such a book as 'Race or Mongrel?' has some scientific basis."[14] Although repulsed by the blatant racism of *Race or*

Mongrel?, Field could not deny its potential significance. Economics in the US may not have been as intertwined with sociology as it was just 15 years earlier, but economists continued to pay attention to developments in the sister-discipline that might influence the course of economic thought.

Field ultimately opted not to review *Race or Mongrel?* but did write a lengthy review of eugenics scholarship that was published in the November, 1911 issue of the *Quarterly Journal of Economics*. Focusing primarily on the history of eugenics research in England and the US, Field's review largely described the work of biologists and eugenics societies that had conducted the initial forays into eugenics research. That man could determine hereditary characteristics was amply proven. The question moving forward, Field concluded, was what to do with the information. Who could determine the most efficient, rational combinations of hereditary characteristics? Enlisting the economist, Field argued, was the next step in translating the benefits of eugenics research to US society, though that next step never quite materialized.

Perhaps owing to its "home" in a different discipline, or its tendency to attract controversy, the study of eugenics in particular failed to attract a dedicated following in professional economics. It was a stroke of luck, as the AEA's insistence on distinguishing itself from sociology and an insistence on institutional neutrality ensured that controversial subjects failed to sink deeper roots within American economic thought. The leading American economics journals reviewed books on eugenics and some economists published on the subject, but with little fanfare, though William Z. Ripley's *The Races of Europe* stands as a stark exception to that general rule. Numerous prominent economists did, to be clear, express interest in the sort of social engineering eugenics promised to make possible. But in keeping with the disciplinary culture then being formed, professional economists were left to promote their viewpoints as individuals and surprisingly few spent enough time on either issue to consider it central to their intellectual legacy (save the aforementioned Fisher and Ripley). In short, the US's professional economics community was largely content with allowing their sociologist colleagues to pursue the controversial subject.

In addition to growing their role within academia, economists also began to explore new roles in both government agencies and private businesses. An increase in the number of public institutions that subscribed to the *American Economic Review*, from four to 55 in the first two decades of the twentieth century, reflected the change. Economists' skill sets made them indispensible to the functions of a growing bureaucratic state, which required personnel capable of translating data into intelligible analysis. The range of American economists' activities in the public sector before World War II suggests they were every bit as active and influential as their post-war counterparts. Economists applied their training in virtually every department of the federal government. The AEA had first recommended advisors to the Census Bureau in the late 1880s and continued to do so for the 1900 and 1910 surveys (although declined to take on official responsibilities as an organization). Johns Hopkins-trained Charles Neill took control of the Bureau of Labor under Theodore Roosevelt following his success as a labor arbitrator and continued as Commissioner through the Taft years. A number of university-trained economists also found work in America's recently acquired territories. Emory Johnson, a former student of Ely's at Hopkins, served on the Isthmian Canal Commission from 1899 to 1904. Jacob Hollander served as a government agent in the Dominican Republic, where his role in the sale of Dominican Republic bonds through New York firm Kuhn & Loeb in 1906 led to a hefty commission and a public reprimand from the Pujo Commission five years later. Princeton's Edwin Kemmerer, a monetary expert known as the "money doctor," served on the Philippines Commission and later traveled throughout Europe dispensing advice on monetary policy to foreign governments. The bulk of economists' influence derived from outside the policymaking process, but they increasingly parlayed their expertise into more direct roles in the process.

The role of economists in the private sector remains much more opaque. But evidence suggests that private businesses were quicker to realize the skill set of professionally trained economists than previously assumed. W.E. Hotchkiss of Northwestern University noted, with some surprise, the enthusiasm of his businessmen-students for theory as a potential guiding rod in their day jobs. In addition to plumbing the discipline for insights that might help their careers, businessmen also employed professional economists. Insurance companies were a natural fit for those trained in both statistical methods and inductive logic. Private bureaus and research organizations that had cropped up in an attempt to cater to businesses that sought every advantage in the competitive American market similarly utilized professional economists. Businesses like the Brookmire Economic Chart Company sought to harness the tremendous growth in statistical knowledge and economic theory to help produce reliable economic forecasts on which businesses could make decisions. Founder and promoter James H. Brookmire embodied the optimism of those who believed in the power of economic analysis to uncover the mysteries of business, as reflected by his 1913 *AER* article on economic forecasting. Publishing in a reputable journal imbued the author with notable authority, Brookmire noted in a letter to *AER* editor David Dewey, and verification of expertise was valuable in the competitive forecasting business.[15]

Early twentieth century AEA conferences continued to attract a mixture of academic, private sector, and public sector participants. The twenty-fifth anniversary meeting, held in 1909, featured a panel on "The Valuation of Public Service Corporations" that drew Henry C. Adams, then with the Interstate Commerce Commission, Frederick W. Whitridge, President of the Third Avenue Railway Company, corporate lawyer Joseph P. Cotton, and E.B. Whitney of the New York Supreme Court. The conference would have featured Andrew Carnegie had the 74-year-old industrialist not slipped and fallen in the same storm that delayed the presence of President Taft.[16] In these and other ways, professional economics in the US, although defined by the work of college and university faculty members, had become significantly engaged with government and the private sector.

The methodological struggle

The vigorous growth of the profession obscured an equally vigorous struggle over theory and ideology. In terms of professionalization, the first two decades of the twentieth century were a clear and unmitigated success, but the path of methodological and ideological development was far less clear. Professional economists, primarily those who served in leadership positions within the AEA, could work to promote the growth of departments, ensure the success of publications, and secure employment so that economists could make use of their training. But by design, those presiding at the top of the profession's most influential organization were still limited in their ability to codify American economics. Continued emphasis on academic freedom and intellectual neutrality negated any attempts to force consensus within American economics. The task of "winning" over intellectual rivals was left to those who published, lectured, and debated, and as the twenty-fifth anniversary of the AEA came and went, it was clear that fundamental disagreements persisted.

In 1898, well-respected Columbia University economist John Bates Clark contemplated the future of economic theory in an article published in the *QJE*. His observations revolved around the struggle to account for what he referred to as "dynamic forces," by which he meant the unpredictable variables that plagued economic theorists. Since debates over the "static" issues of economics had run their course, Clark argued, what remained for professional economics was to reconcile the laws of economics with on-the-ground conditions. Clark's projection into the future reflected both keen foresight and hope-induced short-sightedness. On the one hand, he accurately identified what has long been the bane of the professional economist – the fact that real-world conditions rarely reflect abstract modeling or long-run predictions. On the other hand, Clark overreached in his rush to confront the future. Far from being resolved, the debate over "static" economic theory was as active as it had ever been. Clark and many other economists were ready to declare victory in the debates that had characterized American economics in the 1880s and 1890s, although none of the participants in those debates had conceded defeat. It was soon clear that the ideas of the classical economists, presumably shed in the late nineteenth century, were in fact as relevant as ever.

The two issues that had sparked renewed vigor in American economic thought – deductive versus inductive reasoning and the relationship between economics and policy reform – were never resolved. The debate over the soul and purpose of economics therefore continued, albeit in a modified dialect. On the one side, classicists adopted marginal theory utility in an effort to keep rational economic man center stage. They still assumed a rational economic man, along with market efficiency and a preference for limited state intervention. On the other side, the reform-minded new economists remained fixed on institutional development, but struggled to translate a wealth of evidence into the kind of theoretical order that had served classical economists so well over the previous 100 years. The debate held significance beyond lecture halls and academic journals as the failure to resolve fundamental differences left professional economics vulnerable to criticism that the discipline was hopelessly inconsistent and irrelevant. Moving forward from the debates that characterized the founding of professional economics in the US, it was still debatable what constituted modern economic theory, as well as what role economics would play in American society.

There were some signs that consensus was possible. The AEA's survival eventually attracted the most notable conservative hold-out, J. Laurence Laughlin, who had overseen the growth of a respected economics department at the University of Chicago in addition to crusading against "soft" money. Laughlin was never at risk of being "cut out" of professional economics had he continued to eschew active membership.[17] In fact, the considerable influence he wielded despite his lack of AEA membership concerned the organization's leaders because they worried he might use his professional clout and the resources of the Chicago Department of Economics to discredit their efforts. Such fears seem unfounded, given subsequent accounts of Laughlin's commitment to academic freedom, but it is clear that despite their proclamations of victory the new economists feared what they would characterize as a "back-slide" in American economic thought.

But Laughlin's membership did not reflect a significant change in thinking. He still regretted the reformist impulses that drove the economic theory of his intellectual rivals, a phenomenon he characterized as "the heart leading the head."[18] As a result, his commitment to *laissez-faire* classical economics at times acted as a wedge between himself and others. At the same time, his validation of the AEA's goals might have indicated his willingness to move toward a less divided American economics. Laughlin's participation closed one of the glaring gaps in the US's professional economics network, though his interaction with the AEA remained awkward and limited (as evidenced by soon-to-be AEA president Davis R. Dewey's reluctance to solicit his participation at the 1908 conference).

There were several ironies in the conflict between the conservative stalwarts and their more liberal peers. First, Laughlin's criticism of the new economists' evangelicizing was matched by his equally zealous commitment to promote what he described as a true, scientific form of political economy. The public's perception of political economy in the US was an on-going concern of Laughlin's and he sought to ensure that the public received the proper version – his. It was a case of the pot calling the kettle black, as neither the reformist new economics nor the *laissez-faire* Classical School could credibly lay claim to a completely neutral understanding of the world in which they worked.

Equally ironic was that the conservative old guard in American economics had lost the battle over the goals of economic science the minute they began to argue with their pro-reform colleagues. Engaging with their reform-minded colleagues lent credibility to a series of debates from which new economists drew authority. The classicists had little choice – it was, after all, the tenor of the times that pushed them first into the professionalization process, followed shortly thereafter by a concerted search for economic policy reform. Yet engaging in debates over municipalization, labor legislation, protective tariffs, and similar interventionist policies meant that the conservative *laissez-faire* economists implicitly acknowledged their intellectual rivals' claims to expertise and ensured a place for the reformist impulse within modern American economic thought.

The twenty-fifth anniversary meeting of the AEA in 1909 underscored this civil contentiousness in American economics. The AEA's executive committee took pains to celebrate the progress of American economics by (in part) inviting prominent European economists, influential government figures, and sponsoring a retrospective panel. The event was, in fact, a time for celebration, as the discipline had grown tremendously in the US since industrial growth and European ideas had sparked a revival in American economic thought. Nevertheless, indications that American economics had failed to live up to the lofty ambitions of the "young rebels" who had founded the AEA could not be ignored.

Invitations were extended to economists from each of the major European nations with which the Americans felt an intellectual affinity – Austria, England, France, Germany, Italy, and Holland. Funds were still scarce despite the organization's substantial growth and stability, and invitations were limited to one per nation with an honorarium of $500 per attendee. AEA emissaries were dispatched the summer preceding the conference with a list of potential attendees, ranked by the AEA executive committee in the order of desirability.[19] An aversion to winter travel and reluctance to leave their homes during the Christmas season led all the leading foreign invitees to decline. James Bonar, Maffeo Pantaleoni, and Henry Higgs did present at the conference and a reception for foreign guests suggests there were additional foreign attendees, albeit none of the prominent intellectuals ranked by the executive committee.[20] French economists, curiously, had remained detached from the intellectual camps of American professional economics. That nation lacked an organizational equivalent to the AEA or the Royal Economic Society, and Walter Willcox, the emissary dispatched to ensure the attendance of a prominent French economist, struggled to fulfill his duties before giving up.[21]

Digging deeper into the executive committee's rankings reveals that the intellectual terrain remained largely unchanged since the intensified importation of European economic thought in the 1880s. The German Historical School, despite its advocates' declarations of triumph over the old orthodoxy, certainly did not dominate the list of invitees. Invitations were extended to notable Historical School scholars Lujo Brentano and Gustav von Schmoller, but the "England" list was similarly topped by classicists Alfred Marshall and William Smart. The Austrian School also received its due, with invitations extended to Eugen von Bohm-Bawerk and Frank Philippovich. True to form, the AEA remained committed to an inclusive vision that included space for scholars and scholarship of all types. A rough balance was maintained in order to avoid the sort of academic disenfranchisement the organization so heartily protested.

Ely's commentary on the first 25 years of the AEA, the highlight of the conference's anniversary panel, offered little more than the by-then stale observation that the new economics of the historical school had shaken the discipline in the late nineteenth century. Arthur Hadley followed with a speech suggesting that the new economists had in fact gone too far, saying: "The old orthodoxy is gone – too much gone, some of us think, who, after helping to break down the fences, are a little astonished by the havoc made by the cattle that have come in through the openings."[22]

Such sentiments, along with the mixed nature of conference participants, makes clear that that declarations of professional harmony often overreached. The tension within professional economics, characterized by Frank Fetter as having manifested through the growth of "two wings," was quite noticeable to all but the most casual observer.[23] The mediation of such dissension led to practical concerns, such as the handling of the book reviews in peer-reviewed journals. As University of Missouri economist H.J. Davenport noted to Fetter in a fit of frustration, reviews often depended on the intellectual dispositions of the reviewer and the reviewed.[24] If in ideological agreement, the reviewer praised the work. If ideologically opposed, the reviewer rendered a negative judgment. "Reviewing of this sort," Davenport declared, "degenerates into the sheer puffery and jockeying appropriate to the level of publishers [sic] announcements."

Editors of the *American Economic Review*, sensitive to the fact that competing schools of thought would thus influence the review of scholarship, established a review process designed to mitigate the effects of ideological or personal bias. A "book," reviewers were advised, "should be appraised from the point of view of the school of thought to which the author belongs."[25] The AEA's leadership could only go so far and they still allowed that the review guidelines could not "prevent an appraisal of its [the reviewed material's] value judged by what the reviewer considers to be the cannons of universal truth."[26] Subsequent disputes over the undue criticism and harshness of particular reviews underscore the tension within the community.

Disagreement was perhaps sharpest in the significant debate over the development of marginal utility theory. In fact, the debate over the relevancy of marginal utility theory may be one of the most significant methodological debates in the twentieth century considering its eventual success and primacy in Western economic thought. While the reform-minded new economists of the late nineteenth century celebrated what they perceived as a victory over the musty theory of the old orthodoxy, they ultimately failed to translate their success into a coherent methodology capable of taking root as the dominant intellectual paradigm in American professional economics. Meanwhile, their more conservative rivals continued to adjust classical economic theory. The source of marginalist theory and the speed with which it spread through Western economics remains a matter of debate, but it clearly reached the US by the late nineteenth century. Marginalism's acceptance by prominent economists like John Bates Clark, Frank Fetter, Frank Taussig, Simon Newcomb, and Clark's son, John Maurice Clark, ensured that the theory took root.[27] The marginalist theory of value, which states that prices vary based on changes in the perceived utility of a product, proved useful to those uncomfortable with the German Historical School's emphasis on historical contingency. The theory allowed for the preservation of assumptions about a rational economic man, while at the same time better explaining changes in economic activity. Marginalism could address the demand for a more inductive methodology by using data to verify the veracity of economic laws determined through deductive reasoning. Thus, neoclassical economics was born through evolution, as opposed to the revolution of the new economics, and effectively maintained the philosophical roots of classical economic theory in the US.

Although they by no means considered themselves so, those who advocated neoclassical economics represented a resurgence of the old orthodoxy that the new economists had sought to slay with the formation of the AEA. Opponents of the "old" way of thinking in economics were well aware of the continuities and voiced their criticisms, which recognized marginalism's ability to show how prices were determined, but also its inability to explain how social conditions ultimately created the conditions that determined value. Marginalism contained insufficient predictive powers and little recognition of the strides made in psychology and sociology, critics of neoclassical economics argued. Yet it offered a coherent methodology in the sense that its underlying assumptions about man as a rational pleasure-seeking creature eliminated the need to endlessly categorize and qualify conclusions. Marginalism similarly narrowed the practitioner's focus to market-place transactions – a convenient limitation in a discipline that continued to define itself as distinct from other social sciences.

The problem with the "new economics"

While neoclassicists attempted to rein-in economic theory, the new economists continued to embrace a growing catalog of considerations that complicated heterodox methodology. The intellectual struggles of Robert Hoxie stand as a case-in-point. Hoxie, a dedicated new economist, spent the bulk of his career at the University of Chicago, where he proudly drew from a host of theories to support his arguments about the merits of trade unionism. Institutionalist Walton H. Hamilton's obituary of Hoxie described a complex intellectual development that defied simple categorization. Hoxie was, in turn, influenced by the classicism of Laughlin, the American Psychological School of Frank Fetter, and the Institutional School of Thorstein Veblen. Like many of his reform-minded colleagues, Hoxie viewed the social upheaval of the second industrial revolution as evidence of the old orthodoxy's insufficiency. The rational man of the old orthodoxy and the equilibrium sought by neoclassical marginalism meant little to Hoxie given the rapid and unpredictable manner in which society changed at the turn of the century. Understanding economic life, according to Hoxie, required a more accurate understanding of elusive and ever-changing human nature. Hamilton concluded that Hoxie ultimately failed in his quest and was never able to "add an elaborate piece of work to the literature of economics" because of his unfortunate tendency toward perfection.[28] It is equally plausible, although less polite, to argue that Hoxie failed to significantly influence American economic theory because he eschewed a coherent theoretical framework in favor of a flexible but vague ideology that paradoxically revered economics as a reliable science and human behavior as wholly unreliable.

A brief summary of Hoxie's career does not, of course, serve as an adequate stand-in for the entire body of American heterodox economics – a blanket term used to describe non-neoclassical economics in the twentieth century. But it does illustrate the degree to which the new economists struggled to replace the old orthodoxy's intellectual foundations. Economic historian Geoffrey Hodgson, in his history of the American institutionalism, notes how the failure of the movement's oft-cited leading thinkers Veblen, Commons, and Mitchell failed to produce a "systematic treatise" on institutionalist theory. He also cites the demand for mathematical economics during World War II, the post-war influx of European economists fleeing totalitarian regimes, the chilling effects of McCarthyism, the Great Depression, and the rejection of Darwinian ideas in the social sciences as sources of institutionalism's demise. All of these factors certainly played a role in the decline of institutional economics, but the failure to deliver a "systematic treatise" strongly suggests that American heterodox economists were working on borrowed time. The lack of a clear unifying theory around which the American heterodox new economists could rally was evident by the end of World War I. Those opposed to the deductive simplicity of neoclassical economics agreed that empirical data, human psychology, the development of institutions, and sociology were crucial to a complete understanding of economic behavior. How the many facets of the new economics interacted was subject to individual interpretation, however. It was a far messier approach to economics that was difficult to package and disseminate to students, policymakers, and the general public.

American professional economists in the early twentieth century agreed that a new era had dawned, but the nature and direction of economics remained unclear. Modern economics, despite J.M. Clark's optimistic claims, was not to be wholly defined by the economists' newly found "sense of solidarity and social-mindedness."[29] Not all economists were willing to abandon the rational individualism of the nineteenth century, which far from being radical was in fact considered self-evident by a significant number of American economists – both professional and amateur. The heterodox economists continued to cite their German-inspired methodology and theoretical shortcoming of classical economic thought as justification for leadership within American economics, but their continued disharmony gradually undercut their mandate. To suggest that the heterodox economics in the US lacked vitality would be misleading. The reform-driven heterodox economists enjoyed such strong representation within American economics in the first half of the twentieth century that the term "heterodox" may in fact be an anachronism of sorts. Even so, a failure to translate this success into a consistent and reliable intellectual paradigm ultimately undercut the vitality of their movement. The failure of heterodox economics to unseat the old orthodoxy was as much the result of what the reformers did wrong as it was a case of what conservative economic thinkers did right.

This problem of increasingly complex theories and methodology within heterodox economics was compounded by the loss of connection with religious sensibilities and communities that had played a role in the early success of the new economics. Several important new economists in the first generation of professional economics had moved in religious reform circles. Richard T. Ely had utilized both economic and religious justifications in his fight for labor reform in the late nineteenth century and routinely called on religious leaders to support his reform efforts. Labor economist John R. Commons, one of Ely's most successful recruits at the University of Wisconsin, was less engaged with the religious community but had considered himself a Christian socialist during his early career. Reform drove early heterodox economists, and to some degree religious beliefs justified reform efforts and the spirit of the new economics. As the discipline grew, whatever remained of the religious influence in professional economics faded. Concerns about academic integrity trumped the early moralist impulses that had attracted clergy to professional economics in the late nineteenth century. In 1900, AEA membership included 23 clergymen. By 1919, clergy had disappeared entirely from the membership rolls. Religion supplied little in way of methodology but provided economists on a mission to reform American society with an immeasurable degree of moral authority. As economist Bradley W. Bateman notes, reform-minded economists did continue to interact with the Social Gospel movement up to the 1920s, particularly in regards to conducting social surveys. Still, heterodox economics gradually shed the overt religious impulses of the late nineteenth century. Doing so undoubtedly helped new economists' image as objective and rational thinkers, but at the expense of powerful moral justification.

The void left by stripping heterodox economics of its ideological justifications begged filling. Marxism, or at least broad criticism of American capitalism, clearly motivated some new economists in the early twentieth century. The cultural resistance to European radicalism discussed in the first chapter persisted, however. The professional economics community remained committed to academic freedom and openly discussed the issue, but professional economists were ultimately subject to the whims of administrators and politicians. Commons, like Ely more than a decade earlier, was investigated following allegations that he taught subversive ideas. Additionally, whether through public pressure or careful consideration of their viewpoints (the latter being more likely), several influential scholars drew back their criticism of American capitalism and deprived the Marx-inspired heterodox economists of some key allies. Ely, it was remarked, "softened" in his old age and no longer suggested as forcefully as he once had that the American economic system needed an overhaul. John Bates Clark, perhaps the most influential American economist at the turn of the twentieth century, abandoned his early flirtations with anti-capitalist thought, wholly embraced American capitalism, and became a leading neoclassical economist. Those who persisted with radical critiques of American capitalism or revolutionary economic reform proposals risked the withdrawal of the institutional support necessary to not only carry out their own work, but also to support graduate students who could in turn build upon the work of their heterodox advisor.

Individual personalities may also have played a role in the limited endurance of the heterodoxy. Veblen, one of the brighter critics of American capitalism, was notoriously eccentric and difficult to converse with, and Hoxie similarly had difficulties working with graduate students from chronic medical issues. Shyness, historian Leon Fink has suggested, may have limited labor economist Selig Perlman's ability to expand his intellectual legacy.

The failure to confront subjective issues within the discipline compounded the dilemma presented by ideological drift. Perhaps the more foreboding tendency for the new economics was its symbiosis with powerful, but temporary social movements. A commitment to objective, scientific research continued to be the standard that held the professional economics community together, yet the professional economist was continually compelled to make subjective judgments – such as what constituted "fair," what was an acceptable balance between private property and government intervention, and the proper balance between individual and collective responsibility. Classical-turned-neoclassical economists had resolved the fairness issue by emphasizing the primacies of personal responsibility and private property in their deductive reasoning. Fair, according to the *laissez-faire* orthodoxy, was a relatively free market in which workers were rewarded according to their ingenuity and effort. This is not to say the orthodoxy did not consider issues of income inequality or misdistribution of capital. However, such investigations were often conducted from the viewpoint that the solution lay in improving productivity rather than engineering social equality.

The new economists had derived a significant portion of their momentum from the sudden, but ultimately temporary, social dislocations of the late nineteenth century. Laughlin, the ever-present champion of the capitalist orthodoxy, noted the effects of mass immigration and the growing inequality of wealth in a 1916 defense of capitalism that ran in *The North American Review*. Laughlin explicitly targeted socialism – in particular the oft-cited observation that capitalism produced two classes of people (employers and employees) as evidence of the desirability of a new economic order. Falling back on a time-tested argument, Laughlin appealed to the primacy of the individual and offered a hypothetical example involving a young man, early marriage, and a brood of hungry children. Compelled to feed his lot but lacking marketable skills, Laughlin concluded, the unwise individual decries the American economic system.

Laughlin's example – simplistic and rife of nativist undertones – nevertheless touched on an important dynamic. As long as the American economic system continued to attract unskilled labor, produced significant income inequality, and generated poor working conditions, economists who studied social conditions in order to produce recommendations for social reform would find a ready audience. The new economics was born in an era of historical social upheaval and inequality. Its origins and success was inextricably linked with the type of social discontent Laughlin lamented in his article in *The North American Review*. The elimination of social conditions that had led to rise of heterodox new economics in the US would prove a tough test for those economists who envisioned a more influential profession that would be directly relevant to the policymaking process.

The growing gap

Inconsistencies and disputes aside, professional economics in the US continued to expand through the first decades of the twentieth century. College-level textbooks were increasingly common – so much so that Irving Fisher referred to the production of such as the "inevitable fate of the economist."[30] Laughlin applauded the emergence of useful teaching tools, but also questioned the necessity of so many economists laying down their basic economic philosophies. His reservations hinted at the increasing difficulty of ensuring a consistency in economic instruction in the US that would allow for an open and productive discussion of basic economic principles. In undergraduate education, American economists struggled to achieve the proper balance between the teaching of theoretical economics, which required deep thinking and held the promise of breakthrough, and hard economic facts, the basics necessary to comprehend the mechanics of commerce.

The AEA, aware of the problem, organized a panel on the teaching of elementary economics for the 1908 annual meeting. The response was overwhelming, and what began as a panel grew into a conference hosted by the University of Chicago and a subsequent special volume of the *Journal of Political Economy* in December 1909 that featured three papers and additional commentary from 29 economists with teaching experience.[31] Despite enthusiasm for the topic, neither the conference nor the corresponding journal articles yielded significant results. The problems were easy to agree on – students entered college with too little background knowledge and left having spent too little time studying economics. Solutions were not as obvious. While some rejected the notion that economic theory and "concrete economic facts," as A.B. Wolfe put it, could be separated, a subtle consensus in favor of parsing of the two subjects emerged with the reasoning that theory was best reserved for more mature minds in the advanced courses that attracted future economists. Conference participants said nothing of primary school instruction, nor did the AEA undertake any major campaigns to transmit advances in American economic thought to primary school students.

The limited diffusion of economics was by no means an indicator of explicit exclusionist attitudes. Businessmen, government officials, and reform movement leaders continued to present at annual meetings. The discipline's commitment to attracting the interest and participation of experts in whichever industry they studied dove-tailed with the goal of academic freedom and thorough inquiry. In matters deemed relevant, the discipline was entirely receptive of amateur participation. Nevertheless, the combination of increased specialization and limits on how quickly and efficiently professional economists could spread economic science continued to widen the gap between expert and amateur. The need to further cultivate the discipline's prestige provided professional economists an incentive to ignore the growing gap between amateur and expert.

Such necessity helps explain in part the continued exclusion of female economists. Much like the other professions that coalesced in the late nineteenth century, the professional economics community preserved gender barriers and defined the professional economist as male. Minimizing women's roles in the discipline preserved Victorian notions of propriety and helped build the exclusivity necessary to distinguish between professional and amateur. The AEA continued to admit women, regardless of the personal opinions of some members, but although the number of female members grew in proportion with total membership it still remained low (by 1910, the AEA had grown to 1,205 members, fewer than 100 of whom were women).[32]

Women were instead to be served by home economics, which had emerged as the natural alternative to economics of a more masculine variety. The topics studied and discussed by the two disciplines were quite obviously different in a myriad of ways, and the founders of the American Home Economics Association were well-aware that "economics" was an awkward descriptor. The term was chosen at the organization's inaugural retreat in 1899 because it "most clearly positioned the home in relation to the larger polity," but the subsequent appointment of a naming committee indicates a lack of satisfaction with the term.[33] The difficulty in naming the new discipline reflected the difficulty in explaining what exactly its practitioners hoped to accomplish. Home economics, particularly in the late nineteenth and early twentieth century, struggled to develop a coherent identity. Some supporters felt the discipline ought to be vocational in nature, with an emphasis on cooking and cleaning. Others, including the influential Ellen Richards, envisioned a more complex curriculum that blended scientific research with sociology and microeconomics. She also insisted on breaking the stereotype of home economists as simple housekeepers and sought to imbue the field with scientific principles and methodology. In this regard, home economists shared in common with professional economists a desire to improve Americans' material conditions by better understanding and managing resources. Similarly, both early professional economists and home economists struggled to identify the relationship between academic research and civic engagement.

Still, the professional economics community ignored the discipline. Economic journals and conferences were void of either home economists or discussion of prevalent issues in home economics, and there was no overlap between the memberships of the two groups. There is a lack of evidence to suggest a particular attitude or attitudes economists held toward home economics, and vice-versa, but Alfred Marshall's comment about the vanishing role as elementary economist that women once occupied proved prophetic. The rise of the American Home Economics Association and home economics programs in schools across the country created an alternative to male-dominated economics that was well-suited to prevailing notions regarding gender roles. The home economics community's comparatively narrow focus on issues pertaining to household consumption thus helped solidify the barrier between home economics and economic theory.

Professional economists also paid scant attention to the amateurs who continually challenged the tenants of modern American economics, despite the obvious irony that professional economics lacked a strong, discipline-wide consensus. Folk economics persisted as a powerful force in American public life. Many Americans accepted the emergence of professional economists with a grain of salt and continued to understand the relationship between government, the economy, and themselves in terms that were not always compatible with either neoclassical or the heterodox new economists' theories. Henry George's followers sustained their crusade for land reform despite his passing in 1897, much to the annoyance of both professional economists and those who disagreed with the politics of the movement. Pro-Georgists organized themselves into "single-tax" clubs to debate and mobilize political support. Reprints of *Poverty and Progress*, along with the efforts of single-tax clubs across the nation, kept the populist theory alive and well. George's ideas continued to draw sharp criticism from professional economists, and he found himself posthumously engaged in a battle with prominent economist Frank Fetter.

The AEA's openness could not guarantee that professional economics, as a discipline, would avoid evolving into the arcane and irrelevant intellectual hobby of the few who occupied ivory towers. The discipline was certainly aware of its potential public image problem. The future of professional economics hinged on the projection of expertise and knowledge about the economy as economists fought to maintain their image. In 1909, AEA Secretary Thomas Carver expressed his concern, noting the competition posed by "the business public," which he felt was responsible for the low esteem in which economists were held in some quarters.[34] That the business community and academic economists pulled in divergent directions seems self-evident – the former was concerned almost exclusively with profit margins, while the latter busied itself with a much broader set of concerns, such as efficiency and equitability of distribution. The business community, therefore, sought out a particular type of economic advice. A 1912 letter from James H. Brookmire, founder of the Brookmire Economic Chart Company, highlighted the difference in interest, as he contrasted the business community's fondness for the work of Samuel Benner (an Ohio farmer who published price forecasts) with its comparative disinterest in the theoretical work of professional economists. The development of business cycle theory and subsequent attempts to chart economic fluctuations, as exemplified by Harvard's Economic Service following World War I, illustrates economists' acknowledgment of the business community's particular interests and a sustained effort by some within the discipline to bridge the gap between theoretical and applied economics.

Professional economics had to be careful. If it ranged too far afield from the interests and prerogatives of the business community, the discipline risked appearing aloof and irrelevant. Yet seeming too closely aligned with the business community could be equally damaging. Ely, in a letter to Charles S. Hull discussing possible speakers for the 1901 annual meeting, cited such concerns about public appearances. Another letter from an Ithaca businessman accused the professional economists of having fallen under the influence of powerful business interests. The Department of Economics at the University of Chicago, which was established along with the rest of the University through donations by J.D. Rockefeller, continued to draw accusations that its faculty was swayed by money, although Laughlin quite convincingly revealed the ridiculousness of the charge in an open letter.[35] The Department was remarkably diverse and accusations of influence-peddling never panned out. The letter likely found little audience outside the professional economics community, however, because it was published in Chicago's *Journal of Political Economy*.

Accusations of impropriety aside, economists continued to publicly insert themselves into the policymaking process in a wholly unorganized fashion that was contingent upon individual personalities and prerogatives. English economist James Bonar remarked that the country was overflowing with students of the science. The discipline's ability to create and maintain the aura of professional expertise hinged on the maintenance of high academic standards and the use of an increasingly specialized terminology and methodology, but such exclusionary necessities had their unfortunate side-effects. For starters, such requirements made it difficult to appeal to the general public. Translating cutting-edge economic theory into digestible prose for the non-expert was an increasingly difficult task for economists. Frank W. Noxon, Secretary of the Railway Business Association, hinted at the growing gap between professional economics and the general public in a letter sent to Thomas Carver to congratulate the Harvard economist on the success of *The Distribution of Wealth*. Noxon wrote, long before the emergence of mathematical models notoriously altered the discipline,

> [Y]ou [Carver] employ, in the main, language well calculated to make diffi-
> cult economic conceptions clear to minds not accustomed to close analytical
> thinking. It would seem as if economic compositions held down to the ground
> in point of substance and treated with such clearness and simplicity would
> tend in the long run to diffuse as never before knowledge of economic princi-
> ples, and to encourage political predilections correspondingly enlightened.[36]

Not all professional economists were as adept at measuring their prose, nor were they all sympathetic to the necessity of such efforts. Columbia's Wesley C. Mitchell showed little sympathy for attempts to speak more plainly for lay audiences in a scathing review of Northwestern economist E.D. Howard's *Money and Banking* (1910) – a book intended to transmit expert theory to the general public. In his response to concerns that his review had been too harsh, Mitchell insisted that Howard "deserved to have his feelings hurt" for producing such loose prose.[37]

The discipline was, in fact, becoming more insular. It was a byproduct of the professionalization of economics throughout the Western world. Specialized terminology allowed professional economists to more accurately communicate complex concepts, but increasingly even some professional economists felt uneasy with the proliferation of opaque language. William Warrand Carlile echoed Noxon's sentiment with charges that neoclassical economists in particular were guilty of unnecessary abstruseness, noting "the science [economics] has become every day more encumbered with a mass of phraseology altogether unknown to our fathers."[38]

Professional economics in the US was very much in a period of transition. The organization was no longer a beleaguered minority within academia that struggled to be heard. Nor was the discipline yet an incredibly complex and arcane subject that inadvertently discouraged outside participation (though it was moving in that direction). The AEA clearly cherished academic freedom and believed in the preservation of divergent opinions among its professional members. But as the discipline grew in every respect, it continued to erect barriers between itself, the public, and fellow academics. This intellectual insulation, a requirement of professionalization, would eventually dog the discipline when a lack of understanding translated into criticism and doubt over the professional economist's value. The paradox – a lasting feature of the discipline, as time would reveal – is striking. Economists in the US had successfully built a professional network that ensured the discipline's place on practically every college campus but still struggled to tie their expertise to the economic policymaking process.

Such criticism and doubt already was apparent in the long-running debate over the labor question, which had proven to be the most combustible of the economic issues that faced turn of the century America. Labor reform was a hard-fought issue that reflected the interdisciplinary struggle over the form and content of American economics. The rapid growth of professional economics ensured that the discipline was present throughout reformers' attempts to reshape American labor relations. At the same time, the inability to develop stricter methodological and ethical guidelines left policy recommendations to the individual economist, which continued the uncertain relationship between expertise and public policy. Economists were free to enter the policymaking process, where their professional training and accreditation solicited growing respect, but the connection between their professional status and their growing role as components of American economic policymaking remained unclear. The inability to arrive at an intellectual consensus ultimately limited professional economists' efficacy in the public policymaking process.

Notes

1 The AEA's published lists of doctoral candidates, certainly not an exhaustive source, reported 94 candidates in 1905. The same source saw the number of doctoral candidates rise to 151 in 1911. These lists excluded doctoral candidates whose continuous non-residence exceeded three years, thus precluding a misrepresentation of growth by counting students twice.
2 These numbers reflect individuals and does not include subscribing institutions, which are also listed as members in the AEA handbooks.
3 Thomas N. Carver, "Thomas N. Carver to E. Stanley Abbot," May 14, 1909, American Economic Association Records, 1886– Box 11, Duke University Rare Book, Manuscript and Special Collections Library.
4 Stigler, Stigler, and Friedland cite these publications, along with *Political Science Quarterly*, as a notably common venue for economics papers from 1892–1901. See Stigler *et al.* (1995).
5 Percent of total subscribing members of the AEA, negligible number of individual subscribers not included. Figures rounded to nearest hundredth.
6 Figures for the first 14 years of publication does not include 1886, since the journal only published one issue that year.
7 These figures were calculated by adding original research articles for each year from 1900 to 1904 and 1906 to 1919, then dividing by total number of years, respectively. I omitted discussion and commentary articles that appeared in the "articles" section of the journal. I also omitted 1905 from my calculations because of an anomalously low number of articles, likely because the editorial staff was in the process of preparing for the new publishing schedule in 1906.
8 Untitled and undated, this document from AEA Secretary Thomas N. Carver's correspondence folder for 1909 appears to be a summary of notable events at the 25th anniversary meeting of the AEA. C.B Fillebrown, Winthrop More Daniels, and R.M. Breckenridge, "The Recent Celebration of the Twenty-Fifth Anniversary of the Founding of the American Economic Association," Unknown, American Economic Association Records, 1886– Box 11, Duke University Rare Book, Manuscript and Special Collections Library.
9 "Correspondence Regarding the Proposition for the American Economic Association to Establish an Economic Journal," 1902, 4, American Economic Association Records, 1886– Box 62, Duke University Rare Book, Manuscript and Special Collections Library.
10 This assessment is based on the observation that all three outlets –- the *QJE*, *JPE*, and the AEA's monograph series –- published articles from an ideologically diverse body of scholars over the course of the late nineteenth century. This claim somewhat contradicts Furner's suggestion that the AEA's early publications were effectively an organ of the "Elyite new school," however, her claim is restricted to the year of 1886,

by which point the AEA had only published three articles authored by Edward Bemis, Albert Shaw, and Edmund James, who certainly were within the "Elyite" school.

11 Richard T. Ely, "The American Economic Association 1885–1909," *American Economic Association Quarterly* 11, no. 1 (April 1910): 80. This comment was a reference to the formation of the American Political Science Association in 1903 and the American Sociological Society (which later changed its name to the American Sociological Association) in 1905.

12 Winthrop M Daniels, "Winthrop M. Daniels to Davis R. Dewey," April 9, 1908, American Economic Association Records, 1886– Box 10, Duke University Rare Book, Manuscript and Special Collections Library.

13 James A. Field, "James A. Field to Thomas N. Carver," May 12, 1910, American Economic Association Records, 1886– Box 12, Duke University Rare Book, Manuscript and Special Collections Library.

14 Thomas N. Carver, "Thomas N. Carver to James A. Field," June 3, 1910, American Economic Association Records, 1886– Box 12, Duke University Rare Book, Manuscript and Special Collections Library.

15 James H. Brookmire, "James H. Brookmire to Davis R. Dewey," November 4, 1912, American Economic Association Records, 1886– Box 62, Duke University Rare Book, Manuscript and Special Collections Library. "Says a Great Economist," *Wall Street Journal*, August 14, 1912. Brookmire also advertised his publications extensively and occasionally used in his ads a brief testimonial from an unidentified, but satisfied, economist.

16 "Carnegie Is Crippled," *The Washington Post*, December 28, 1909.

17 Members of the AEA still respected Laughlin despite his apparent lack of interest in the organization and it is clear the AEA was more interested in Laughlin's participation for its own aggrandizement than the other way around.

18 J. Laurence Laughlin, "The Study of Political Economy in the United States," *Journal of Political Economy* 1, no. 1 (December 1892): 1–19.

19 As listed in the Executive Committees Report: England – Alfred Marshall, Robert Griffin, William Smart, J.S. Nicholson, Edwin Cannan, F.Y. Edgeworth. France – Emil Levasseur, Paul Leroy-Beaulieu, Charles Gide, M. de Foville, Stourm, Adolphe Landry. Germany – Brentano, Schmoller, Cohn, Conrad, Knapp, Sering, Dietzel, Lexis. Austria – Eugen von Bohm-Bawerk, Frank Philippovich. Italy – Maffeo Pantaleoni, Luigi Bodio, Achille Loria, Luzzati. Holland – Pierson.

20 The reception, titled "Breakfast, with Reception to Foreign Guests, and Brief Address" lacks a description in the conference program and AEA post-conference reports lack further details concerning foreign attendance and the perceived quality of the foreign guests.

21 W.F. Willcox, "W.F. Willcox to Davis R. Dewey," August 11, 1909, American Economic Association Records, 1886– Box 11, Duke University Rare Book, Manuscript and Special Collections Library.

22 Richard T. Ely, "The American Economic Association 1885–1909," *American Economic Association Quarterly* 11, no. 1 (April 1910): 96.

23 Frank Albert Fetter, "Frank Fetter to D.R. Dewey," May 24, 1911, American Economic Association Records, 1886– Box 62, Duke University Rare Book, Manuscript and Special Collections Library.

24 H.J. Davenport, "H.J. Davenport to Frank A. Fetter," October 10, 1908, American Economic Association Records, 1886– Box 62, Duke University Rare Book, Manuscript and Special Collections Library.

25 "American Economic Review," 1911, American Economic Association Records, 1886– Box 62, Duke University Rare Book, Manuscript and Special Collections Library.

26 Ibid.

27 Fetter's inclusion is odd, as he was known as the founder of the American Psychological School (also referred to as the Modern School) and argued for a deeper reading of

psychology in the market place. It remains, however, that Fetter wholly embraced marginal utility value and that the concept was central to his economic philosophy. See Hoxie (1905).

28 Walton H. Hamilton, "The Development of Hoxie's Economics," *Journal of Political Economy* 24, no. 9 (November 1916): 882.

29 John M. Clark, "The Changing Basis of Economic Responsibility," *Journal of Political Economy* 24, no. 3 (March 1916): 210.

30 Irving Fisher, "Irving Fisher to T.N. Carver," October 27, 1910, American Economic Association Records, 1886– Box 12, Duke University Rare Book, Manuscript and Special Collections Library.

31 Papers were presented by A.B. Wolfe (Oberlin College); Simon Litman (University of Illinois); F.M. Taylor (University of Michigan); attendees (institution in parenthesis) J. Laurence Laughlin, R.F. Hoxie, L.C. Marshall, William Hill, John Cummings, C.W. Wright, J.A. Field (University of Chicago), John Gray (University of Minnesota), Frank T. Carlton (Albion College), William A. Scott (University of Wisconsin), George Groat (Ohio Wesleyan University), Ulysses Weatherly, U.H. Smith (Indiana University), W.E. Hotchkiss, M.S. Wildman, E.D. Howard, F.S. Deibler, F.R. Mason (Northwestern University), A.S. Johnson (University of Texas), Robert C. Chapin (Beloit College), H.H. Freer (Cornell College), E.H. Johnson (Emory College), Spurgeon Bell (University of Missouri), E.B. Patton (University of Rochester), C.C. Arbuthnot (Western Reserve University) Elliot Whipple (Wheaton College), H.S. Smalley, C.E. Perry (University of Michigan), and F.R. Fairchild (Yale University).

32 As with my analysis of female membership in Chapter One, I determined gender by looking at first names in the AEA's published list of members, which is reliable but not infallible. I identified fifty-six female members using this approach. In some instances, only an initial appears in place of a first name. If all such cases were assumed to be female members, women would only account for 120 of the 1,205 total members.

33 Sarah Stage and Virginia Bramble Vincenti, *Rethinking Home Economics: Women and the History of a Profession* (Ithaca, NY: Cornell University Press, 1997), 5.

34 Thomas N. Carver, "T.N. Carver to John L. Stewart," June 16, 1909, American Economic Association Records, 1886– Box 11, Duke University Rare Book, Manuscript and Special Collections Library.

35 In his account of the first 20 years of the department historian William Barber similarly discounted the suggestion that the school was captive of big business. See Barber (1988).

36 Frank W. Noxon, "Frank W. Noxon to Thomas N. Carver," October 13, 1911, American Economic Association Records, 1886– Box 12, Duke University Rare Book, Manuscript and Special Collections Library.

37 W.C. Mitchell, "W.C. Mitchell to Davis R. Dewey," January 12, 1911, American Economic Association Records, 1886– Box 62, Duke University Rare Book, Manuscript and Special Collections Library. W.C. Mitchell, "Money, Prices, Credit, and Banking," *The American Economic Review* 1, no. 1 (March 1911): 115–17.

38 William Warrand Carlile, "The Language of Economics," *Journal of Political Economy* 17, no. 7 (July 1909): 434.

Bibliography

"American Economic Association." *Publications of the American Economic Association, 3rd Series* 1, no. 1 (February 1900): 7–36.

Andelson, Robert V., ed. *Critics of Henry George: A Centenary Appraisal of Their Strictures on Progress and Poverty*. Rutherford, NJ: Fairleigh Dickinson University Press, 1979.

Barber, William J. *Breaking the Academic Mould: Economists and American Higher Learning in the Nineteenth Century*. Middletown, CT: Wesleyan University Press, 1988.

Bateman, Bradley W. "Make a Righteous Number: Social Surveys, the Men and Religion Forward Movement, and Quantification in American Economics." *History of Political Economy* 33, no. Winter Supplement (Winter 2001): 57–85.

Bernstein, Michael A. *A Perilous Progress: Economists and Public Purpose in Twentieth-Century America*. Princeton, NJ: Princeton University Press, 2001.

Bornemann, Alfred. *J. Laurence Laughlin: Chapters in the Career of an Economist*. Washington: American Council on Public Affairs, 1940.

Brookmire, James H. "Methods of Business Forecasting Based on Fundamental Statistics." *The American Economic Review* 3, no. 1 (March 1913): 43–58.

Carlile, William Warrand. "The Language of Economics." *Journal of Political Economy* 17, no. 7 (July 1909): 434–47.

Carver, Thomas N. *The Distribution of Wealth*. New York: MacMillan, 1911.

Chernow, Ron. *Titan: The Life of John D. Rockefeller, Sr.* New York: Random House, 1998.

Clark, John B. "The Future of Economic Theory." *The Quarterly Journal of Economics* 13, no. 1 (October 1898): 1–14.

Clark, John M. "The Changing Basis of Economic Responsibility." *Journal of Political Economy* 24, no. 3 (March 1916): 209–29.

Coats, A.W. "The Educational Revolution and the Professionalization of American Economics." In *Breaking the Academic Mold: Economists and American Higher Learning in the Nineteenth Century*, edited by William J. Barber, 340–75. Middletown, CT: Wesleyan University Press, 1988.

——. "The First Two Decades of the American Economic Association." *The American Economic Review* 50, no. 4 (1960): 556–74.

Commons, John R. *Myself: The Autobiography of John R. Commons*. New York: The Macmillan Company, 1934.

——. *Races and Immigrants in America*. New York; London: Macmillan, 1907.

Downey, E. H. "The Futility of Marginal Utility." *Journal of Political Economy* 18, no. 4 (April 1910): 253–68.

"Eight List of Doctoral Dissertations in Political Economy in Progress in American Universities and Colleges." *The American Economic Review* 1, no. 1 (March 1911): 212–19.

Elias, Megan J. *Stir It Up: Home Economics in American Culture*. Philadelphia: University of Pennsylvania Press, 2008.

Ely, Richard T. *Ground Under Our Feet: An Autobiography*. New York: The Macmillan Company, 1938.

——. *Social Aspects of Christianity*. Boston: W.L. Greene & Co., 1888.

——. "The American Economic Association 1885–1909." *American Economic Association Quarterly* 11, no. 1 (April 1910): 47–111.

Field, James A. "The Progress of Eugenics." *The Quarterly Journal of Economics* 26, no. 1 (November 1911): 1–67.

Fink, Leon, ed. "A Memoir of Selig Perlman and His Life at the University of Wisconsin." *Labor History* 32, no. 4 (Fall 1991): 503–25.

Forget, Evelyn L., and Craufurd D. Goodwin. "Intellectual Communities in the History of Economics." *History of Political Economy* 43, no. 1 (2011): 1–23.

Fox, Daniel M. *The Discovery of Abundance: Simon N. Patten and the Transformation of Social Theory*. Ithaca, NY: Cornell University Press, 1967.

Friedman, Walter. "The Harvard Economic Service and the Problems of Forecasting." *History of Political Economy* 41, no. 1 (2009): 57–88.

Furner, Mary O. *Advocacy & Objectivity: A Crisis in the Professionalization of American Social Science, 1865–1905*. Lexington, KY: The University Press of Kentucky, 1975.

"Geographical Index of Members and Subscription." *The American Economic Review* 9, no. 3 (September 1919): 67–110.

Glazer, Penina Migdal, and Miriam Slater. *Unequal Colleagues: The Entrance of Women into the Professions, 1890–1940*. New Brunswick, NJ: Rutgers University Press, 1987.

Goldstein, Carolyn M. *Creating Consumers: Home Economics in Twentieth-Century America*. Chapel Hill, NC: University of North Carolina Press, 2012.

Goodwin, Craufurd D. W. "Marginalism Moves to the New World." In *The Marginal Revolution in Economics: Interpretation and Evaluation*, edited by R.D. Collison Black, A.W. Coats, and Craufurd D.W. Goodwin, 285–304. Durham, NC: Duke University Press, 1973.

Grossman, David Michael. "Professors and Public Service, 1885–1925: A Chapter in the Professionalization of the Social Sciences." Ph.D Dissertation, Washington University, 1973.

Hamilton, Walton H. "The Development of Hoxie's Economics." *Journal of Political Economy* 24, no. 9 (November 1916): 855–83.

Harris, Barbara J. *Beyond Her Sphere: Women and the Professions in American History*. Westport, CT: Greenwood Press, 1978.

Hodgson, Geoffrey M. *The Evolution of Institutional Economics: Agency, Structure, and Darwinism in American Institutionalism*. London; New York: Routledge, 2004.

Howard, E. D., and Joseph French Johnson. *Money and Banking: A Discussion of the Principles of Money and Credit*. New York: Alexander Hamilton Institute, 1910.

Howard, Stanley E., Frank D. Graham, David A. McCabe, and Frank Albert Fetter. "Edwin Walter Kemmerer 1875–1945." *The American Economic Review* 36, no. 1 (March 1946): 219–21.

Howey, R.S. *The Rise of the Marginal Utility School, 1870–1889*. New York: Columbia University Press, 1989.

Hoxie, Robert F. "Fetter's Theory of Value." *The Quarterly Journal of Economics* 19, no. 2 (February 1905): 210–30.

Johnson, Alvin S. "Robert Franklin Hoxie." *The New Republic*, July 8, 1916.

Johnson, Edgar H. "The Economics of Henry George's 'Poverty and Progress'." *Journal of Political Economy* 18, no. 9 (November 1910): 714–35.

Judson, Harry Pratt, J. Laurence Laughlin, John H. Gray, *et al.* "Discussion." *Journal of Political Economy* 17, no. 10 (December 1909): 703–27.

Laughlin, J. Laurence. "Academic Liberty." *Journal of Political Economy* 14, no. 1 (January 1906): 41–43.

——. "Capitalism and Social Discontent." *The North American Review* 203, no. 724 (March 1916): 403–12.

——. "The Study of Political Economy in the United States." *Journal of Political Economy* 1, no. 1 (December 1892): 1–19.

Leonard, Thomas C. "Retrospectives: Eugenics and Economics in the Progressive Era." *Journal of Economic Perspectives* 19, no. 4 (Autumn 2005): 207–24.

"List of Members." *American Economic Association Quarterly, 3rd Series* 11, no. 2 (May 1910): 6–48.

"List of Members." *The American Economic Review* 9, no. 3 (September 1919): 5–66.

Longawa, Vicky M. "Episodes in the History of the Journal of Political Economy." *Journal of Political Economy* 100, no. 6 (December 1992): 1087–91.

Marshall, Alfred. "The Old Generation of Economists and the New." *The Quarterly Journal of Economics* 11, no. 2 (January 1897): 115–35.

McCann, Jr., Charles R. *Order and Control in American Socio-Economic Thought: Social Scientists and Progressive-Era Reform.* New York: Routledge Press, 2012.

Mitchell, W.C. "Money, Prices, Credit, and Banking." *The American Economic Review* 1, no. 1 (March 1911): 115–17.

"Purposes of the American Economic Association." *The American Economic Review* 12, no. 2 (June 1922): 1–2.

Ripley, William Z. *The Races of Europe: A Sociological Study.* London: K. Paul, Trench, Trübner & Company, 1899.

Rubin, Paul H. "Folk Economics." *Southern Economic Journal* 70, no. 1 (July 2003): 157–71.

Samuels, Warren J., ed. *The Founding of Institutional Economics: The Leisure Class and Sovereignty.* New York: Routledge Press, 1998.

Stage, Sarah, and Virginia Bramble Vincenti. *Rethinking Home Economics: Women and the History of a Profession.* Ithaca: Cornell University Press, 1997.

Stigler, George J., and Claire Friedland. "The Pattern of Citation Practices in Economics." *History of Political Economy* 11, no. 1 (1979): 1–20.

Stigler, George J., Stephen M. Stigler, and Claire Friedland. "The Journals of Economics." *The Journal of Political Economy* 103, no. 2 (April 1995): 331–59.

"The Seventh Annual Meeting." *Publications of the American Economic Association* 10, no. 3 (March 1895): 39–50.

"The Twenty-Second Annual Meeting." *American Economic Association Quarterly, 3rd Series* 11, no. 2 (May 1910): 49–79.

"Third List of Doctoral Dissertations in Political Economy in Progress in American Universities and Colleges, January 1, 1906." *Publications of the American Economic Association, 3rd Series* 7, no. 3 (August 1906): 43–48.

Veblen, Thorstein. "The Limitations of Marginal Utility." *Journal of Political Economy* 17, no. 9 (November 1909): 620–36.

4 Economists and the search for industrial order

By 1900, the professional economics community had made little progress toward consensus on the constellation of economic questions that had perplexed the Western world since industrialization had upended traditional social arrangements. The discipline provided a general understanding in regards to monetary theory and tariffs, but remained sharply divided over what constituted proper industrial and labor policy. Conflict between employers and employees intensified throughout the second wave of industrialization and had in more than one instance ended in violent confrontations. Fifteen years had passed since the founding of the American Economic Association signaled a dramatic increase in the number of economists studying the issue, yet the ideological divide remained strikingly obvious during talk of labor reform. At the same time that professional economists failed to find a rigorous, scientific consensus on straightforward issues such as the role of labor unions or the need for worker's compensation laws, progressive reformers organized and pushed for protective legislation with great success.

More so than any other issue, the mixing of professional "new economists" and the Progressive Era reform movements with which they identified make it difficult to draw a clear line between those ideas developed within academia and those shaped by reformers' political rhetoric. Compounding the challenge is the fact that there was no clear goal around which a majority of economists rallied when debating labor policy. The AEA continued to abide by its commitment to avoid propagandizing (in 1907, the AEA's executive committee sent representatives to the National Peace Conference, but that would be the exception that proved the rule).

As with the money question, the labor and monopoly questions were more than an academic exercise. Industrial relations, as the 1912 Commission on Industrial Relations declared in its final report, dictated the pace and quality of life for millions of Americans. Furthermore, the labor question evoked questions about American identity and citizenship. The ability to secure economic independence through work was a prerequisite for active citizenship and the fluidity of the labor market that accompanied industrialization and increased immigration raised the specter of a much more diversified and unpredictable American society.

The monopoly question was equally fraught with implications. Long concerned with the security of the democratic process, Americans feared that the large businesses that grew out of second-wave industrialization might subvert the economic independence necessary for a healthy republic. As Louis D. Brandeis, the well-known progressive attorney and eventual Supreme Court judge, once opined: "We may have democracy, or we may have wealth concentrated in the hands of a few, but we can't have both."[1] The unrestrained power of large businesses, whose resources dwarfed those of the federal government, was perceived by some Americans to be unsustainable and immoral. Journalists, novelists, and attorneys alike built careers on the public condemnation of unsavory business practices and any economist looking to influence the debate would have contended with much more than peer reviews.

Professional economists' training did imbue them with a degree of social prestige that granted direct access to the policymaking process. Nevertheless, it is apparent that the discipline's influence in the Progressive Era debates over labor and monopoly reform was mitigated by continued public skepticism, interdisciplinary strife, and ambiguity about the relationship between expertise and governance in a democratic society. Seemingly only those economists who could successfully mix academic authority with political savvy could hope to shape public discourse, and this attempted mixing was particularly pronounced in Wisconsin, where the university's leading economists claimed a distinctly activist research agenda.

The Wisconsin School

Professional economists' first attempt to muster a response to the labor and monopoly questions began on the East coast, but by the turn of the twentieth century the University of Wisconsin had emerged as the center for reform-minded economics. Both labor and economic historians have long noted the significant influence of the Wisconsin School in the development of American labor economics. However, the discrepancy between the Wisconsin School's influence at the state and federal levels sheds light on the factors that ultimately diminished economists' influence over federal economic policy. Wisconsin School economists played a direct role in transforming Wisconsin into one of the more labor and consumer friendly states of the Progressive Era. Translating that success to the national level proved a difficult and untimely process – many of the Wisconsin School's recommendations for economic reform were not implemented until the economic crisis of the 1930s forced federal reform nearly 20 years later. The discrepancy in influence was a product of differences between Wisconsin and national politics. The Wisconsin economists' pro-labor activism cultivated powerful allies within the state, but marked them as untrustworthy and un-American on the national scene.

The Wisconsin School eventually attracted the "institutionalist" label on account of Wisconsin economists' tendency to emphasize the influence of public and private institutions on economic conditions. But the most observable theme in the first several decades of the Department's existence was a dual commitment to the German Historical School-inspired new economics and the progressive reform movement of the early twentieth century. Richard T. Ely and his equally prolific colleague and successor, John R. Commons, built the first economics department in the US that not only taught a particular approach to the discipline, but also instilled the belief that academic training ought to be applied to practical problems.

Ely's appointment as head of the economics program by the University of Wisconsin's Board of Regents proved to be a shrewd decision, despite the professor's aforementioned brush with public controversy two years after his arrival (see Chapter 1). The "socialism" controversy did little to curb Ely's enthusiasm for the new economics and he continued to advocate for economic reform. The same year he faced Wells' accusations, Ely published "On Natural Monopolies and the Workingman in America" in the *North American Review*, in which he sketched the rationale behind the interventionist economic policy that the Wisconsin School came to promote. Written for the general public, the article eschewed both private ownership and regulation in favor of public ownership of several key industries that had emerged during the late nineteenth century (namely railroad, telegraph, and gas networks).[2] Ely justified his position by arguing that these industries were natural monopolies for which duplicate network construction was enormously wasteful. Their privatization had led to "unearned income" for those who presided over the new, large industrial corporations that had come to dominate American business.[3]

Ely went on to yoke the issue of labor rights to that of private ownership, arguing:

> The monopolist is not likely to be a good employer of labor. His power is so great, and that of a single wage-earner so small in comparison, that the former is exposed to the danger of becoming an arbitrary and arrogant employer.[4]

Public ownership, Ely reiterated, would resolve the most explosive labor disputes because representative government by its nature is more responsive to workers' demands than private owners. Ely built Wisconsin's economics program around this sentiment.

It was a perfect fit for a state led by the progressive icon Robert La Follette. "Fighting Bob's" career, which included two terms as governor of Wisconsin (1901–1906) followed by a run in the US Senate (1906–1925), overlapped with the peak of the Wisconsin School's influence over state economic policy.[5] Undeterred by the often-harsh criticism from his conservative opponents, La Follette sought out academic experts to study the state's problems and recommend policy solutions. Such a system could only work provided the proper civil servants and policy experts were in place, and Wisconsin was one of the few states that fit the bill in the early 1900s.

The idea of calling on knowledgeable professionals to help craft economic policy, dubbed the "Wisconsin Idea" by legislative librarian Charles McCarthy in *The Wisconsin Idea*, was by McCarthy's account not as much a rigid philosophy as an ethos. A shoemaker and sailor, McCarthy obtained a bachelor's degree from Brown University before coaching the University of Georgia's football team to pay his way through law school. While at Georgia, McCarthy studied economics and the power dynamics of slavery, at which point he saw the issue of economic control in a new light. Attracted to Ely's new economics, he headed north in 1899 to enroll at the University of Wisconsin, where he obtained a Ph.D. in history and was a ready convert to Ely's vision of activist scholarship. Advocates of the Wisconsin Idea, McCarthy explained, sought to use the state to temper the power of big business and ensure a more equitable distribution of wealth. Achieving this goal required state leaders to tap into the community's collective knowledge and resources in order to become "efficiency experts." The professional economists at the state's flagship university, naturally, loomed large in such a system.

Wisconsin was neither the first nor the only state to view its school system as a potential driver of civic improvement. The first colleges in America were prized for their ability to produce a steady stream of clergy whose instruction would uplift the communities in which they preached. State assemblies and the founders of numerous post-secondary schools in the nineteenth century had spoken of more direct bonds between education and civic activism, though such lofty ambitions never moved beyond the theoretical. Several factors converged to set Wisconsin apart. In addition to La Follette's support from his position of power, the state capital stood literally down the street from the university campus. This geographic proximity put Wisconsin legislators in direct contact with the academic experts whose intellectual capital figured so largely in the Wisconsin Idea. McCarthy founded a legislative library in 1901 to cement the connection and serve as a non-partisan resource for lawmakers engaged in the process of drafting legislation.[6] He promoted the library's use and oversaw its expansion over the succeeding 20 years.

In addition to aiding the legislative library's reference center, the Wisconsin economists and their students promoted and delivered lectures in the Assembly chamber, bringing the two houses of state government together to hear lectures from experts on state issues as often as three times a week at the height of their involvement in 1911. The state assembly members, labor economist Selig Perlman later recalled,

> were so friendly to the university experts. They appreciated the aid which they got from such men as Commons and others and, of course, we must not overlook the great role played by Dr. Charles McCarthy who was, well, who was really the lobbyist for the people.[7]

Wisconsin economists benefited from more than just La Follette's support and McCarthy's enthusiasm, however. The Wisconsin Idea also derived considerable support from a constituency of farmers and industrial workers of German and Scandinavian extraction, whose thick accents colored the Assembly's meetings and left a strong impression on Perlman (who was then working as Commons' graduate assistant). Demographics were of great consequence; McCarthy referred to Wisconsin as a "fundamentally a German state" – a point he unscientifically, yet convincingly demonstrated by referencing the family names in the University of Wisconsin's student and faculty directory.[8] The political traditions of the German and Scandinavian immigrants that flowed into Wisconsin throughout the nineteenth and early twentieth centuries lent valuable popular support to the push for increased state involvement in economic affairs. It was a reciprocal relationship, as the University's economics faculty helped Wisconsin's political activists sharpen their impulses into more specific ideas. This dynamic made Wisconsin an especially liberal, pro-labor state in which the University's labor-friendly economic theories could be readily tied to policy reform.

By the time La Follette assumed the governorship in 1901, Ely already had more than 15 years of teaching, research, and public service under his belt – more than enough to market himself as an expert advisor. The Wisconsin Idea received an additional boost with Commons' arrival in 1904. Together, Ely and Commons refined the Department's dual commitment to teaching and community outreach. Commons' appointment proved shrewd. *The Distribution of Wealth* (1893), Commons' first contribution to American economics, hinted at enthusiasm for the sort of economic activism practiced by his mentors at Johns Hopkins University (where he had studied under Ely and Sidney Sherwood). Commons downplayed the significance of marginal utility theory and echoed the belief that particular industries in a modern economy tended toward monopolization and required public ownership. Yet *The Distribution of Wealth* was a largely dry effort directed at the professional economics community. *Social Reform and the Church* (1894), published with an enthusiastic foreword from Ely, better reflected Commons' strong commitment to social activism rooted in religious principles. Furthermore, Commons' second effort was a combination of lectures delivered to lay audiences, thus reflecting his desire to extend his influence beyond academia. The tone and arguments of *Social Reform and the Church* removed any potential doubts about Commons' intellectual disposition left by *The Distribution of Wealth*.

After brief stints teaching at Oberlin College and the University of Indiana, Commons moved to Syracuse and taught at the University until 1899, when his unconventional opinions about Sunday activities ran afoul of the school's more pious boosters and led to his dismissal. Unemployed and unsure of where to go, Commons was offered a position at the Bureau of Economic Research by George H. Shibley – the self-taught lawyer who had appealed to populists with his call for free silver, as described in Chapter 2. Shibley persuaded Commons to head the Bureau, which was Shibley's project to acquire and disseminate statistical data on commodities prices. But the arrangement was short-lived and Commons soon found himself unemployed once more. The situation was quickly remedied by an offer from E. Dana Durand, Commons' former student at Oberlin College and the Secretary to the United States Industrial Commission. Durand enlisted Commons to complete a report on Immigration. This work was followed by a stint as assistant to Ralph M. Easly, the then secretary of the National Civic Federation. This series of academic and practical training, combined with Commons' enthusiasm for reform-focused economics, made him a perfect candidate to join the faculty at Wisconsin and Ely secured a position for his former student in 1904.

Like Ely, Commons helped pioneer labor economics in the US and attempted to transform the discipline from an intellectual movement based on moral convictions to a movement more grounded in empirical science. Within several years of Commons' arrival, the state's reputation as a liberal laboratory had stretched across the nation. Newspapers and journals made note of the phenomenon and attracted sympathetic intellectuals, including the aforementioned Perlman, who described the following decades as "the golden age of Wisconsin, both intellectually and politically."[9]

To be effective, the Wisconsin Idea required a bureaucracy staffed by researchers and assistants versed in the skills necessary for gathering and processing large amounts of information. To meet the demand, Ely and Commons trained students who embodied both the public-mindedness and technical know-how necessary to pursue progressive legislation. From 1893 to 1920, Wisconsin conferred 65 doctorate degrees, an average of 2.4 per year at a time when obtaining a bachelor's degree was still a rare accomplishment. Of those degrees, nearly half listed Ely, Commons or William A. Scott as an advisor.

Doctoral students accounted for only a fraction of total students trained in economics by Ely, Commons, Scott, and their successors, of course. Exact figures are elusive, but it is safe to conclude that Wisconsin conferred approximately 75 undergraduate degrees in economics in 1902 with the number per year rising gradually to 231 in 1920.[10] Graduates went on to promote the Wisconsin Idea through teaching, research, and public service. Among the most influential graduates were Helen Sumners Woodbury, who worked for a series of federal agencies on a contract basis before accepting a position with the Children's Bureau, and John B. Andrews, who founded the American Association for Labor Legislation – an organization whose influence one-time AEA president and *AER* editor Davis Dewey claimed was on par with that of the AEA's activities or Laughlin's efforts to maintain the gold standard. Andrews also ran the organization's journal, the *American Labor Legislation Review*, and throughout his career pursued progressive federal labor legislation. Additional graduates included John Fitch, who worked for the New York Department of Labor and edited the social workers' magazine *Survey* following his contribution to Paul Kellogg's landmark study of steel workers in Pittsburgh, *The Pittsburgh Survey*; Henry C. Taylor and John D. Black, both of whom went on to promote policy reform to prop up the agricultural industry; and Selig Perlman, Frederick S. Deibler, Ezekiel H. Downey, and Warren M. Persons, all of whom enjoyed long careers in academia. The Wisconsin School also produced key economists of the generation that were to help oversee the creation and implementation of New Deal programs, such as Edwin Witte, "the father of social security."[11] These men and women carried on the spirit of the new economics and public service so ingrained at Wisconsin, and in doing so, pressed professional economics farther into the policymaking process at both the state and federal levels.

With the support of a strong research staff, Commons coordinated closely with the La Follette faction in Wisconsin politics in order to promote economic reform through legislation. The list of reforms, many of them either firsts or among the first of their kind, included a public utilities law, workmen's compensation, progressive taxation, unemployment compensation, employer's liability law, and railway rate regulation. The Wisconsin School was also instrumental in the formation and operation of the Industrial Commission of Wisconsin, which served the interests of state reformers and passed numerous regulations for businesses in the state.

The Wisconsin Idea goes national

The Wisconsin School reached beyond the state's borders, but it is their attempt to apply the Wisconsin Idea's principles at the national level that highlights the fragility of professional economists' influence. In addition to serving as an exemplar of state action for progressives throughout the nation, Commons and his team of research assistants intervened in national matters on two fronts. On the academic front, Commons oversaw the research and writing of *A Documentary History of American Industrial Society*, a landmark study in labor economics. Commons and his graduate assistants also played a significant role on the 1912 Commission on Industrial Relations, better known as the Walsh Commission. Neither endeavor was without its successes, but both efforts made clear that the Wisconsin School's influence at the state level was an exceptional, and not necessarily replicable, phenomenon.

Writing and editing *A Documentary History of American Industrial Society* occupied Wisconsin's economics department well before the Walsh Commission demanded attention. The ten-volume undertaking was housed at the University of Wisconsin, but backed by more than $30,000 in funding from the American Bureau of Industrial Research (ABIR) and a mixture of industrialists with whom Ely and Commons were acquainted.[12] The project also received notable support from the Carnegie Institution's labor history project. All of this made *Documentary History* one of the nation's most generously funded projects of its kind.

The series was a culmination of several decades' work that stretched back to the publication of Ely's *The Labor Movement in America*. Frustrated by what he saw as a lack of appreciation for economic records, Ely had endeavored to gather as many primary sources on the labor movement as possible. His personal collection had at times struck his colleagues as peculiar and unnecessary, but Ely had finally realized his scholarly vision through the formation of the ABIR and the publication of its most prominent series. The series was important in itself, but it also represented a larger commitment to creating a depository of source material from which future economists could reliably draw evidence – a national legislative library of sorts.

True to the form of the German Historical School that had inspired Commons, *A Documentary History of American Industrial Society* was intended to provide solutions to America's labor dilemma through methodological analysis of how the American economy had developed over the previous century (the previous two centuries in the case of the South). Labor was indeed the central focus of the series despite its more inclusive title. The series relied on noted Southern historian Ulrich B. Phillips to describe plantation culture and the frontier. The eight remaining volumes of the series were organized by Commons and his assistants from the ABIR, and contained documents relevant to labor conspiracy cases and labor movements from 1806 to 1842 and 1820 to 1880, respectively. Ely's preface conveyed the familiar conviction that overcoming the challenges of industrialization was largely a matter of research, education, and action. *The Documentary History*, it was hoped, fulfilled two of the prerequisites for reform.

The series' positive reception reinforced the Wisconsin economists' recognized status among professional economists as leading experts on the issue of labor relations. The University of Pennsylvania's Emory R. Johnson declared: "This 'Documentary History' ... outranks all other publications upon American labor, both because of the value of the documents to students of history, and because of the illuminating economic analyses . . ."[13] University of Illinois economist Ernest L. Bogart met the release of the first two volumes with a similarly effusive review in *The Economic Bulletin*, where he declared the series a "significant event in the history of economics in the United States."[14] Naturally, there were minor quibbles. Bogart's review of later volumes noted skepticism regarding Commons' interpretation of labor's role in securing homestead legislation in the mid-nineteenth century. Johnson also criticized the last four volumes of the series on account of Commons' obvious interest in Horace Greely and subsequent narrow reading of the mid-nineteenth century labor movement.

The project failed to garner much attention outside the professional economics community, however. Newspaper coverage of the ABIR's accomplishment was limited to a handful of publication notices and short reviews. The project was a distinctly academic endeavor and would serve as a valuable resource for researchers in the years to come, but the editors' failure to recommend policy reform, the lack of a clear narrative, and its length placed the series beyond the reach of all but the most dedicated public officials. The series' limited influence points to the general dilemma that economists began to face with growing regularity. Such endeavors were necessary to build disciplinary expertise, but academic research was also a costly process that typically produced specialized products tailored to the professional economics community, which surely lent merit to charges that the discipline was slowly becoming an arcane field of inquiry. The documentary series was an intellectual triumph, but translating it into an answer for the labor question was another matter.

On the applied economics front, the Wisconsin economists found themselves in a strong position to affect national change, though conditions proved unfavorable to the national emulation of the Wisconsin Idea. Theodore Roosevelt's glowing praise of Wisconsin's economic policies in his introduction to McCarthy's *The Wisconsin Idea* – a system he described as the practical application of "sane radicalism" – reflected growing interest in harnessing the power of experts to engineer economic reform and the Wisconsin School's association with that possibility. In 1913, members of the American Political Science Association's Committee on Practical Training, in conjunction with representatives from the American Economic Association, compiled a report to analyze how the recent enthusiasm for expertise was being applied across the country. The report's authors identified a growing belief that the knowledge accumulated by economists and political scientists ought to be applied to public policy, noting:

The scientific student has well equipped laboratories provided for him, and considerable laboratory work required of all students of the natural sciences, even in elementary courses. The student of geology has his field excursions to make surveys .... The student of astronomy has his observatory .... Engineering students have their summer camps and their assignment to business establishments .... Thus, the college and university has long recognized, in several departments of learning, the need for personal contact with actual problems of the various fields of experience."[15]

A handful of university-supported research bureaus sprang up in the years following the establishment of the Wisconsin reference library, although not enough to suggest that the push to meld academic expertise with public governance was ubiquitous. The committee's report identified nine reference bureaus with university ties. In addition to Wisconsin, the Universities of Oregon, Texas, Washington, California, Cincinnati, and Iowa had each moved to provided reference services for public. Harvard University established two such institutions – one dedicated to municipal research and the other business research (both of which preceded the creation of the Harvard Economic Service in 1917).

Yet professional economists' lack of formal procedure and passive role in the policymaking process meant that there was little chance of them exerting a strong, consistent influence on the policymaking process in most states. The idea behind reference libraries and bureaus of research was to support the democratic process by providing the information necessary to make sound decisions when crafting policy. In Wisconsin, state legislators often consulted with professional economists owing to a combination of geographic convenience, political culture, and assertive leadership within the Department of Economics at the University of Wisconsin. Outside Wisconsin, arrangements were less clear. In his 1914 survey of reference libraries in the United States, librarian Jon B. Kaiser noted an emerging tendency to place reference work "directly under the control of university authorities," or at least to coordinate with such experts.[16] But the movement to establish such institutions was carried out simultaneously by public librarians and cities without university support.

Kaiser's observation dove-tailed with the sentiments of a report issued by the joint APSA-AEA Committee on Practical Training. "The New Democracy," the report's authors concluded, required public servants versed in the details of governance and capable of supplementing elected officials. The report's authors were unable to deliver clear recommendations for how to translate ideals into action, however. The report only vaguely described the criteria that defined reliable public servants and made no recommendation for the standardization of course work. Hands-on experience, it was assumed, made the expert. The vagueness of professional economists' role in the policymaking process, underscored from the beginning by the fact that the report was the initiative of American Political Science Association, was further illustrated by the fact that research bureaus employed a mixture of social scientists.

That economists were recognized as necessary but only vaguely relevant, and certainly not privileged, components of the policymaking process was echoed by Commons' experience with the Walsh Commission.[17] Formed in 1912, the Commission was a response to President Howard Taft's call for an investigation of the on-going conflict between labor and capital – a conflict underscored by the bombing of the *Los Angeles Times'* offices in response to their perceived antipathy toward labor. The Walsh Commission (named after Commission Chairman and labor lawyer Frank P. Walsh), held the potential to place professional economists on the national stage and demonstrate the usefulness of economic expertise to lawmakers and to the public. Although it was tasked with purely investigative powers, the Commission provided a national platform and the ample resources to support careful investigation of the labor problem. Over the course of its two-year investigation, the Commission interviewed Commons' former students and by-then-established professional economists John. B. Andrews, John A. Fitch, and William M. Leiserson, in addition to Charles McCarthy and members of the Wisconsin Industrial Commission. McCarthy and Perlman also served on the Commission as support personnel. The Commission's research staff, headed by Commons and McCarthy, solicited studies by economists George E. Barnett, D.A. McCabe, Leo Wolman, Sumner Slichter, Henry Hoagland, Robert Hoxie, and Carl Hookstadt.

What began as a great opportunity, both in terms of Commons' career and the discipline as a whole, gradually lapsed into great disappointment. Commons later recalled his work with the Commission as one of the "tragic events" of his academic life, a point underscored by Perlman's observation that the Commission's work "robbed him [Commons] of his sleep and peace of mind … he really grieved over the whole business."[18]

Commons' grief stemmed from Walsh's decision to ignore his opinion, which also happened to be the majority opinion of the Commission's board. By June 1915, the Commission had interviewed more than 700 witnesses and was ready to complete its investigation into the sources of industrial unrest. The Commission had polarized opinions with its at times aggressive investigative techniques – particularly Walsh's cross-examination of John D. Rockefeller, Jr., following the Ludlow Massacre in April 1914. The Commission adopted an increasingly confrontational tone that undoubtedly polarized those who followed the Commission's progress, which in turn placed the professional economists involved with the Commission's work in an awkward position. Ostensibly tapped as neutral specialists, the economists interviewed and employed by the Commission, as with any expert eyewitness, could be easily dismissed as either socialist radicals or "bought men" working on behalf of moneyed interests.

The Commission's investigative strategy failed to take full advantage of the abilities of its professional economists on staff. Of the 740 witnesses called, only 20 were economists or sociologists. Rather than utilizing the testimony of the Commission's economic experts, who were listed in the final report as "non-affiliated" witnesses, Walsh relied on sensational testimony to underscore the severity of labor discord. Commons, meanwhile, led the Commission's private research staff and observed the public hearings from a distance. These differences in temperament and methodology led Walsh and Commons to two very different conclusions, which clashed in the summer of 1915 when Commission members began drafting a report for Congress.

To Commons' frustration, Walsh rejected his report, opting instead to submit a report drafted by a staff member and signed by a minority of the Commission's members. To work around the fact that Commons' report had attracted the signature of five Commission members and was, in fact, the majority report, Walsh referred to his as the "staff" report and insisted on its supremacy. The difference between the two reports was stark, as evidenced by the introduction to Commons' "minority report," which stated:

> We find ourselves unable to agree with other recommendations and resolutions for legislation that would be enforceable, or because they are directed to making a few individuals scapegoats, where what is needed is serious attentions to the system that produces the demand for scapegoats, and with it the breakdown of labor legislation in this country.[19]

Walsh's "majority" report pulled no punches in its criticism of the nation's industrial and financial elite, citing the uneven distribution of wealth and poor working conditions as the root of labor turmoil. The conclusions were largely well-founded, but the tone evoked a strong negative reaction in conservative circles. The sharpest criticism portrayed the report as hopelessly biased. Former President Taft chastised Walsh for his lack of "judicial poise," while the *Los Angeles Times* decried the call for a national minimum wage and legalization of sympathy strikes.[20] Most papers chose to focus on the Commission's lack of consensus, which implicitly undercut the influence of its work.

Commons' report agreed with the "majority" report's findings regarding the abuses that required addressing. But rather than calling for the restructuring of American industrial relations and the redistribution of wealth, he called for the establishment of federal agencies capable of investigating labor relations and enforcing the laws and codes already on the books, reasoning that dramatic reform was unlikely and that the failure to enforce existing labor laws was as harmful to labor relations as any other concern. Later, in his autobiography, Commons described the difference in opinion, reflecting, "I thought, at that time, that the three labor representatives were being misled by the general labor unrest into throwing their movement into politics. I wanted them to avoid politics" and instead focus on setting up federal labor boards so as to meet employers at the bargaining table.[21]

Commons' recommendations were arguably more practical than Walsh's and reflected his expertise and experience crafting policy in Wisconsin. Additionally, Commons' insistence on the establishment of federal agencies – staffed by neutral experts as well as labor and employer representatives – was a reasonable proposal that had worked in Wisconsin. But Commons' standing as the board's only economic expert carried little weight and his recommendation was consequently ignored. The Commission successfully exposed labor conflict, but failed to take the next step toward action.

Obstacles to influence

The Wisconsin School's failure to translate its success to the national stage raises questions about the efficacy of economic expertise in general during the Progressive Era. It is tempting to dismiss the Walsh Commission as an exceptional incident and to focus instead on the continued diffusion of professional economists throughout government agencies as evidence of the discipline's increased influence. But Commons' experience demonstrates that presence did not necessarily translate to influence. As Perlman reflected, the disappointment about missed opportunities and unfulfilled visions that he and others endured in Wisconsin resonated in other states that tried to import the Wisconsin Idea and make use of expertise in the policymaking process. Policymakers' reluctance or unwillingness to accept the input of professional economists likely stemmed from institutional inertia and political expediency. The economic expert was still a relatively new concept and it would take time to work such figures into the policymaking process.

Additionally, the public's concerns regarding political bias and subjectivity continued to be powerful factors and help account for the reluctance to accept professional input. It is clear that accusations from conservative Americans concerning the Wisconsin School's political leanings hounded the profession in general and made it difficult to refine and export the Wisconsin Idea. Wisconsin School members and their colleagues were burdened by accusations of ideological extremism. The issues of academic freedom and public animosity toward anything that so much as hinted toward socialist origins continued to weigh on the minds of heterodox economists. The Wisconsin crowd kept close tabs on cases of academic censure, as evidenced by the collection of materials related to freedom-of-speech cases maintained by Ely, Commons, John Fitch, and Helen Woodbury Summers throughout their careers. Periodic incidents did little to assuage public fears about the connection between radicalism and heterodox economic thought. Socialist candidates for office boasted of their study of political economy as a qualification. Political economics professors endorsed socialist candidates. Political assassins cited their study of political economy as a moment of awakening. To counter the fall-out, members of the Wisconsin School became adept at distancing themselves from the hot-headed activists who invoked political economic theory as justification for their view and actions.

Throughout the early twentieth century, the Wisconsin School economists were careful to avoid overt sympathy with the socialist cause but the label stuck nevertheless. Following his brush with controversy, Ely made sure to espouse the virtues of American democracy and freedom in an effort to expunge from the public's mind any recollection of his association with socialism. His caution was such that the impression emerged, according to Perlman, that Ely had turned conservative by the 1910s. There is no evidence that Ely's dismissal of communist and socialist solutions was anything but genuine, nor that he eschewed his earlier progressive ideology. Ely continued to ensure that his students studied and understood Marx, but encouraged the rejection of Marxist solutions to American labor issues. Marx's *Communist Manifesto* was common reading for graduate students at Wisconsin.

Wisconsin was hardly a hot-bed for reactionary radicalism. A critique of the *Communist Manifesto* prepared under Ely by John Fitch, then a new graduate student with strong populist leanings, speaks volumes. Fitch agreed with Engels and Marx's general assessment of the problems posed by industrialization, but rejected the prophetic warnings of a vanishing middle class that invoked a need for radical reform. When accusations of socialist-leanings dogged David Saposs during his tenure as chief economist on the National Labor Relations Board, his supporters balked at the notion and insisted that the Wisconsin-trained economist came from a tradition of "old-line Wisconsin liberals" who had fought communists at the state level for some time.[22]

Commons' decision to invite controversial anarchist activist Emma Goldman to speak to his class in 1910 raised eyebrows, and concerns, yet it is hardly an indicator of a radical bent. Commons did not condone Goldman's views and, like Ely, stridently opposed socialism as a political movement, yet felt the need to grant Goldman an audience. Edward Ross – the controversial sociologist who had been dismissed from Stanford for controversial statements regarding railroad and Asian labor – actively supported Goldman's visit by introducing her at a socialist gathering following a tour of the campus. Ross was censured by the Board of Regents for giving the impression that he condoned radicalism. Curiously, Commons avoided a reprimand from University authorities, and his autobiographical account of Goldman's visit is the only one that suggests the economist played more than an informed spectator's role in the whole affair. In this instance, the leader of the Wisconsin School may have overstated his role as an iconoclast.

Helen Sumner Woodbury, a frequent collaborator of Commons' and a well-known labor economist in her own right, believed that the study of economics was intertwined with the pursuit of broader social justice, particularly when it came to child labor and women's issues. Woodbury supported the defense of *Lucifer the Light-Bearer*, an anarchist periodical that ran afoul of highly restrictive indecency laws in 1905 and demonstrated a similar commitment to progressive causes through donations to the Sanger Defense Fund ten years later.[23] Fitch, for his part, publicly supported the League of Free Nations Association's efforts in to reinstate a New York Assembly member that had been ousted in 1920 because of his socialist convictions.[24]

The Wharton School's 1915 dismissal of Scott Nearing, a young and promising economist who enjoyed the support of his former teacher and highly respected colleague Simon P. Patten, reinforced what most reform-minded new economists understood. Addressing the labor question was more than simply an academic exercise. Debates over the proper relationship between the state and labor evoked powerful emotions from all parties involved. Nor could the labor question easily be separated from broader debates over the character and conduct of state and federal government in general. Reform required public sympathy, and the new economists' reputation as radicals, warranted or not, rendered it difficult to gather the broad support necessary translate their expertise into progressive economic policies at the national level. Just as economists who engaged in debate about monetary policy were dogged by suspicions about their motivations many of those who sought labor and anti-monopoly legislation were subject to dismissal as hopelessly biased sources.

It is beyond question that both labor and anti-monopoly legislation were strengthened from 1900 to 1917. Likewise, it is clear that professional economists exerted some measure of influence over the public policymaking process in select states and at the federal level. The work of the Wisconsin School economists was, despite its impressive scope, only a fraction of the work done by professional economists at the state and federal level during the period in question. From 1900 onward, state and federal politicians and agencies increasingly found it necessary to call on trained economists to both advise and to serve within the growing state bureaucracy.

Yet as close examination of the Wisconsin School's early twentieth century efforts makes clear, the degree of influence economists exerted on the policymaking process was limited by concerns over the integrity and ability of the profession. The voting public and policymakers alike turned to professional economists in the most sparing of fashions by invoking economists' expertise when convenient and ignoring it when it was expedient. The discipline's refusal to establish specific goals or endorse economic policies was perhaps necessary in a culture that claimed to prize freedom of expression and the open exchange of thought. But it also created an environment that allowed for the outright dismissal of labor economists' opinions because they were either too radical, or not radical enough. As with the money issue, it quickly became clear the Congress' failure to heed the advice of Commons and his "minority" report represented a missed opportunity. The leading labor economist of the era watched in frustration as the nation turned away from his proposed solution of government-mediated collective bargaining at a time when its speedy adoption seemed an eminently reasonable alternative to the often bitter confrontations that persisted instead.

Notes

1 Irvin Dilliard, *Mr. Justice Brandeis, Great American: Press Opinion and Public Appraisal* (Modern View Press, 1941), 42.
2 Richard T. Ely, "On Natural Monopolies and the Workingman in America," *The North American Review* 158, no. 448 (March 1894): 294–304.
3 Ibid., 298. Ely clarified his position on unearned income by stating "When it is said that there is such a thing as unearned income, it is meant individually unearned; that is, unearned by him who receives it. Of course, no one enjoys any income for which someone does not toil, and the individually unearned income is socially earned."
4 Ibid., 299.
5 La Follette died several months following his fourth appointment.
6 Interestingly, Melvil Dewey also had ties to the home economics movement and provided the open remarks at the 1900 meeting of the Lake Placid Conference on Home Economics. Wisconsin was not the first state to establish a legislative library. Dewey established the first legislative reference library in the United States for the state of New York in 1890, but that reference library lacked ties to an institution of higher

learning and its patrons did not pursue original research. The Wisconsin legislative library was to explicitly harness the resources of the State's schools and in doing so placed the professional economists at Wisconsin in direct contact with those who voted on policy issues. See Rothstein (1990); Elias (2008).

 7 Selig Perlman, "Tape No. 1," April 13, 1950, 10, Papers, circa 1909–1998, Wisconsin Historical Society.
 8 Charles McCarthy, *The Wisconsin Idea* (New York: The Macmillan Company, 1912), 20.
 9 Perlman, "Tape No. 1." Perlman referenced a specific article in *Scribner's Magazine* (referred to as "Skidmore's" in a separate letter), however, an extensive search failed to turn up the referred to article. Given the late date of Perlman's recollection, it is likely that he had read about the Wisconsin project in a separate magazine altogether and mistakenly referred to *Scribner's* (Perlman 1950).
10 This approximation was made by comparing the number of economics courses offered in 1920 (when the number of undergraduate degrees in economics is known) to the number of courses offered in 1902 and 1912 (Lampman 1993).
11 Additional graduates of note include Harry Jerome, George S. Wehrwein, Jacob Perlman, Harold Groves, Edward Moorehouse, and Arthur Altemeyer.
12 The most significant donors, in terms of money provided, were V. Everit Macy, Stanley McCormick, Robert Fulton Cutting, P. Henry Dugro, and Ellison A. Smyth.
13 Emory R. Johnson, "A Documentary History of American Industrial Society," *Annals of the American Academy of Political and Social Science* 36, no. 2 (September 1910): 211–16.
14 Ernest L Bogart, "A Documentary History of American Industrial Society," *The Economic Bulletin* 3, no. 1 (March 1910): 26–29.
15 Charles McCarthy, "Preliminary Report of the Committee on Practical Training for Public Service," *The American Political Science Review* 8, no. 1 (February 1914): 305–306.
16 John Boynton Kaiser, *Law, Legislative and Municipal Reference Libraries an Introductory Manual and Bibliographical Guide* (Boston: The Boston Book Company, 1914), 232.
17 For additional information on the Walsh commission see Fink (1996); Kaufman (1993); McCartin (1997).
18 John R. Commons, *Myself: The Autobiography of John R. Commons* (New York: The Macmillan Company, 1934), 181. Perlman, "Tape No. 3," 5.
19 Basil M. Manly and John R. Commons, *Final Report of the Commission on Industrial Relations, Including the Report of Basil M. Manly, Director of Research and Investigation, and the Individual Reports and Statements of the Several Commissioners* (Washington, DC: Government Printing Office, 1916), 171.
20 "A Report and a Farce," *Los Angeles Times*, August 24, 1915."Value of Judicial Poise," *Los Angeles Times*, August 18, 1915.
21 Commons, *Myself: The Autobiography of John R. Commons*, 167.
22 Saposs had come under scrutiny following accusations by Mapes Davidson, trial lawyer for the National Labor Relations Board, that he was a dedicated communist.
23 M. Harman, "M. Harman to Dear Honored Friend," February 10, 1906, Helen Laura Sumner Woodbury Papers 1896–1933 Box 1, Wisconsin Historical Society. Leonard D. Abbot, "Leonard D. Abbot to Friend," April 2, 1915, Helen Laura Sumner Woodbury Papers 1896–1933 Box 1, Wisconsin Historical Society.
24 "A Fight for Elementary Americanism," *The Bulletin of the League of Free Nations Association* 1, no. 1 (March 1920).

Bibliography

Bogart, Ernest L. "A Documentary History of American Industrial Society." *The Economic Bulletin* 3, no. 1 (March 1910): 26–29.
——. "A Documentary History of American Industrial Society." *The Economic Bulletin* 3, no. 4 (December 1910): 414–16.

——. "A Documentary History of American Industrial Society: Volumes VII and VIII, Labor Movement, 1840–1860 by John R. Commons." *The American Economic Review* 1, no. 1 (March 1911): 86–87.

Brøndal, Jørn. *Ethnic Leadership and Midwestern Politics: Scandinavian Americans and the Progressive Movement in Wisconsin, 1890–1914.* Northfield, MN; Urbana and Chicago: Norwegian-American Historical Association; Distributed by the University of Illinois Press, 2004.

——. "The Ethnic and Racial Side of Robert M. La Follette Sr." *Journal of the Gilded Age and Progressive Era* 10, no. 3 (2011): 340–53.

Carstensen, Vernon. "The Origin and Early Development of the Wisconsin Idea." *The Wisconsin Magazine of History* 39, no. 3 (Spring 1956): 181–88.

Cohen, Wilbur J. "Edwin E. Witte (1887–1960): Father of Social Security." *Industrial and Labor Relations Review* 14, no. 1 (1960): 7–9.

Commons, John R. *Myself: The Autobiography of John R. Commons.* New York: The Macmillan Company, 1934.

——. *Social Reform and the Church.* New York: Thomas Y. Crowell & Company, 1894.

——. *The Distribution of Wealth.* New York; London: Macmillan and Company, 1893.

Commons, John R., Ulrich B. Phillips, Eugene A. Gilmore, John B. Andrews, and Helen L. Sumner, eds. *A Documentary History of American Industrial Society.* 10 vols. Cleveland, OH: The A. H. Clark Company, 1909.

Dilliard, Irving. *Mr. Justice Brandeis, Great American: Press Opinion and Public Appraisal.* Modern View Press, 1941.

Elias, Megan J. *Stir It Up: Home Economics in American Culture.* Philadelphia: University of Pennsylvania Press, 2008.

Ely, Richard. *The Labor Movement in America.* New York: T.Y. Crowell, 1886.

Ely, Richard T. "On Natural Monopolies and the Workingman in America." *The North American Review* 158, no. 448 (March 1894): 294–304.

Fink, Leon. "Expert Advice: Progressive Intellectuals and the Unraveling of Labor Reform, 1912–1915." In *Intellectuals and Public Life: Between Radicalism and Reform*, edited by Leon Fink, Stephen T. Leonard, and Donald M. Reid, 182–213. Ithaca, NY: Cornell University Press, 1996.

Fitzpatrick, E.A. "McCarthy of Wisconsin." *The Wisconsin State Journal.* April 10, 1921.

——. *McCarthy of Wisconsin.* New York: Columbia University Press, 1944.

Friedman, Walter. "The Harvard Economic Service and the Problems of Forecasting." *History of Political Economy* 41, no. 1 (2009): 57–88.

Hansen, W. Lee. *Academic Freedom on Trial: 100 Years of Sifting and Winnowing at the University of Wisconsin-Madison.* Chicago: University of Chicago Press, 1998.

Hill, Joshua Benjamin. "Touching Vitally the Principles of Democracy Itself: John A. Fitch and the Progressive Response to Industrialization." Timothy Dwight College, 1999.

Johnson, Emory R. "A Documentary History of American Industrial Society." *Annals of the American Academy of Political and Social Science* 36, no. 2 (September 1910): 211–16.

——. "Documentary History of American Industrial Society. Volumes VII, VIII, IX and X by John R. Commons: Ulrich B. Phillips: Eugene A. Gilmore: Helen L. Sumner: John B. Andrews." *Annals of the American Academy of Political and Social Science* 38, no. 2 (September 1911): 335–36.

Kaiser, John Boynton. *Law, Legislative and Municipal Reference Libraries an Introductory Manual and Bibliographical Guide.* Boston: The Boston Book Company, 1914.

Kaufman, Bruce E. *The Origins & Evolution of Industrial Relations in the United States.* Ithaca, NY: ILR Press, 1993.

——. "John R. Commons and the Wisconsin School on Industrial Relations Strategy and Policy." *Industrial and Labor Relations Review* 57, no. 1 (October 2003): 3–30.

Kellogg, Paul Underwood. *The Pittsburgh Survey.* New York: Charity Organization Society of the City of New York, 1909.

Lampman, Robert, ed. *Economists at Wisconsin 1892–1992.* Madison, WI: University of Wisconsin Press, 1993.

Manly, Basil M. *Final Report and Testimony Submitted to Congress by the Commission on Industrial Relations.* Vol. 1. 11 vols. Washington, DC: Government Printing Office, 1916.

Manly, Basil M., and John R. Commons. *Final Report of the Commission on Industrial Relations, Including the Report of Basil M. Manly, Director of Research and Investigation, and the Individual Reports and Statements of the Several Commissioners.* Washington, DC: Government Printing Office, 1916.

McCarthy, Charles. "Preliminary Report of the Committee on Practical Training for Public Service." *The American Political Science Review* 8, no. 1 (February 1914): 301–56.

——. *The Wisconsin Idea.* New York: The Macmillan Company, 1912.

McCartin, Joseph Anthony. *Labor's Great War: The Struggle for Industrial Democracy and the Origins of Modern American Labor Relations, 1912–1921.* Chapel Hill, NC: University of North Carolina Press, 1997.

Miller, Harold L. "The American Bureau of Industrial Research and the Origins of the Wisconsin School of Labor History." *Labor History* 25, no. 2 (1984): 165–88.

Perlman, Selig. "Tape No. 1," April 13, 1950. Papers, circa 1909–1998. Wisconsin Historical Society.

——. "Tape No. 2," April 13, 1950. Papers, circa 1909–1998. Wisconsin Historical Society.

——. "Tape No. 3," April 13, 1950. Papers, circa 1909–1998. Wisconsin Historical Society.

Phillips, Ulrich B., ed. *Plantation and Frontier Documents, 1649–1863.* 2 vols. Cleveland, OH: The A. H. Clark Company, 1909.

Rothstein, Samuel. "The Origins of Legislative Reference Services in the United States." *Legislative Studies Quarterly* 15, no. 3 (August 1990): 401–11.

5 Obscured irrelevance

Economists in the boom years

John R. Commons' failure to drive the Walsh Commission's conclusions underscores the vagaries of professional economists' influence in the early decades of the twentieth century. The passive approach to reform, which depended on lawmakers to tap recognized experts for advice while crafting economic policy, assumed that lawmakers' desire to deliver sound policy would trump political pressure. Leading economists' continued support for the American Economic Association's role as a passive facilitator of the exchange of economic thought reflected this noble commitment to democratic ideals, but left the discipline's relevance to the American economic policymaking process uncertain at best.

Both then and now, this systemic barrier to influence was obscured by signs of success. Economics graduate programs continued to thrive in response to demand for more dismal scientists. Woodrow Wilson's presidency and the exigencies of World War I masked the tenuous connection between economic experience and economic policy and suggested that, setbacks aside, the new economists' vision of a technocratic democracy was starting to take shape. However, the events of the 1920s make clear that even as the discipline reached advanced stages of professionalization, the connection between professional economics and economic policy remained fuzzy. Thus a paradox emerged: professional economics in the US matured as a distinct discipline with a strong institutional foundation, yet professional economists struggled to see their rough consensus on key issues translated into economic policy in a consistent and timely fashion.

False promise

Wilson owed his rise to the White House in 1912 in part to his reputation as an enlightened progressive who advocated for the "new economics." Americans acknowledged "Professor Wilson's" academic credentials and, by extension, those of professional economists he had learned from and consulted with. Wilson's study of political economy and political science at Johns Hopkins University was noted from the outset of the race and helped to distinguish him from the rest of the pack. Few could claim, as Wilson could, to have worked alongside Richard T. Ely and progressive intellectual John Dewey on a textbook covering the history of US political economy. Although the book was never published, Wilson did produce his portion of the manuscript, which biographer Henry Bragdon notes for its clear embrace of economic progressivism. Following short terms teaching political economy and political science at Bryn Mawr College and Wesleyan University, Wilson accepted a position at Princeton University and eventually assumed the presidency. As president of the university, he instituted reforms to modernize the curriculum that were not unlike those his former teacher Ely had encouraged decades prior at Hopkins. The combination of his intellectual heritage and support of Ely's "radical" first draft of the AEA's constitution left no doubt that Wilson was sympathetic to the ideas of the new economists.

While previous US presidents had called on economic advisors in the past, Wilson was the first to fully harness the social prestige of professional economics. His public persona rested on the notion that he was in league with experts in the discipline who pursued reform for the sake of the public's welfare. Wilson's academic training was a cause for derision in the eyes of his opponents and a fount of confidence among his supporters. As the *The Baltimore Sun* noted, "In the early days of the republic men like Thomas Jefferson retired from the Presidency to become college presidents. Wilson resigned the presidency of Princeton to go into politics."[1] It seemed as if Americans were slowly warming to the idea of academic expertise driving government, and Wilson's ascent to the White House suggested a bright future for economists in particular. Americans apparently saw some benefit in electing a political leader familiar with the expertise of trained economists. His presidency, to be clear, was not the first sign that modern economists' ideas had an influence on federal economic policy. Rather, Wilson's election served as a symbolic victory and suggested missed opportunities such as the Indianapolis Monetary Commission's failure to endorse a centralized banking system or the Walsh Commission's rejection of federal arbitration boards might soon be failures of the past.

After some political maneuvering to avoid credit falling to the Republicans, Wilson signed the Federal Reserve Act that had emanated from the efforts of the bankers and economic advisors on the National Monetary Commission. The establishment of the Federal Reserve System was not without its critics within the professional economics community, but after 15 years Washington had finally delivered a central banking system not unlike those the majority of economists called for during the "Battle of the Standards." The Federal Reserve Act was followed by a series of additional legislative measures that built on recommendations from professional economists. The Revenue Act of 1913, which is best known for imposing a federal income tax, also dramatically lowered tariffs. The move toward freer trade reflected the general consensus of the discipline, as most economists had abandoned the protectionist impulses of Henry Carey by the 1880s. The Clayton Anti-Trust Act (1914) strengthened federal anti-monopoly laws and exempted unions from anti-trust regulations. The passage of the Federal Trade Commission Act (1914) established the infrastructure necessary to ensure the federal government could actually enforce the rules laid out by the Clayton Anti-Trust Act and formed yet another federal agency in need of professional economists' expertise. Labor economists had further reason to celebrate following passage of the Keating–Owen Act (1916), which sought to eliminate child labor (although the law was later deemed unconstitutional in 1918).

The drift toward the new economists' vision accelerated rapidly during Wilson's second term, as war mobilization drew hundreds of professional economists to Washington, DC. The rush to organize the American economy in support of the war effort suggested unlimited possibilities and *The New Republic*, overestimating the enthusiasm for government intervention, went so far as to call for the rejection of the profit motive and complete government coordination. The nation, it seems, caught a glimpse of what a planned economy managed by professional economists and business leaders might look like. By the end of the war, federal officials had taken over the operation of the nation's railroads and shipbuilding, as well as the distribution of commodities deemed essential to the war effort. Business leaders dominated the War Industries Boards that managed these takeovers, but economists played an important role, too.

By 1917, the US had a substantial pool of trained economists (unlike Britain, where the small number of economists meant marginal contributions to the war effort). The AEA, having shaken out interlopers through increased dues and membership drives that focused on the academic community, counted nearly 2,500 members. Irving Fisher estimated that no fewer than 120 members of the AEA worked in Washington, D.C. during the conflict, to say nothing of those who contributed at the state level. Professional economists consulted and served on numerous committees and commissions, including the Federal Trade Commission, the War Savings Section of the Treasury Department, the War Industries Board, and the Food Administration.

But the most noteworthy wartime development for professional economists was the temporary shift in how they viewed the discipline and its role in American society. For the first time, the AEA mobilized as a bloc and attempted to rally its members, and in effect the professional economics community, behind a specific goal. There was, after all, no guarantee that the professional economics community would pull together to support the war. The conflict evoked a strong response from pacifists and isolationists and certainly qualified as the kind of partisan issue that the AEA typically avoided at all costs. Influenced by a strong sense of patriotism, the Association worked toward consensus building owing to the leadership of Irving Fisher and the economic ramifications of the conflict.

World War I proved to be a war of attrition not only in terms of manpower, but also financial resources. The conflict stressed European markets, and economists clearly understood that US entry would necessitate a massive financial commitment. The warring nations' reliance on financing through debt was particularly troubling to economists and to the financial community. Both groups feared that over-reliance on borrowing would raise inflation to dangerous levels, as had been the case in England, although professional economists had extra cause for concern. Historical precedent, in particular Secretary of the Treasury Salmon Chase's attempt to finance the Civil War through short-term loans, was a worrying reminder that proper policy was crucial. General sympathy with the views of Hume, Smith, Ricardo, and Mill, all of whom preferred taxation over borrowing to finance a war effort, imbued the community with additional concerns. The potential for economic catastrophe pushed a significant portion of the professional economics community to abandon their reservations and lobby as a group.

The US officially entered the war on April 6, 1917. Three days later the Treasury Department approached Congress with a request to raise $5 billion through the sale of government bonds. With great speed, economists organized under E. Dana Durand, chair of the Department of Economics at the University of Minnesota, to draft a memorandum. The "Minnesota Memorial," as it came to be known, implicitly rebuked the Treasury's request to sell bonds and argued in favor of financing the war through taxation. It warned that ruinous inflation would accompany reliance on bonds to cover wartime spending. In addition to avoiding inflation, the Memorial asserted, taxation would force greater industrial efficiency and provide a sense of social justice. Nearly 250 economists at 43 schools – including Harvard, Yale, Cornell, and the Universities of Chicago, Minnesota, and Illinois – signed the document. In addition to furnishing copies at a press conference, Durand sent the Memorial to every member of Congress as well as to the president and his cabinet.[2]

Although not every economist supported the Memorial's plan to fund the war through taxation, resistance was moderate and limited to the argument that bond issues would be necessary at some point to cover the gap between tax revenues and war expenses – a point acknowledged in the memorial itself and by Durand in a later journal article. The chief "opponent" to the taxation policy, Columbia University's Edwin Seligman, agreed that financing the war exclusively through bonds was "short-sighted."[3] His criticism of the Memorial rested on the belief that war expenditures would simply outstrip tax revenues more quickly than the pro-tax crowd realized. Even so, Seligman did not object to the principle of steeply increased war-time taxes to mitigate inflation. Such concerns were echoed during a roundtable discussion on war finance at the annual AEA meeting in 1916, where criticism of the "pay as you go" policy also rested on concerns that tax revenue may not be able to cover total expenses.[4] Conservative economists one might expect to object to increased taxes and to the expansion of government largess were notably silent. Overwhelmingly, however, the professional economics community supported steep tax increases to fund as much of the war effort as possible.

The public declaration was an even more notable departure because it cut across political lines and delivered clear economic advice on an issue that held the potential to divide the nation. The Democratic Party had fought a difficult battle to increase tax revenue from the outset of the conflict in an effort to offset aid to European allies, likely owing to the fact that a war bond drive was not politically viable while Wilson campaigned on a policy of neutrality. The Wilson administration's earlier push for a large bond drive raised the possibility that the war would need to be financed on credit after all. Within a month of the Memorial's distribution Wilson and Secretary of the Treasury William McAdoo began to promote the "fifty-fifty theory," which proposed to meet war expenditures through equal parts tax revenue and loans.[5] At the very least, the Memorial and any subsequent commentary or lobbying from its signatories generated political leverage for those seeking to raise taxes. Seligman, it appears, agreed: his post-mortem of the war financing effort referred to the Memorial and Wilson's plan in conjunction.

The formation of the AEA's Committee on the Economic Problems of the War and the Committee on the Purchasing Power of Money offers another example of the organization's temporary erosion in policy neutrality. Irving Fisher, who assumed the Presidency of the AEA in 1918, encouraged the organization to do its "bit" for the war effort. Fisher's enthusiasm for public lobbying and his willingness to risk controversy in the name of promotion promised an active leadership willing to side-step the organization's traditional reluctance to directly promote action. Indeed, it was Fisher's lament of the discipline's lack of influence in 1902 that helped start the process of establishing a flagship journal for the AEA. Fisher took control of the AEA immediately preceding the years of his career that were marked less by economics than by activism. A Yale graduate and professor of political economy, Fisher built a multi-faceted career as an academic reformer. His promotion of eugenics-inspired legislation and efforts to regulate Americans' diets were well-known throughout the country. Unlike many of his colleagues, Fisher eschewed government commission work, but nevertheless believed in the discipline's ability to change society for the better. His leadership ensured the AEA's support of the war effort in the form of committee work and one-off measures, such as using the organization's mailing list to encourage members "as individuals" to promote the purchasing of savings stamps. The AEA's leadership authorized committees on the "Economic Problems of the War" and "Purchasing Power," in addition to committees charged with carrying out investigations in "War Finance," "Foreign Trade," "Price Fixing," "Marketing," and "Labor." It is unclear how many AEA members studied mobilization through these new committees. To avoid duplication and help coordinate these efforts, Walton Hamilton urged the creation of a disciplinary clearing house, but the war concluded before any such work could be completed.

The discipline had shown a willingness and ability to help manage the economic response to the war, but at a little more than one-and-a-half years the conflict was too short to muster a more substantive response, as reflected in the AEA's committee reports several months following the cessation of hostilities. Anticipating a brief war, Fisher's Committee on Purchasing Power had restricted its actions to the dissemination of information to encourage reduced consumption and increased production. The Committees on War Finance and Price-Fixing, similarly recognizing time constraints, adapted their work to include an analysis of appropriate post-war policies.

As it was, economists' wartime roles were limited to those associated with technical expertise. By staffing commissions and boards established to coordinate mobilization, economists were essentially charged with managing resources, a task for which they were well-trained. In fact, economists' data and statistical analysis had proven so valuable during mobilization that Harvard economist Edwin Gay managed to solicit support from the charitable Commonwealth Fund in order to establish the National Bureau of Economic Research (NBER) in 1919. The NBER went on to develop "gross domestic product" and equally valuable metrics that are still used to monitor and evaluate the national economy.

Although their suggestions percolated up to decision-makers, such an arrangement was a far cry from the sort of preventative influence the new economists had envisioned. Professional economists did well to demonstrate their value in solving problems by assisting in the management of programs such as the Liberty Bond drive or the Food Administration's purchasing program, but had little success in conveying broad, systemic principles that could prevent problems in the first place. As Allyn A. Young noted in his AEA presidential address years after the war, most Americans still conceived of war as a natural function of economics. The perception that nations would engage in armed conflict as a matter of economic self-interest struck Young and most of his fellow economists as odd, considering the cost of war ultimately detracted from a nations' net wealth. Yet economic necessity continued to be a popular explanation for the cause of the war.

Interestingly, H.C. Engelbrecht and F.C. Hanighen's *Merchants of Death*, the popular anti-war exposé that fed isolationist settlement, failed to garner significant attention from the professional economics community when it was released a little over a decade later. Engelbrecht and Hanighen's charge that economic incentives drove certain industries to encourage global conflict would have presumably piqued the interest of the nation's economic experts, yet no economics journal reviewed the work and there is no evidence that economists engaged with the thesis in the public sphere. Far from evolving into sages and society builders, economists found themselves cast as technicians called on to solve problems rather than prevent them.[6]

The discipline's involvement with the peace process further highlighted the dynamic. Economists from around Europe and the US were included in peace talks in the hope that their advice might help ensure that economic conditions were conducive to long-term stability – a hope that gradually disappeared, as famously recorded by British economist John Maynard Keynes in the oft-referenced *The Economic Consequences of Peace*. Like Keynes, Harvard economist and tariff specialist Frank Taussig advised his government as a member of the US Commission to Negotiate Peace in Paris, where his frustrations with the political maneuvering came through in his correspondence. Taussig's statements regarding tariffs and his review of Keynes' famous critique of the terms of peace make clear that he encouraged generous terms of peace on the grounds that economic isolationism and uncertainty regarding Germany's ability to handle exorbitant reparations would crash the global economy and harm already fragile relations. The treaty that was subsequently negotiated failed to take into account such concerns.

Despite his reservations, Taussig offered support for the terms of peace as a member of the AEA's Committee on Foreign Trade. The AEA executive committee supported the Treaty of Versailles from an early date, including its call for a League of Nations, and created the Committee on Foreign Trade as part of its inquiry into the economic basis of peace. The first report of its Committee on Foreign Trade, printed in March 1919, emphasized the need for a measured peace process to restore economic balance. The Committee's second report, written and released after the terms of the Treaty of Versailles had been set, concurred that the economic necessities of peace called for a "league of nations of some sort."

Entry into the League of Nations proved to be a contentious proposition in the US owing to the return of isolationist sentiment. Rejection of the Treaty of Versailles threatened the viability of the League of Nations, since US entry depended on its recognition. Both Taussig and the AEA executive committee were silent on the issue after the release of the Committee on Foreign Trade's second report, which left Irving Fisher as the *de facto* representative of American professional economists on the issue.[7] As a lecturer for the League of Nations Association of New York, Fisher argued that US support for the League was necessary to ensure the political and economic conditions conducive to peace. Fisher's claim that recently deceased President Harding secretly had confided in him his support for the League led to a brief uproar that damaged what little persuasive powers Fisher held in the debate. Underwhelmed and unmoved by the professional economist community's largely invisible support for the League of Nations and content with isolationist policy, the American public closed the door on economic cooperation and never ratified the Treaty of Versailles.

The First World War capped an ambiguous few years for professional economists in the US Wilson's election and the changes in federal economic policy that followed, in addition to mobilization, offered signs that the new economists and their vision of a more closely managed economy were ascendant. The rapid mobilization created a hinge, to borrow a term from sociologist Andrew Abbott, between the professional economics community and government. On one level, economists benefited from supporting mobilization because it granted them greater access to the policymaking process and allowed the discipline to better demonstrate its abilities. On another level, government officials benefited from the good will generated by the more efficient management of public resources during a particularly difficult time. This mutually beneficial hinge certainly suggested there was much more room for further collaboration between professional economists and government agencies in the coming years.

But economists' newfound willingness to lobby for specific policy as a discipline, in this case financing the war through taxation, produced ambiguous outcomes. Seligman's doubts about the ability of tax revenues to keep pace with war expenditures proved well-founded. Despite dramatic income and luxury tax increases, tax revenues covered less than one-third of the costs associated with fighting the war and the heavily promoted Liberty bond drive proved vital. The report of the AEA's War Finance Committee noted the "laudable effort ... to secure as large a revenue as possible from taxation," but did not dwell on the claims of so many AEA members that such revenues could offset total costs.[8] In these and other ways, the economists' public "stand" was a double-edged sword. On one edge, a large body of professional economists organized and used their social prestige as economic experts to help sway public policy in a direct manner. On the other, they asserted that taxation would address most of the nation's financing needs during the war – and they were wrong. Worse yet, neither the AEA nor any other body of professional economists followed the Minnesota Memorial with a similar effort during the peace process. Economic policy advocacy continued to be a contentious process in which consensus-building was elusive and intellectual camps thrived.

A new era with old dilemmas

The public zeal for reform that had slowly grown during the Progressive Era and the more recent turn to economic management during World War I faded quickly. Republican Presidential candidate Warren G. Harding's popular 1920 campaign slogan, which called for a "Return to Normalcy," alluded to a popular desire to unravel the sort of changes new economists had sought. Enthusiasm for progressive reform, although never entirely dormant, was weakened in the decade that followed, illustrating how the institutions that professional economists had established were vulnerable to shifts in public sentiment. While the new economists faced further challenges to their influence, in the 1920s their more conservative colleagues and folk economists continued to build on traditional cultural values and on the classical intellectual heritage. The Red Scare that followed the war intensified attacks on those economists perceived to threaten the economic order and placed new economists under particularly sharp scrutiny.

The perennial problem of academic censure garnered renewed attention during and after the war. In 1913, Edwin Seligman was named head of an AEA committee to "examine and report upon the present situation in American education institutions as to liberty of thought, freedom of speech, and security of tenure for teachers of economics ...." The Committee quickly evolved into a joint committee with members from the American Political Science Association, the American Sociological Society, and eventually committee from the newly formed American Association of University Professors (AAUP).[9]

The immediate impetus to form a committee on academic freedom in December 1913 is unclear. The controversy surrounding Emma Goldman's visit to the University of Wisconsin campus had died down several years prior, and there were no significant cases regarding any scholars, let alone an economist, drawing national attention at the time. The Committee's final report was an abstract discussion of the merits of academic freedom – including its section on "practical proposals" that offered general guidelines for institutional conduct. The report provided a starting point for discussion at the inaugural meeting of the American Association of University Professors (AAUP) in January of 1915, but failed to garner public notice despite the Committee's professed interest in publicizing the public benefits of academic freedom. The AEA, having conducted its joint report and expressed support for the AAUP, stepped back from the issue of academic freedom in the study of economics just as the pressure on scholars, including economists, was set to increase.

Irving Fisher's presidential address at the annual AEA meeting in December 1918 underscored the conservative turn. Concurring with the "radical" assertion that economists ought to serve someone, Fisher focused on the question of "whom."

It was in answering this question that Fisher decried the German influence on the new economics, declaring that American heterodox economists' admiration for the German Historical School was unforgivable given that German academics had "prostituted their professional services to serve Germany's criminal purposes." Fisher went on to combine German responsibility for the war with the Bolshevik uprising in Russia, cautioning economists against the impulse to wave the "red flag of class war" and against getting carried away by the interests of America's laborers. He reserved his harshest criticism for economists who acted as "champions or apologists" for trade unionism, socialism, Bolshevism, syndicalism, and I.W.W.-ism (the latter referring to the Industrial Workers of the World).[10] Of course, neither Fisher's speech nor public outcry forced the new economists "underground." Most new economists preached what they considered minor adjustments to the American free market system – collective bargaining rights, municipalization of select utilities, or farm subsidies for beleaguered communities – all of which were assumed to strengthen democracy and private property rights, rather than ushering in a new system of socialistic governance. Relatively few professional economists fit the stereotype of the wild-eyed revolutionary, but they had reason for concern given that past experience had demonstrated the public's tendency to render judgment based on a mistaken understanding of economists' ideas.

The tightening intellectual climate undoubtedly narrowed the discipline and discouraged overt challenges to the status quo. Thorstein Veblen, no stranger to public pressure, noted his concern in *The Higher Learning in America*. His criticism focused on the trustee system, which Veblen lamented for granting control to non-academic board members whom he believed inevitably conformed to the views of the nation's business class, thus restricting the economists' ability to pursue broader knowledge. The book elicited a mixture of condemnation and praise. Administrators at the University of Chicago, a prominent target in Veblen's critique, dismissed the book as both satire and bolshevism. Academic reviews were generally positive, although cautioned against taking too seriously Veblen's charges regarding the business community's influence over higher education. Popular social critic Upton Sinclair offered a more widely circulated critique in *The Goose-Step: A Study of American Education*, which similarly suggested that the nation's universities were beholden to corporate donors. Reviews of *The Goose-Step*, both in academic and popular publications, charged Sinclair with oversimplifying academia, but acknowledged the dilemma posed by academic censure. As one commenter noted, by focusing exclusively on the top-down authority Sinclair ignored the fact that "Faculties dominated by men fighting for their own survival afford examples of suppression by means of a community terror and a tyranny of opinion as flagrant as can be found on the part of president and trustees."[11] Subject to such pressures, economists' hopes that the discipline might follow an unhindered path of development seem overly optimistic and naive.

By continuing as an affiliate of the AAUP, the AEA effectively outsourced its commitment to academic freedom. None of the three leading American economics journals reviewed Veblen's *The Higher Learning in America* or Sinclair's *The Goose-Step*, nor did they comment on academic censure. To be sure, the type of administrative backlash against radical economic theory Veblen and Sinclair warned about had peaked by the mid-1920s. But lessons about socially controlled limits on the form and conclusions of economic study persisted. As individuals, US economists were vehemently opposed to academic censure and sensitive to the harm it might cause. As a discipline, they did little to explore how external pressure might shape the evolution of economic thought and how that evolution might in turn shape the course of US economic policy.

Defining the indefinable

In addition to pressure from a more politically conservative society, the new economists struggled to move past criticism of classical economics and offer a model of economic theory that rivaled the simplicity and neatness of neoclassical theory. In 1919, Walton H. Hamilton, Robert Hoxie's aforementioned eulogist and an economist at Amherst, attempted to organize the new economics in an *AER* article that outlined the American "institutional approach." He bluntly rejected neoclassical theory on the grounds that its practitioners failed to concern themselves with social customs and conventions. Instead, he offered a five-plank platform that asserted: (1) economic theory should unify economic science; (2) economic theory should be relevant to the modern problem of control; (3) the proper subject matter of economic theory is institutions; (4) economic theory is concerned with matters of process; and (5) economic theory must be based on an acceptable theory of human behavior.

It was yet another declaration of intent, similar in spirit to Ely and the "young rebels'" call for a more practical and scientific economics in 1885. The underlying causes of their continued failure to forge a new, historically and culturally aware chapter in American economic thought remained, however. The search for a unifying economic science was wildly optimistic at best, considering the fact that the longstanding gap between orthodox and heterodox camps in American economics and the assertion that economics ought to concern itself with the problem of control flew in the face of *laissez-faire* tradition, which remained strong in both American politics and economics. The success of neoclassical economics defied Hamilton's claim that institutions were the only "proper" subject matter for economists.

The new economists' assumption of constant change in both economic processes and human behavior rendered it impossible to deliver definite conclusions. The argument that people and customs change over time rang true. Indeed, that was in part why heterodox economics enjoyed such broad support in the wake of changes wrought by the second industrial revolution. But stating that change has taken place and explaining how such changes should affect economic regulation proved much more difficult. Hamilton was upfront about the challenge, noting:

> [I]t is doubtful whether at this time a general description of the economic order can be given. It may require a decade or more for a process of trial and error to produce a relatively consistent body of [Institutionalist] thought.[12]

Historical revision has since allowed for envisioning a coherent American Institutionalist School of economic thought. But as economic historian Marc Blaug notes, the founders of American Institutionalist School made strange bedfellows. The American heterodoxy – now defined by Institutionalists and their still-diffuse focus – remained relevant but lacked the coherency and direction of neoclassicism.

It was not that the newly labeled Institutionalists were incompetent or fundamentally wrong in their analysis of the economy. Rather, their difficulty in establishing Institutionalism stemmed from their lack of galvanizing intellectual leadership and poor marketability. Unlike their neoclassical colleagues, who could continue to use the classical canon as a foundation for agreement on baseline economic philosophies, the Institutionalists struggled to establish a compelling intellectual heritage. A combination of the conservative social climate and academic competitiveness made it difficult for a scholar or small cohort of scholars to emerge as an appealing alternative to neoclassicism and its respected icons. Furthermore, new economists' decision to eschew economic laws and advocate for the use of case studies, psychology and sociology to analyze economic problems made it difficult to establish principles on which Institutionalism could be built. Such an approach held the promise of delivering specific policy recommendations, but could also appear highly subjective and unreliable. The new economists' attention to detail and a commitment to interdisciplinary research proved to be both Institutionalism's strength and its weakness.

The neoclassical school, having continued to focus on the "classical line" of inquiry, continued to build-out the assumptions of the classical masters, adapting old theory to new practice. Unlike the Institutionalist School, its members pronounced no dramatic declarations of a neoclassical resurgence, nor did they call for a systematic re-imagining of what neoclassical economics might offer society. The neoclassicists simply continued with their focus on marginal utility, distribution, and measuring efficiency. Although they were not as provocative as their Institutionalist colleagues, neoclassical economists' ideas and arguments remained well within the accepted norms of American political economy and they maintained their influence over the discipline.

Heterodox economists' attempts to force a breakthrough regarding economic theory became wearying and increasingly futile. The AEA executive committee rejected a proposal to establish a committee to once more act as a clearing house for economic definitions, citing as the reason a likely lack of agreement. Many economists' excitement regarding the status and future of theory was high, but the enthusiasm frustrated those within the discipline who saw the ongoing debates as fruitless.[13] After a decade of gestation, the discipline took stock of the Institutionalist movement through a series of conference panels and journal articles. Commons' assessment reflected the on-going ambiguity of Institutionalism. As he noted, "The difficulty in defining a field for the so-called institutional economics is the uncertainty of meaning of an institution."[14] In yet another attempt to forge some sort of order, Commons argued somewhat vaguely that "Institutional economics is the assets and liabilities of concerns, contrasted with Adam Smith's *Wealth of Nations*."[15] Commons called for the further investigation of human psychology – the continued pursuit of the sort of elusive concepts that continually invoked disagreement and placed Institutional economics beyond the pale for many Americans. A roundtable on economic theory at the AEA's forty-fourth annual meeting and subsequent responses furthered the feeling that Institutionalism had failed to develop a coherent identity. Cornell's Paul T. Homan dismissed the field outright, declaring that "a distinguishable body of economic knowledge or theory properly to be called institutional is an intellectual fiction."[16] Undeterred, Institutionalists responded to their critics and persisted in their mission to reshape the way Americans approached economic problems. Ultimately, their failure to deliver a theory as simple and consistent as that of the neoclassical school ensured that classical thought in American economics would persist to a degree unimaginable to the new economists of the late nineteenth century.

Despite the fears of some, professional economists in the US were largely divided by methodology rather than ideology. The distinction was ignored at times and rather than presenting a unified front by building on general consensus regarding issues such as free trade or the necessity of a central bank, the discipline remained divided. Neoclassical and heterodox economists' tendency to drift apart and engage in academic debates damaged the discipline's authority in the public sphere, as it made economists seem as subjective as the politicians to whom they offered advice. It became clear that without concerted effort, such as commission work, or an emergency response brought on by financial panic or war, economists would continue to focus on differences as a matter of academic discourse. As a result, professional economics retained the appearance of a confused and highly subjective discipline.

Amateurs and businessmen

Continued conflict among professional economists implicitly legitimized fringe economists – both professional and amateur. As a result, folk economists continued to play a role in shaping American economic thought and economic policy, likely unaware of the intellectual battles within academia beyond the observation that the discipline could not seem to agree on much. For many Americans, access to formal education remained beyond reach and economic theory was scoffed at as the unnecessary obfuscation of simple truths. Public discourse continued to shape widespread opinions about proper economic policy, and as memories of Wilson's Presidency faded, so did any illusions that Americans readily understood or recognized the distinction between professional and amateur economists.

The gap between trained, professional economists and amateur theorists had indeed continued to widen. AEA membership in the 1920s grew mainly through new economics graduate students and junior faculty members, a trend encouraged by the Membership Committee following the observation that lasting members were those "whose interests are intimately tied to economic work of some kind."[17] AEA membership reached 3,746 by 1926 and the organization was justifiably confident in continued growth. A 1929 report on the overlapping between the four main social science organizations in the US – the American Political Science Association, American Sociological Society, American Statistical Association, and the AEA – affirmed economists' position at the top of the social sciences in terms of membership and draw. The organizational overlap indicated that economists played a leading role in the social sciences, though there was no guarantee that expansion within the academy would translate into recognition in the public sphere.

The insulation that had begun with the alienation of clergy in the early 1900s continued with the gradual estrangement of businessmen and amateur economists. E.S. Cowdrick, an employee of Colorado Fuel & Iron, relayed the mutual concerns he and a business associate harbored about the reception of non-professional economists at the annual meetings, stating "The attitude of the representatives of industry whom I knew seemed to be that it was the professors' party and that it was good policy to stay out of the discussions."[18] Secretary Frank Deibler received the criticism with grace and promised to bring the matter to the attention of the Program Committee, but denied its merit. Deibler's denial and professional economists' best wishes notwithstanding, the AEA and its academic members would need to separate expert from non-expert to create an intellectual domain that conferred prestige.

Despite the very real distinction between amateur and professional, those in positions of power could simply claim the title of economist. Such was the case with Deputy-Secretary of the Nebraskan Department of Agriculture Grant Shumway, who declined an invitation to join the AEA, declaring:

I have practiced "economics" so long as I can remember and the last three years just a little bit more than all other previous years. In fact I feel like a practical and economical man at the present time, so much so that the fees indicated would be one of the deterring influences in becoming a member of the Association unless I were convinced of its benefits.[19]

Shumway could wear an economist's credentials with no real consequences. The AEA would never refute the claim and the public seemed unlikely to note the distinction between a trained economist and a politician in charge of economic policy.

Professional economists had consolidated their intellectual turf within academia and the AEA, but folk economists and business leaders continued to exert influence over the policymaking process. The Georgist movement of the late nineteenth century proved to pose a particularly resilient challenge to the professional economics community, as populist clamoring for an economic panacea showed no sign of diminishing. In the aftermath of World War I it was clear that the US was the industrial powerhouse of the world, and populists sought to elevate small businesses (along with independent farmers) as the virtuous economic building blocks of American society. This served to update George's single-tax theory, which continued to resonate with many Americans owing to its simplicity and perceived benefit to small entrepreneurs.

Promoters and pamphlets touting the "single-tax solution" were commonplace. Single-tax advocates' enthusiasm and penchant for monopolizing discussion wore on some academic economists – including Royal Meeker, who, in a letter to Edwin Kemmerer, declared he was "frankly afraid of cranks in general and

S.T.'s [single-taxers] in particular."[20] Still, the movement enjoyed several supporters within the US professional economics community, namely MIT-trained Stuart Chase and Yale's Harry Gunnison Brown. The mixture of populist support, a handful of academic champions, and victories at the local level of government encouraged many within the single-tax movement that theirs was an unstoppable cause driven by logic and the laws of economics.

Despite this modicum of legitimacy, the single-tax movement remained at arm's length from the professional economics community, mainly because its most vocal advocates persisted in presenting their cause as the only logical conclusion of economic reasoning. Their unyielding commitment to a national single-tax policy as a universally beneficial policy meant that the group found little sympathy within the professional economics community. Interest groups routinely contacted the AEA in the hope of attracting professional economists' support through the aegis of academic inquiry. But single-tax organizations were unable to build such a relationship because of their reputation as propagandists – a point made clear by Frank Deibler in response to the Henry George Foundation's request for AEA associate status. Such rebuttals encouraged the long-held opinion among single-taxers that the AEA represented "vested interests" committed to obfuscating economic truths. To Americans skeptical of authority or resentful toward the educated class from which they felt excluded, folk economists continued to be an alternative source for economic policy proposals. Undeterred by its rejection, the Henry George Foundation and similar organizations both outside of and on the fringes of academia continued to promote George's message through lectures and conferences.[21]

The Manufacturers and Merchants Federal Tax League, in contrast, adopted more confrontational tactics, turning the quest for single-tax policy into a shrill attack in what became a repeat of the populist crusade against professional economics in the late nineteenth century. Ironically, Richard T. Ely became the center of the group's attention in 1924 as a result of his work on the Institute for Research in Land Economics and Public Utilities. Once decried as a socialist bent on abolishing private property, Ely was painted as a front-man for monopolies bent on punishing the working class.

The Institute, devoted to the "study of the economic relationships arising from the ownership and use of land and the administration and regulation of public utilities," eschewed individual research in favor of a collective approach, which Ely felt was in line with the reputable Harvard Bureau of Business Research and the National Bureau of Economic Research.[22] The decision to form the Institute in 1920 – one year after the Federal Tax League began campaigning for federal tax reform – proved to be unfortunate timing because it fed fears that "landed interests" had mobilized to counter the single-tax movement.[23]

The Federal Tax League seized on the Institute's private funding and Ely's rejection of a single-tax solution. The 30,000-member-strong organization circulated the accusations of Emil O. Jorgensen (the group's Bureau of Information director) in its newsletter and disseminated a pamphlet titled "Prof. Richard T. Ely Exposed!" In both instances, Jorgenson purported to show how a "gigantic, nation-wide scheme" had been erected to deceive the public regarding the "right solution" to the nation's economic problems.[24] As with the populists' criticisms of professional economists during the "Battle of the Standards," Jorgensen's charges rested on a small degree of fact bolstered by unsubstantiated conjecture. The underlying assumption of his claims was that actual evidence of wrong-doing was unobtainable owing to the inherent secrecy of such cabals – an argument virtually impossible to refute.

There is little doubt that the Institute possessed the same integrity as any other academic research organization of the era. Correspondence between Ely and Henry C. Taylor, a noted agricultural economist and the Institute's first Secretary, illustrates concerns about maintaining a balanced staff and research program. Furthermore, contrary to being a well-funded front for the public utilities and land speculators, the Institute struggled to find and maintain financial support throughout its first decade. If Ely and the Institute's widely respected staff were bought, then their price was exceptionally low. As Jorgenson correctly noted in his attack pamphlet, the Institute secured annual funding of around $50,000, but this sum had to cover the costs of ten staff members, administrative staff, and the publication of monographs and the Institute's journal. The financial strain was such that Ely and the Institute had to move from the University of Wisconsin to Northwestern University in 1925 for the promise of stable funding (where continued difficulties eventually led Ely to move the Institute to New York).[25]

Despite the tenuousness of the charges – a point John R. Commons took the time to illustrate in a letter to Jorgensen following his initial charges in late 1924 – the Federal Tax League continued to publicly attack Ely and the Institute.[26] Department of Agriculture economist S.W. Mendum reviewed a book-length version of Jorgensen's accusations in the *Journal of Farm Economics*, but Mendum's attempt to establish a productive scholarly dialogue was an exercise in futility. The Federal Tax League's rigid prerogatives and personal attacks soured the potential for a meaningful discussion between the single-tax movement and the professional economics community. The Federal Tax League presented the AEA with a formal appeal to assemble a special committee to investigate Ely and the Institute, but the AEA refused to get involved. The Executive Committee declined "on the grounds that such an investigation would lie outside the function of this organization."[27] Although technically true, the AEA's refusal to publicly confront The Federal Tax League for its bullying tactics represented another missed opportunity to act as an authoritative body on economic policy.

The Federal Tax League's campaign against Ely, although certainly never significant enough to threaten either his job or the Institute's existence, was not entirely superfluous. Members of the American Teacher's Federation seized on the accusations, arguing that the Institute's stance on decreased land taxes placed it at odds with the interests of laborers who would be forced to assume a higher burden when the taxation of goods inevitably rose instead. The ATF, a member of the larger American Federation of Labor, went so far as to call for a ban on Ely's textbooks in classrooms at the AFL's convention in 1927, although the measure failed following a heated debate on the floor.[28] The fringe Federal Tax League had successfully carved out a place in American economic thought, however marginal, and in doing so challenged the authority of professional economists.

Ironically, the campaign to discredit Ely likely hurt the single-tax movement in the long run. Ely and the Institute promised to renew interest in land as a unique factor in economic theory at a time when many professional economists were gradually treating it as synonymous with capital. Had the various groups that composed the single-tax movement directed their resources toward engaging in a dialogue with the Institute and with the academic community in general, it is conceivable that George's ideas may have found traction within mainstream economic theory at a crucial period for federal farm and housing policy. As it was, Georgists continued to campaign as an alternative to professional economists and were therefore relegated to stoking dissent and suspicion.

The Georgists were joined by a potpourri of businessmen and business organizations of varying motives and degrees of efficacy. In a decade when many found the "gospel of business" appealing, the opinions of those who carried the cachet of being a successful businessman warranted attention. Such faith was not without reason. In many cases, business leaders demonstrated an understanding that was in line with the prevailing principles of modern economic theory. But not all business leaders seemed to grasp the challenges of modern economic theory in relation to public policy.

The simplicity of business leaders' policy proposals could be astounding, as demonstrated by Thomas Edison or Henry Ford when they spoke on monetary policy. The two warned of the perils of a gold standard in the early 1920s, when the debate over post-war monetary policy evolved into a general debate about growth policies. Edison dismissed the precious metal as wholly unsuited for its assigned task as a standard of value. He preferred instead a system of barter based on fixed-price commodities.[29] Ford demonstrated a similarly simplistic understanding of the issue when he urged the federal government to print money outright, reasoning that it made little sense for the government to issue bonds and incur the cost of interest since they were the original source of money from the outset.[30] John R. Commons, having shifted from his traditional focus on labor issues to serve as president of a pro-gold standard lobbying group, the National Monetary Association, visited both men in an attempt to change their opinions – with little success. The two business leaders were joined by W.H. Coin Harvey, author of *Coin's Financial School* and the prominent figure in the populist push for free silver in the 1880s and 1890s. The National Honest Money Association seized on Ford and Edison's public comments to lend credibility to their renewed efforts at overturning the US monetary status quo. Perhaps understanding that an anachronistic cry for "free silver" might eliminate the already-marginal organization's appeal, the group instead expressed an interest in a national currency backed by bonds.[31]

This is not to suggest that cranks, charlatans, or the unjustifiably confident represented the only challenge to professional economists' reputation as the nation's economic advisors. If such were the case, then identifying the line between expert and amateur would have been easy. Rather, the line between professional and non-professional economist proved genuinely permeable. Paul Warburg, a successful banker and advocate of the Federal Reserve Act, routinely promoted positions within the realm of reason according to most professional economists. His stance on war finance, his work as advisor of to the Federal Reserve, and his work with the Institute of Economics (later named the Brookings Institute) reflected a deep interest in the work of the discipline. Likewise, Warburg was engaged in an active dialogue with academic economists – publishing several books and articles in the AAPSS regarding his experiences with and opinions on banking and monetary policy. Frank Vanderlip, William McKinnley's Assistant Secretary of the Treasury and President of the National City Bank of New York, similarly managed meaningful engagement with the professional economics community throughout his career. In addition to publishing in scholarly journals, Vanderlip maintained an active membership in the AEA and served as Vice-President of the organization in 1918. It was certainly possible for a non-academically trained economist to not only find acceptance within the realm of professional economics, but also to find a genuine understanding of the discipline and its nuances.

The increasing sophistication of business groups that exerted pressure on lawmakers and public opinion further complicated the process of identifying expertise in the policymaking process. Historians have noted the rise and influence of public relations and advertising campaigns, both of which enhanced business leaders' ability to mount campaigns in favor of desired policy to sway voters and politicians. Meanwhile, growing numbers of economists were employed in the private sector, which also complicates any attempt to parse academic versus "business" economics. The National Industrial Conference Board, an umbrella organization for major trade organizations, solicited recommendations from the AEA to staff its economic research staff. Trade associations continued to participate in the annual AEA meetings, often sending representatives to present alongside labor representatives and professional economists. Increased corporate and trade association employment of professional economists began to further blur the line between the archetype dispassionate economic experts that early professionalizers had hoped to create and the sort of "bought economist" the public had long decried.

Such challenges to the authority and expertise of professional economists presented the public and policymakers with a difficult situation as they sought to identify and employ expertise in a consistently contentious field. Even though by this time professional economics was a firmly entrenched fact of the American intellectual landscape, the discipline was already locked into a frustratingly ancillary role in the economic policymaking process. The public, it seemed, lacked a clear understanding of what the discipline could offer, in part because professional economists themselves were still uncertain after 40 years of organizing.

Despite these shortcomings, professional economics in the US appears to have reached maturity. Significant changes loomed in the future, to be sure. The discipline would continue to expand in size and scope as more men and women attended college and pursued advanced degrees in the discipline. The methodological toolkit of these later generations also would expand greatly and lead to mathematical models so complex that they stretched the gap between professional and layman further than early twentieth century economists feared possible. At the same time, the creation of federal agencies and advisory groups would seemingly draw professional economists and the nation's lawmakers closer together.

Yet much of what gives professional economics its professional veneer was firmly in place by the end of the 1920s. The discipline's leading organization, the AEA, its top journals, and the nation's leading economic departments were well-entrenched by the end of the decade. These institutions arguably fulfilled their duties as well in 1925 as at any other time in the twentieth century. They enhanced communication among economists, distinguished economics from its sister disciplines, and allowed economists and non-economists alike to distinguish between trained professionals and untrained laymen. Yet although these key institutions maintained the discipline's contours, they could not eliminate internal dissent or the external criticism that made it difficult for professional economists to successfully influence economic policy. These shortcomings were not a sign of the discipline's immaturity, but rather stemmed from the fact that the majority of US economists continued to believe that the discipline must necessarily limit its role to that of the neutral advisor in order to maintain respectability within the relatively democratic American system.

In his Presidential Address at the AEA's 1926 meeting, Edwin Kemmerer – the "money doctor" who had famously travelled the world to advise foreign governments on monetary policy – decried the "widely accepted economic fallacies" he had encountered, particularly in "economically new countries."[32] His speech suggested that the US, unlike those upstart nations, had overcome anachronistic approaches to policymaking. The irony in Kemmerer's speech became abundantly clear a short decade later when strict US adherence to the gold standard – the sort of monetary policy Kemmerer was promoting abroad – lengthened and deepened the Great Depression worldwide. More striking is the false dichotomy Kemmerer portrayed between developing nations that ignored professional economists' advice and industrial powerhouses like the US, which, he argued, prospered through the adoption of such advice.

In fact, as the US moved through the generally prosperous 1920s, politicians continued to employ economic theory in a haphazard and makeshift fashion. Americans and those engaged in the economic policymaking process recognized the social prestige of professional economists, but did not necessarily understand how to act on the discipline's consensus, when one emerged. Continued disagreement within the discipline, as well as continued challenges to academic freedom, often undercut the image of the academically trained economist as an authoritative and objective guide in the policymaking process. At the same time, the illusion emerged that the realm of commerce had been tamed through the application of economic science.

Notes

1 "Defeated Candidates Send Congratulations to Governor Wilson," *The Sun*, July 3, 1912.
2 "Economists Ask U.S. to Meet War Cost by Taxation," *New York Tribune*, April 19, 1917. "Taxation Is Favored To Meet War Expenses," *The Atlanta Constitution*, April 19, 1917. "Taxation for War Cost Urged," *The Christian Science Monitor*, May 14, 1917.
3 "Financing of War Divides Political Scientists' Opinion," *New York Tribune*, November 3, 1917. Edwin R. Seligman and Robert Murray Haig, *How to Finance the War* (New York: Division of Intelligence and Publicity of Columbia University, 1917).
4 The "tax first, bonds in an emergency" approach was echoed once more at the discussion of the Committee on War Finance's report in December 1918.
5 "Holland's Letter," *Wall Street Journal*, May 19, 1917. Edwin R. Seligman, "The Cost of the War and How It Was Met," *The American Economic Review* 9, no. 4 (December 1919): 739–70.
6 Interestingly, H.C. Engelbrecht and F.C. Hanighen's *Merchants of Death*, the popular anti-war exposé that fed isolationist settlement in the mid-1930s, failed to garner significant attention from the professional economics community. Engelbrecht and Hanighen's charge that economic incentives drove certain industries to encourage global conflict would have presumably piqued the interest of the nation's economic experts, yet no economics journals reviewed the work and there is no evidence that economists championed or criticized Engelbrecth and Hanighen's thesis in the public sphere.
7 As biographer Loring notes, from 1920 till 1924 Fisher's promotion of US entry into the League at times consumed a significant amount of his energy and ultimately detracted from his scholarly pursuits.
8 Ernest L Bogart *et al.*, "Report of the Committee on War Finance," *The American Economic Review* 9, no. 1 (March 1919): 1–127.
9 Edwin R. Seligman *et al.*, "Preliminary Report of the Joint Committee on Academic Freedom and Academic Tenure," *The American Economic Review* 5, no. 1 (March 1915): 316–23. Edwin R. Seligman, "Edwin R Seligman to A.A. Young," April 16, 1915, American Economic Association Records, 1886– Box 14, Duke University Rare Book, Manuscript and Special Collections Library. The initial committee members were: Edwin Seligman, Richard T. Ely, Frank A. Fetter (AEA); F.N. Judson, J.Q. Dealey, Herbert Croly (APSA); U.G. Weatherly, James P. Licthenberger, Roscoe Pound (ASS).
10 Irving Fisher, "The Red Flag of Class War," *New York Tribune*, January 7, 1919. Irving Fisher, "Economists in Public Service: Annual Address of the President," *The American Economic Review* 9, no. 1 (March 1919): 5–21.
11 "Two Professors Quit as Amherst President Goes," *The Christian Science Monitor*, June 21, 1923.
12 Walton H. Hamilton, "The Institutional Approach to Economic Theory," *The American Economic Review* 9, no. 1 (March 1919): 309–18.
13 Royal Meeker, "Royal Meeker to E.W. Kemmerer," February 21, 1926, American Economic Association Records, 1886– Box 21, Duke University Rare Book, Manuscript and Special Collections Library.
14 John R. Commons, "Institutional Economics," *The American Economic Review* 21, no. 4 (December 1931): 648.

15 Ibid., 650.
16 Paul T. Homan, "An Appraisal of Institutional Economics," *The American Economic Review* 22, no. 1 (March 1932): 10.
17 Frank S. Deibler, "Report of the Membership Committee," *The American Economic Review* 15, no. 1 (March 1925): 146.
18 E.S. Cowdrick, "E.S. Cowdrick to Frederick S. Diebler [sic]," January 22, 1929, American Economic Association Records, 1886– Box 24, Duke University Rare Book, Manuscript and Special Collections Library.
19 Grant Shumway, "Grant Shumway to Ray B. Westerfield," July 1, 1924, American Economic Association Records, 1886–Box 19, Duke University Rare Book, Manuscript and Special Collections Library.
20 Meeker, "Royal Meeker to E.W. Kemmerer."
21 The most notable of these organizations is the Robert Schalkenbach Foundation, which was founded with funds from businessman Robert Schalkenbach's estate following his death in December 1924. The organization continues to promote George's ideas through dissemination of his works and the commissioning of original research on single-tax theory. The foundation has also supported the publication of *The American Journal of Economics and Sociology* since 1941.
22 Richard T. Ely, "Research in Land and Public Utility Economics," *The Journal of Land & Public Utility Economics* 1, no. 1 (January 1925): 1–6.
23 S.W. Mendum, "False Education in Our Schools and Colleges by Emil O. Jorgensen," *Journal of Farm Economics* 8, no. 2 (April 1926): 277–79.
24 Emil O. Jorgensen, "Emil O. Jorgensen to E.W. Kemmerer," July 31, 1926, American Economic Association Records, 1886– Box 22, Duke University Rare Book, Manuscript and Special Collections Library. Emil O. Jorgensen, "Emil O. Jorgensen to E.W. Kemmerer," September 30, 1926, American Economic Association Records, 1886– Box 22, Duke University Rare Book, Manuscript and Special Collections Library. "Keller Land Tax Bills Indorsed [sic]," *The Christian Science Monitor*, June 9, 1921.
25 Ely, Commons, and Perlman's recollections of Ely's departure make clear that some degree of bad blood did encourage the move, but the Department's subsequent move to turn Ely's Madison home into a memorial space for economics graduates suggests that Ely's comments to the press about placid relations in 1925 were not wholly lacking in truth. In the late 1920s, the Institute was once more embroiled in controversy when its relationship with the National Electric Light Association was revealed. The resultant controversy and onset of the Great Depression dried up funding and the Institute died in New York City after a vain attempt to relocate in search of greener pastures.
26 John R. Commons, "John R. Commons to Emil O. Jorgensen," September 23, 1924, Henry C. Taylor Papers, 1896–1968 Box 10, Wisconsin Historical Society.
27 Edwin W. Kemmerer, "Edwin W. Kemmerer to Emil O. Jorgensen," December 30, 1926, American Economic Association Records, 1886– Box 22, Duke University Rare Book, Manuscript and Special Collections Library.
28 George Shaffer, "Northwestern U. Center of Labor Meeting Battle," *Chicago Daily Tribune*, October 14, 1927.
29 "Says Gold Almost Useless, Edison Urges Fixing Prices," *Boston Daily Globe*, February 19, 1922. John R. Commons, "Hobson's 'Economics of Unemployment'," *The American Economic Review* 13, no. 4 (December 1923): 638–47.
30 "Ford's Energy Dollar Useless, Treasury View," *New York Tribune*, December 17, 1921.
31 "Oppose Gold Money Basis," *The Washington Post*, December 17, 1921. Carol W. Gelderman, *Henry Ford: The Wayward Capitalist* (New York: Dial Press, 1981), 313. Israel Rubin and Thomas Alva Edison, "Thomas Alva Edison's 'Treatise on National Economic Policy and Business'," *The Business History Review* 59, no. 3 (Autumn 1985): 433–64. Although Rubin rightly acknowledges the energy with which Edison engaged

the issue of monopolistic behavior, his praise seems to derive from surprise that the industrial magnate would spend the time writing such a treatise, rather than from the quality of the ideas themselves. Edison's plan to allow businesses to enter legally sanctioned price-fixing agreements hardly constituted an innovative or realistic plan of action.

One could argue that Ford, Edison, and Harvey alike were simply visionaries ahead of their time. Indeed, economist Israel Rubin suggests that Edison possessed a cunning economic mind, as evidenced by his unpublished 1891 treatise on "National Economic Policy." The gold standard, after all, was eventually abandoned in the depths of the Great Depression, and punitive monetary policies have been cited as a source of animosity leading up to the hostilities of World War II. But none of the three men ever demonstrated a strong understanding the nation's monetary system post-1913. Ford harbored a particularly strong distrust of bankers, driven in part by his anti-Semitism, and argued that such financial institutions ought to be limited to the holding of customer deposits. Their criticism did not reflect a careful engagement with the realities of the political economic situation, but rather impulses of a folk economist – beholden to absolute truths and unwilling or unable to acknowledge the context in which policy had to be formed.

32 Edwin W. Kemmerer, "Economic Advisory Work for Governments," *The American Economic Review* 17, no. 1 (March 1927): 1–12. The list of national governments Kemmerer advised includes the Philippines, Mexico, Guatemala, Colombia, Germany, South Africa, Chile, Poland, Ecuador, and Bolivia.

Bibliography

Abbott, Andrew. "Linked Ecologies: States and Universities as Environments for Professions." *Sociological Theory* 23, no. 3 (September 2005): 245–75.

Allen, Robert Loring. *Irving Fisher: A Biography*. Cambridge, MA: Blackwell Publishers, 1993.

Alvord, Clarence W. "The Goose-Step by Upton Sinclair." *The Mississippi Valley Historical Review* 10, no. 3 (December 1923): 336–37.

Bailey, T.P. "The Goose-Step by Upton Sinclair." *The Sewanee Review* 31, no. 4 (October 1923): 508–9.

———. "The Higher Learning in America by Thorstein Veblen." *The Sawanee Review* 28, no. 1 (January 1920): 119–20.

Bernstein, Michael A. *A Perilous Progress: Economists and Public Purpose in Twentieth-Century America*. Princeton, NJ: Princeton University Press, 2001.

Blaug, Mark. *Great Economists before Keynes: An Introduction to the Lives & Works of One Hundred Great Economists of the Past*. Atlantic Highlands, N.J.: Humanities Press International, 1986.

Bogart, Ernest L, Edwin W. Kemmerer, Edwin R. Seligman, *et al*. "Report of the Committee on War Finance." *The American Economic Review* 9, no. 1 (March 1919): 1–127.

Bragdon, Henry W. *Woodrow Wilson: The Academic Years*. Cambridge, MA: Belknap Press of Harvard University Press, 1967.

Cairncross, Alec. "Economists in Wartime." *Contemporary European History* 4, no. 1 (March 1995): 19–36.

Commons, John R. "Hobson's 'Economics of Unemployment'." *The American Economic Review* 13, no. 4 (December 1923): 638–47.

———. "Institutional Economics." *The American Economic Review* 21, no. 4 (December 1931): 648–57.

———. *Myself: The Autobiography of John R. Commons*. New York: The Macmillan Company, 1934.

Davenport, H.J. "The War-Tax Paradox." *The American Economic Review* 9, no. 1 (March 1919): 34–46.

——. "War Finance and American Business." *Journal of Political Economy* 24, no. 2 (February 1916): 97–125.

Deibler, Frank S. "Report of the Membership Committee." *The American Economic Review* 15, no. 1 (March 1925): 146.

——. "Report of the Secretary of the American Economic Association." *The American Economic Review* 16, no. 1 (March 1926): 331–35.

Durand, E. Dana. "Taxation Versus Bond Issues for Financing the War." *Journal of Political Economy* 25, no. 9 (November 1917): 888–916.

Eichengreen, Barry J. *Golden Fetters: The Gold Standard and the Great Depression, 1919–1939.* New York: Oxford University Press, 1992.

Ely, Richard T. "Research in Land and Public Utility Economics." *The Journal of Land & Public Utility Economics* 1, no. 1 (January 1925): 1–6.

Engelbrecht, H. C., and Frank Cleary Hanighen. *Merchants of Death; A Study of the International Armament Industry.* New York: Dodd, Mead & Company, 1934.

Farrer, David. *The Warburgs: The Story of a Family.* New York: Stein and Day, 1975.

Fisher, Irving. "Economists in Public Service: Annual Address of the President." *The American Economic Review* 9, no. 1 (March 1919): 5–21.

Fogel, Robert William, Enid M. Fogel, Mark Guglielmo, and Nathaniel Grotte. *Political Arithmetic: Simon Kuznets and The Empirical Tradition in Economics.* Chicago, IL: University of Chicago Press, 2013.

Friedman, Elisha M., David Friday, A. Barton Hepburn, Phillip B. Kennedy, Thomas W. Lamont, Jason A. Neilson, J. Russell Smith, O.M.W Sprague, and F.W. Taussig. "Report of the Committee on Foreign Trade." *The American Economic Review* 10, no. 1 (March 1920): 241–47.

Friedman, Elisha M., O.M.W Sprague, Paul Warburg, David Friday, Burwell S. Cutler, F.W. Taussig, A. Barton Hepburn, Jason A. Neilson, and Horace Secrist. "First Report of the Committee on Foreign Trade of the American Economic Association." *The American Economic Review* 9, no. 1 (March 1919): 366–68.

Gelderman, Carol W. *Henry Ford: The Wayward Capitalist.* New York: Dial Press, 1981.

Gloriosus, Miles. "The Goose Step by Upton Sinclair." *The Journal of Educational Research* 8, no. 1 (June 1923): 74–76.

Hamilton, Walton H. "The Institutional Approach to Economic Theory." *The American Economic Review* 9, no. 1 (March 1919): 309–18.

Harvey, W.H. *Coin's Financial School.* Chicago: Coin Pub. Co., 1894.

Holmes, George E., John Cummings, Kingman Nott Robins, Willford I. King, and Ernest L Bogart. "Report of the Committee on War Finance: Discussion at the Richmond Meeting." *The American Economic Review* 9, no. 1 (March 1919): 129–42.

Homan, Paul T. "An Appraisal of Institutional Economics." *The American Economic Review* 22, no. 1 (March 1932): 10–17.

Howard, Stanley E., Frank D. Graham, David A. McCabe, and Frank Albert Fetter. "Edwin Walter Kemmerer 1875–1945." *The American Economic Review* 36, no. 1 (March 1946): 219–21.

Jorgensen, Emil O. "The Progress of the Singletax Movement." *The Libertarian* 5, no. 5 (November 1925): 330–49.

Kemmerer, Edwin W. "Economic Advisory Work for Governments." *The American Economic Review* 17, no. 1 (March 1927): 1–12.

Keynes, John Maynard. *The Economic Consequences of the Peace.* New York: Harcourt, Brace, and Howe, 1920.

"Memorial of American Economists to Congress Regarding War Finance," n.d. American Economic Association Records, 1886– Box 3. Duke University Rare Book, Manuscript and Special Collections Library.

Mendum, S.W. "False Education in Our Schools and Colleges by Emil O. Jorgensen." *Journal of Farm Economics* 8, no. 2 (April 1926): 277–79.

Milonakis, Dimitris, and Ben Fine. *From Political Economy to Economics: Method, the Social and the Historical in the Evolution of Economic Theory*. London; New York: Routledge, 2009.

Mitchell, W.C., Royal Meeker, Edwin W. Kemmerer, Irving Fisher, W.M. Persons, and B.M. Anderson. "Report of the Committee on the Purchasing Power of Money in Relation to the War." *The American Economic Review* 9, no. 1 (March 1919): 364–65.

Rice, Stuart A., and Morris Green. "Interlocking Memberships of Social Science Societies." *Journal of the American Statistical Association* 24, no. 167 (September 1929): 303–6.

Rubin, Israel, and Thomas Alva Edison. "Thomas Alva Edison's 'Treatise on National Economic Policy and Business'." *The Business History Review* 59, no. 3 (Autumn 1985): 433–64.

Rutherford, Malcolm. *The Institutionalist Movement in American Economics, 1918–1947: Science and Social Control*. New York: Cambridge University Press, 2011.

Seligman, Edwin R. "Loans Versus Taxes in War Finance." *Annals of the American Academy of Political and Social Science* 75 (January 1918): 52–82.

———. "The Cost of the War and How It Was Met." *The American Economic Review* 9, no. 4 (December 1919): 739–70.

Seligman, Edwin R., and Robert Murray Haig. *How to Finance the War*. New York: Division of Intelligence and Publicity of Columbia University, 1917.

Seligman, Edwin R., Richard T. Ely, Frank Albert Fetter, Charles E. Bennett, and Henry W. Farnam. "Report of the Committee on Academic Freedom and Academic Tenure." *The American Economic Review* 6, no. 1 (March 1916): 230–46.

Seligman, Edwin R., Richard T. Ely, Frank Albert Fetter, F.N. Judson, J.Q. Dealey, and Herbert Croly. "Preliminary Report of the Joint Committee on Academic Freedom and Academic Tenure." *The American Economic Review* 5, no. 1 (March 1915): 316–23.

Sinclair, Upton. *The Goose-Step: A Study of American Education*. Pasadena, CA: The Author, 1923.

Skidelsky, Robert Jacob Alexander. *John Maynard Keynes, 1920–1937, V. 2, The Economist as Saviour*. London: Papermac, 1992.

Sprague, O.M.W, E.T. Miller, H.L. Lutz, and Edmond E. Lincoln. "Loans and Taxes in War Finance: Discussion." *The American Economic Review* 7, no. 1 (March 1917): 214–23.

Straus, Oscar S., Samuel Gompers, Edward A. Filene, Henry A. Atkinson, and William H. Short. "League to Enforce Peace to H.J. Davenport," January 7, 1920. American Economic Association Records, 1886– Box 17. Duke University Rare Book, Manuscript and Special Collections Library.

Taussig, F.W. "Germany's Reparation Payments." *The American Economic Review* 10, no. 1 (March 1920): 33–49.

———. "Keynes, The Economic Consequences of the Peace." *The Quarterly Journal of Economics* 34, no. 2 (February 1920): 381–87.

"The Higher Learning in America: A Memorandum on the Conduct of Universities by Business Men by Thorstein Veblen." *The American Historical Review* 24, no. 4 (July 1919): 714–15.

"The Higher Learning in America by Thorstein Veblen." *The North American Review* 209, no. 760 (March 1919): 417–20.

Veblen, Thorstein. *The Higher Learning in America: A Memorandum on the Conduct of Universities by Business Men.* New York: B.W. Huebsch, 1918.

Warburg, Paul. "Political Pressure and the Future of the Federal Reserve System." *Annals of the American Academy of Political and Social Science* 99 (January 1922): 70–74.

——. "Some Phases of Financial Reconstruction." *Annals of the American Academy of Political and Social Science* 82 (March 1919): 347–73.

Young, Allyn A. "Economics and War: A Presidential Address." *The American Economic Review* 16, no. 1 (March 1926): 1–13.

——. "Report of the Secretary for the Year Ending December 19, 1916." *The American Economic Review* 7, no. 1 (March 1917): 284–85.

6 Stuck in the middle

Economists, agricultural reform, and crisis[1]

To many in the early 1920s, growth in manufacturing and finance fed the illusion that Americans had managed to translate economic expertise into effective economic policy. The confidence Princeton's Edwin Kemmerer expressed in his presidential address at the American Economic Association's 1927 gathering suggested that the systemic market failures of the nineteenth century were a thing of the past now that professional economists were on the case. Agricultural economists and farmers knew otherwise. US economic growth had masked a slow-burning disaster in rural communities and America's professional economists began to worry about how farmers would adjust to unprecedented productivity in the face of declining agricultural prices as wartime mobilization wound down. Professional economists' influence remained sporadic and incomplete, however, as politicians and the public alike questioned the wisdom of America's presumed economic experts.

The fight over agricultural reform echoed the "Battle of the Standards" that had given professional economists their first taste of the policymaking process in the 1890s. Price-guaranties replaced free silver as the rallying cry of folk economists throughout rural America, and professional economists struggled to discourage lawmakers from pursuing such schemes. Misinformation and misunderstanding once more occluded debate, as agricultural economists found themselves pushed and pulled between Farm Bloc Democrats and Hooverite Republicans. Professional economists delivered consistent criticism of price-guaranty proposals, but failed to rally behind a clear alternative in a timely fashion. As with the money, labor, and monopoly questions, professional economists addressed the issue of declining rural standards of living through a program of research and advising. Once more, they found that applying economic expertise to on-the-ground problems in a timely manner proved to be extremely difficult. The three maladies that had undercut effective economic reform since 1885 – the public's skepticism of economic expertise, the discipline's insularity and internal dissent, and the unpredictable nature of networking – exposed the monumental challenges to developing and deploying expertise in democratic society.

The state of agricultural economics

The groundwork for a robust economic sub-field devoted to the economic issues of farming was laid in the decades preceding the 1920s price-level crisis. The

Morrell Land-Grant Act's emphasis on practical education ensured that state colleges pursued agricultural sciences as early as the 1860s, although such work typically focused on what is better described as crop and livestock management than agricultural economics. The rise of agricultural economics in the US (as it was known in the 1920s) came several decades later, when the discipline as a whole expanded rapidly. Although there was always a degree of interest in agricultural issues, professional economists in the 1880s and 90s seemed interested in farmers as a subplot in the larger story of industrial expansion. By 1907, a handful of economists had seized upon what was gradually recognized as agricultural economics. Henry C. Taylor taught the subject within the Wisconsin Department of Political Economy. George F. Warren (Cornell), Andrew Boss (Minnesota), and Thomas F. Hunt (Pennsylvania State) similarly lectured on farm management and rural economics. In 1909, the University of Wisconsin established the nation's first department of agricultural economics and placed Taylor in charge. Public and private universities soon responded in kind – Minnesota and Cornell most notably.

Passage of the Smith–Lever Act in 1914 ensured federal funding for state-level farm bureaus, which supported "country agents" tasked with distributing information and organizing farmers.[2] The agents provided crucial statistical information for the discipline and additional employment opportunities for agricultural economists who emerged from the nascent graduate programs. The state bureaus were organized under the American Farm Bureau Federation in 1919, adding to the growing number of farmers' groups that had opened offices in Washington, DC, during World War I. In that same year, the American Farm Management Association merged with the American Association of Agricultural Economists and established the *Journal of Farm Economics*. Although never as prestigious as the leading US economics journals, the *Journal of Farm Economics* served as an additional scholarly forum for agricultural economists.

The confluence of professional economists' research and the growing demand for government support led to the creation of the Bureau of Agricultural Economics (BAE). As a branch within the Department of Agriculture, the BAE consolidated the Bureaus of Crop Estimates and Markets, as well as the Office of Farm Management and Farm Economics. The work of its agricultural economists and sociologists was directed by Taylor, who continued the Wisconsin economists' tradition of pursuing public service work. Taylor, in turn, reported to Secretary of Agriculture Henry C. Wallace, whose reputation as editor of *Wallaces' Farmer* made him popular with Mid-Western farmers in particular. The BAE's 1,800 employees received in-service training on economics and statistics, in effect turning the service into a graduate research program of sorts. Under Taylor's guidance, the BAE established its role as an aggregator and processor of the information obtained by state agricultural researchers. Its purpose, as Taylor later noted in his history of agricultural economics, "was to give information and render service which would enable farmers to see the fabric of economic life of which they are a part and to adjust their production and marketing accordingly" – an ideal of passive persuasion that echoed his former advisor, John R. Commons.[3]

Under Taylor, the BAE refined its system of collecting real-time information from farm communities nationwide, which was in theory then used to inform federal agricultural policy. The BAE tasked researchers not only with collecting data on crop production, but also with producing comprehensive "quality of life" reports by utilizing the "door-to-door" techniques Taylor had pioneered as a graduate student with the help of the newly arrived Model-T ten years earlier.[4] The agency utilized a standardized questionnaire book, although researchers were given considerable autonomy. Topics of inquiry included the measurement of price levels in farm communities and fluctuations in farm property prices. This loose research methodology, in conjunction with the Bureau's field researchers from across the country, provided the Department of Agriculture with a flexible and educated research staff.

Public sector agricultural economists were supplemented in 1917 by the formation of the American Association for Agricultural Legislation, which sought to organize and make available information regarding agricultural reform. Once more, Richard T. Ely exerted his influence over American economics, in this case as co-founder of the AAAL alongside Elwood Mead, Taylor, and Cornell's George F. Warren. In typical fashion, under Ely's guidance the organization appealed to notions of progress through research and declared that it was high-time that the nation's farmers paid attention to scientific and economic thought to resolve their growing crisis.

Defining the problem

The immediate source of the farmer's troubles was clear. Agricultural commodity prices had dropped as a result of overproduction in the wake of World War I, squeezing farmers and rural communities that relied on their income. Secretary of Agriculture Edwin Meredith's annual report for 1920 succinctly captured the dilemma – American farmers had increased crop production, yet could expect 2.7 billion dollars less than they had received for the previous year's smaller crop (a decline of 17 percent).[5] At the same time, the prices of industrial products that farmers required remained steady. The net result was a transfer of wealth from rural to urban America.

Beyond this simple observation were broader questions about equality and national identity that would impassion both sides of the impending debate over farm policy reform. The allure of cities, which attracted growing numbers of Americans seeking economic opportunity, upended the demographic scales. In 1920, for the first time, the number of urban Americans exceeded the number living in communities of 5,000 or fewer (which the US census then defined as rural). This demographic shift, combined with the long-standing tendency to think of society as being composed of Manichean halves – the placid rural and chaotic urban – fueled concern about the future of American society throughout the early twentieth century. The countryside was perceived as the simpler stabilizing force that was built on irreplaceable tradition and it was unclear how the demographic transition might affect future generations. Although some considered agriculture merely a "means to industrial greatness," others held fast to an idealized notion of rural life.[6]

These subjective cultural issues emerged in the work of professional economists and complicated the seemingly straightforward application of their expertise. In his assessment of post-war problems, Warren cautioned that an unbalanced economy would push talent from farms to factories, the knock-on effect of which he argued would be a gradual decline in national talent because farm families were larger than those in the city. Warren's concern may strike modern readers as clearly flawed, but such thoughts nevertheless shaped debates about agricultural policy, as sympathy for a romanticized notion of rural laborers, as well as sentiments held by the farmers themselves, made agricultural reform an issue of national character as much as economic prosperity. It was not unreasonable to ask, as Nourse did, whether the nation would

> show herself capable of formulating a policy for the epoch upon whose threshold we now stand, which shall rest upon the impartial judgments of a sound social economy and not be the partisan program of commercial or agrarian or manufacturing interests.[7]

The nation's professional economists, with agricultural economists naturally at the forefront, attempted to confront the issue of declining rural fortunes and to deliver the impartial policies Nourse had hoped for. There was some disagreement not only about the appropriate cure, but also about the best diagnosis. Economists provided a host of explanations that included increased global competition, excessive transportation costs, and a lack of credit. By 1925, the Department of Agriculture's Charles J. Brand could identify eighteen factors that had been cited as contributing to the decline of agricultural prices. That many causes made it difficult to offer definite solutions since each problem demanded its own unique response.

Despite the potential for crippling confusion, the debate quickly focused on the desirability of direct government intervention and the discipline proved reasonably consistent in its conclusions. Immediately after the War, some raised questions about the viability of reinstituting federally imposed price controls; they had, after all, presumably prevented predatory trade during mobilization. The professional economics community was aware of the potential pitfalls associated with such schemes, having participated in and discussed the relatively successful price-control programs (then called price fixing) during mobilization. But the government's haphazard approach to controlling prices and the brevity of the War made it difficult to gauge the long-term viability of any such system.

In essence, economists' arguments against price-fixing programs rested on long-standing classical theory arguments against government intervention, particularly in light of the dynamic nature of the agricultural sector. The University of Minnesota's John D. Black noted regional differences and disparities in the economics of individual crops that made blanket principles exceedingly difficult. Furthermore, conditions on individual farms and the desires of individual farmers varied greatly, defying efforts to craft a "one-size-fits-all" policy. John D. Willard, an agricultural economist at the Massachusetts Agricultural College who had served on the Massachusetts Food Commission during the war, was familiar with the challenges of price-fixing. His experiences led him to conclude that a policy as direct as price-fixing all but guaranteed disaster, which in turn led him to endorse the push for self-regulating reform through research and education.

Economists raised additional questions regarding the sustainability of price-fixing schemes in the face of political pressure. In theory, administrators could regulate prices toward an equitable balance between the interests of the producer (farmers) and the consumer (urban workers). Yet how to determine what constituted an equitable balance? The question raised a host of political and social issues that made professional economists uneasy. Because the very premise of price-fixing flew in the face of basic supply-and-demand logic, any such proposal was unlikely to attract the support of more than a few heterodox economists – a point highlighted by Walton H. Hamilton's failure to rally support for a price-fixing scheme later in the decade.

In keeping with marginal theory, which continued to appeal to a majority of professional economists in the U.S, the farm crisis was best understood in terms of supply and demand. America's farmers simply produced more than consumers demanded, and until the two reached equilibrium, economic suffering was bound to persist. "Adjustment" and "readjustment" – buzz words used to describe painful economic contractions in the years following the War – were readily employed to explain the agricultural crisis. The terms succinctly conveyed the argument that agriculture production and consumption simply were out of balance as a result of abnormally high war-time demand and of the structural shifts that had followed industrialization over the previous decades.

The first critical step, professional economists determined, lay in the accumulation of better data that could in turn be presented to farmers and government agencies, then translated into action. As director of the BAE, Taylor had seized on this principle and pushed the agency to provide the sort of economic overview necessary to allow farmers to better understand and react to shifting markets. Cooperative marketing agencies were widely touted for their potential to help farmers apply economic theory to practice. Willard's analysis of milk prices in New England illustrated this kind of non-interventionist solution to the agricultural crisis that would enjoy widespread support. In the case of the New England dairy farmers, cooperative sorting and storage facilities allowed the farmers to withhold their goods from market until favorable prices returned. Willard also argued that proper price forecasting could theoretically reveal the ideal time to bring their milk to market. By this method, the dramatic expansion of agricultural markets that had previously worked against farmers could be exploited. But, Willard also recognized that cooperative selling raised additional issues that needed addressing, and disciplinary consensus on a definite plan was elusive and not aggressively pursued. Rising railroad rates still threatened to undercut any increase in profits, and there was always the threat that a producers' cooperative might engage in price-fixing or otherwise bully small members of the association.

The prospect of adjusting unfavorable tariffs, long a sore subject for farmers who were forced to sell on the open international market and buy in a protected domestic market, was cited as one potential solution. Opinions were decidedly mixed, however. Nourse cited an imbalanced tariff policy as problematic in his analysis of agriculture in an industrial society, but seemed unsure of the proper solution. He both cautioned against and suggested a need for protective tariffs, citing England's mercantilist policies in both cases.[8] But as tariff expert Jacob Viner noted, engaging in tariff manipulation would ultimately fail to address the excessive prices of manufactured goods that had cut into farmers' profits. An international tariff was also impractical for commodities produced in surplus of domestic demand, as was the case with many American-produced farm goods, because it was the lack of demand rather than foreign competition that drove prices downward. Warren suggested a potpourri of programs to directly improve rural living standards; building hospitals, schools, and transportation networks, for instance, might better close the gap between the rural and urban populations. Anything, he urged, that would make the farmer's life more appealing to the growing numbers of men and women flocking to cities in search of higher pay was worth considering.

Rather than proposing simple panaceas, professional economists offered a frank and thorough assessment of the agricultural crisis. They identified a number of factors that conspired to drive down farmers' income, overproduction being the most notable. The general solution was clear – since price fixing and tariffs would inevitably fail, a combination of cooperative marketing and voluntary adjustment was necessary to resolve the crisis. And yet the complexity and depth of the problem combined with divergent opinions about state intervention to produce a confused mass of well-informed opinions regarding specifics.

A half-baked solution

The gulf between the discipline's reasoning and farmers' desires was captured by the disparity of opinions John D. Black encountered while polling agricultural college presidents and state commissioners of agriculture. The responses, he concluded, fell into two general camps: those who embraced *laissez-faire* policies that focused on education and those who believed a mercantilist approach that regulated production was a more appropriate solution.[9] As with the money, labor and monopoly questions, the nation was split.

By 1922, the crisis had deepened. Farm commodity prices continued to fall and the foreclosure rate on farms had begun to creep upward. Whereas the period from 1913 to 1920 saw a farm foreclosure rate of 3.2 per 1,000, from 1921 to 1926 that number increased to 10.7 per 1,000, with Western states accounting for an alarmingly high percentage of the increase. Eager to reverse the situation, Secretary Wallace obtained permission from President Harding to hold a National Agricultural Conference. The conference, which lasted four days, was organized by Taylor and the staff of the BAE. Of the 336 participants, only six were identified as economists: Theodore Price, Warren, Ely, Nourse, Alexander E. Cance

(Massachusetts Agricultural College), H.C. Filley (University of Nebraska), and Wesley C. Mitchell (National Bureau of Economic Research). An additional 25 participants were identified as delegates from agricultural colleges who straddled the fence between agricultural economics and fields such as animal husbandry and dairy science.

On the surface, the conference appeared to be a repeat of the Indianapolis Monetary Commission at which economists were in the overwhelming minority and their input was largely secondary to that of the business community (although in the case of the IMC, the interests of both communities' dovetailed in the end). However, unlike the IMC, or the Walsh Commission for that matter, the National Agricultural Commission was organized by Taylor and his staff of professional economists with input from Ely, Commons, Mitchell, and Warren. Professional economists clearly played a larger role than in previous conferences of a similar nature. Of the six economists in attendance, all but Mitchell served on one of the Conference's twelve committees. Furthermore, the relatively few economists who attended played significant roles in organizing discussion. Ely, Mitchell, and Warren delivered three of the conference's 24 presentations, and Nourse served as secretary for the Committee on Costs, Prices, and Readjustments.[10] An additional paper on finance was presented by Eugene Meyer, Jr., a well-to-do financier whose profession, long-term membership in the AEA, and position as head of the War Finance Corporation placed him closer to the professional economics community than most. Taylor was made "available for consultation at all times" and therefore played an ambiguous yet undoubtedly instrumental role beyond that of conference organizer.[11] For arguably the first time ever, the professional economics community had a significant presence at a state-sponsored economic conference.

Those in the agricultural sector watched the conference with interest as farmers, farm officials, and farm business group leaders met under the guidance of professional economists and attempted to forge a plan to rescue the agricultural sector. The resulting recommendations were straight out of the leading economics journals. Delegates called for improvements in the collection of agricultural statistics, reductions in transportation costs, and short-term financing for struggling farmers. Farmers were also encouraged to reduce overhead costs, diversify their crops, and "adjust farm operations to market demands."[12]

The "Farm Bloc" in Congress and its constituents – already skeptical of the conference and convinced that the endeavor was a political ploy to delay real action – criticized the recommendations as insufficient. Denunciations from key conference participants like William Jennings Bryan and Samuel Gompers fueled suspicions that the conference was political showmanship and its conclusions nothing more than the desires of the urban Republican elite.[13] Ely's adamant stand against price-fixing solutions during his speech on land use no doubt added to suspicions that the event was "rigged."[14] Less than a week after the Conference concluded, reports began to circulate that a guaranty bill (i.e. price-fixing bill) would soon be floated despite a lack of endorsement in the conference's final report.

The reports proved accurate. Among the conference delegates unsatisfied with the final recommendations was George N. Peek, president of the Moline Plow

Company. Like many businessmen before and since, Peek attempted to leverage his experience as a businessman into qualification as an economic policymaker. His concern about the farm crisis had been aroused by the realization that sales of his company's farm implements were in peril as a result of farmers' declining incomes. Unsatisfied with the results of the National Agricultural Conference, Peek and his colleague Hugh S. Johnson approached Taylor with a plan to guarantee price levels through government subsidies. Unsure of such a solution, but willing to play the role of the dispassionate economic expert at the disposal of policymakers, Taylor reviewed Peek's proposal and offered feedback.

Peek and Johnson, who as part of their campaign had co-authored a book on agricultural reform, sought out additional support for a price-guaranty program. In February 1922, Secretary Wallace hosted a conference to discuss the merits of such a plan. The Peek–Johnson plan proposed to raise the purchasing power of agricultural commodities to pre-war levels by establishing two markets for crops – one a domestic market protected by a tariff, the other an export market managed by a government agency. Key to the plan was an excise tax (alternatively described by Johnson as an "assessment") on growers and processors that would in theory offset the loss incurred by the government agency when exported crops were sold at lower than domestic prices.

The Conference ended without a concrete plan of action, but the seed had been planted. Over the course of the next year, the Peek–Johnson plan spread throughout farm communities and its authors continued to search for support of their proposal. Taylor soon found himself tied to the growing agitation for a price-guaranty program, much to his surprise. He had expressed cautious optimism about the plan's ability to address root causes of farmers' problems, but was hardly a vocal or consistent champion of the measure.[15] As Taylor traveled through the West in an attempt to better understand the "wheat problem," agitation for a price-guaranty program mounted in Washington. The White House was soon convinced that Taylor's fact-finding mission had evolved into a campaign trip for the Peek–Johnson plan. Taylor had in fact remained skeptical of any such scheme, and continued to promote readjustment through farmers' cooperatives, education, and low-cost financing. The strongest evidence of Taylor's support for McNary–Haugen – a 1922 internal report in which Taylor tentatively approved of a program to raise prices – is hardly compelling evidence of endorsement. The diary of assistant chief of the BAE Niles Olsen further contradicts the notion that McNary–Haugen enjoyed widespread support among agricultural economists. Olsen did not record any run-ins with pro-MacNary–Haugen economists until the 1930s, at which point he identified Taylor as a supporter, while also noting Charles J. Brand's comment that Taylor would not publicly acknowledge his support for the measure. Nonetheless, by 1923 the Peek–Johnson plan had taken on a life of its own, secured support in Congress, and become the McNary–Haugen plan. Consequently, McNary–Haugen dominated the debate over agricultural reform for the next four years.

Virtually every professional economist who bothered to contemplate the farm crisis acknowledged that action was necessary to stabilize farm communities. Yet the direct assistance programs and indirect tariff manipulations urged by the farm lobby and outlined in McNary–Haugen were clearly at odds with basic, dominant economic theory on supply-and-demand. The price-fixing mechanism that defined McNary–Haugen worried professional economists because it proposed to implement in peacetime a program of stabilization that had just barely worked during the war.[16] Price supports would undoubtedly relieve pressure on farmers by raising the prices paid for their crops; but overproduction would continue and inevitably overwhelm the purchasing agency without an incentive for farmers to stop growing. Similarly, tariffs might offer short-term relief, but such hopes were speculative at best, and fighting one bad policy (industrial tariffs) with yet another struck professional economists as shortsighted. Warren, the principal supporter for either solution within the professional economics community, proved to be a rather soft advocate. In his 1924 account of the agricultural situation, Warren neither dismissed the principles of McNary–Haugen nor endorsed the measure. Likewise, his public lobbying was sparse, rendering his voice of relative dissent unheard.

Scholars have previously noted the business community's resistance to McNary–Haugen. The marginal and reluctant support of the professional economics community arguably is more noteworthy. Whereas resistance from urban business groups was to be expected, lack of support within the professional economics community revealed both the raw political motivation behind the bill and the powerful Farm Bloc's outright dismissal of reasonably non-vested experts. Barring a collapse in non-US production, or a dramatic uptick in consumption, the American farm crisis could only be solved through a reduction in production. There was little hope that European production would drop to war-time levels; and it was equally hard to conceive of already well-fed urbanites suddenly consuming far more than necessary. No one – least of all the agricultural economists who worked with rural communities – was eager to tell farmers that the boom was over and it was time to adjust expectations. But the professional economists' weak enthusiasm for McNary–Haugen was revealing, as was their failure to push debate past an economically unsustainable solution.

Pursuing the panacea

Many rural Americans had either little faith in or little patience for the cooperative marketing schemes professional economists endorsed, despite their potential. The allure of price-guaranties, which promised parity with urban communities without dramatic changes at home, was powerful. The findings of a National Bureau of Economic Research study noted that although 30 percent of Americans worked in agriculture, the industry received only 17 percent of the national income and each year brought additional evidence of the inequity that undoubtedly stoked farmer resentment and frustration. It did not help that the *Wall Street Journal*, the popular organ of eastern financial elites, routinely invoked economists' opinions when criticizing the bill. Worse still was the public criticism of Benjamin N. Anderson, Jr., an economist at Chase National

Bank whose employment at one of the leading eastern financial institutions automatically rendered him suspect in the eyes of rural America.

From the introduction of the McNary–Haugen bill onward professional economists' voices were drowned out by politicians, lobbyists, editors, farmers, and business groups. The American Association for Agricultural Legislation, which Ely and his colleagues had started with so much optimism six years prior, had failed to make much of a mark. Ely biographer Benjamin Rader suggests that the AAAL may have influenced federal farm policy during World War I and provides several convincing quotations from politicians to demonstrate as much. However, references to the AAAL and its activities were quite rare at the time, and accounts of the group's contributions to the debate over farm policy in the early 1920s are non-existent. The organization had issued a handful of bulletins and met in conjunction with the much larger AEA several times, but lacked any recognizable public influence. The AAAL merged with the American Farm Economic Association (AFEA) in 1924, which meant that the only non-governmental agency staffed by economic experts and dedicated to translating the lessons of economic research into policy reform ceased operation just as McNary–Haugen was presented to Congress. The AFEA, like the AEA, operated under a constitution that limited its activities to research and education. The decision affirmed early economists' faith in the belief that the free exchange of ideas would inevitably lead policymakers to the correct policy solutions, but as previously noted such an approach required an understanding between professional economists, policymakers, and the American public that had proven difficult to achieve.

Farm reform remained firmly an issue of political gamesmanship. The economist as an abstract concept was still conspicuously present, however. In what would be a shining example of the problems associated with identifying and acknowledging economic expertise, Secretary of Commerce Herbert Hoover cultivated his image as a technocratic leader who was not only in tune with cutting-edge economic theory, but also its application to policy. In doing so, he became in the eyes of millions of Americans an economist on par with those who taught, researched, and advised from their posts in academia and research bureaus. As the fight for farm relief continued, President Hoover seemingly embodied all that was modern about economics – the astute vision, ambiguous messaging, and the enviable but fickle social prestige.

Hoover entered the debate over McNary–Haugen with a strong reputation as an expert administrator. There is no doubt that he believed in a cooperative approach to policymaking, but the Midwest native also feared overexpansion of government and readily dismissed ideas that he felt threatened Americans' sense of individualism. A mining engineer by training, he had honed his administrative skills through the management of food relief efforts during World War I and service as head of the Food Administration. In the years immediately following the war, Hoover contemplated a run for the presidency, but chose instead to back Republican candidate Warren Harding. Harding, in turn, offered Hoover the much-maligned Secretary of Commerce post, which at the time possessed relatively limited powers and little promise of greatness. Hoover accepted, but only after assurances that his powers were to be wide-ranging and absolute.[17]

Judging from what little evidence there is regarding the matter, the professional economics community appears to have generally approved of Hoover's appointment as Secretary of Commerce. His aggressive purchasing plans during the war indicated that he was beyond the antiquated *laissez-faire* dogmatism of so many New Era Republicans. Although journalists did not seek commentary from the economics community as they later did during Hoover's Presidential campaign, economic journal articles throughout the war and the years prior to his appointment as Commerce Secretary reinforced Hoover's credentials as a practicing economist.[18]

His strong opposition to McNary–Haugen exacerbated friction between Secretary of Agriculture Wallace and President Harding (and later President Coolidge). Hoover, who tended to focus on issues surrounding industrial production and the elimination of waste, viewed the price-guaranty program as un-American and a perpetuation of the sort of haphazard practice that had led farmers to trouble in the first place. Nearly 30 years later Hoover still characterized Wallace as a fascist and McNary–Haugen as a radical proposition designed to control farmers' production.

His rhetoric and enthusiasm for a large federal bureaucracy indicate that his thinking had advanced beyond notions of a *laissez-faire* economy. But as illustrated in *American Individualism*, Hoover remained firmly wed to traditional notions about self-sufficiency and personal responsibility. He stressed the need to encourage "individualism" in order to "provide opportunity for self-expression, not merely economically, but spiritually as well."[19] He also warned against the pitfalls of socialism, foreshadowing his lifelong tendency to equate government authority with unequivocal despotism. Although Hoover clearly believed that the federal government ought to provide some measure of protection against the concentrated control of industry and capital, his pursuit of theoretical solutions ended with a slightly modified version of classical theory that was seemingly flexible only under his personal supervision.[20]

The gap between Hoover and the professional economics community was obscured by the dynamics of the debate over farm policy reform. On that particular matter, both Hoover's opinion and the discipline's consensus about farm policy aligned rather nicely. Neither group thought the price-fixing mechanism in McNary–Haugen workable and instead encouraged cooperative marketing backed by financing relief. The combination of Hoover's popularity and apparent symbiosis with the discipline's thinking precluded a public outcry on the part of the professional economics community. But frustration with Washington's failure to act gradually mounted.

Political stand-off

Ineffective politicking certainly frustrated professional economists engaged with the farm question. President of the American Farm Association Thomas P. Cooper, in a thinly veiled reference to McNary–Haugen, expressed frustration with the continued dismissal of economists' research, noting that "Instances, too, have been known where the presumed 'failure' has been that of refusing support to 'pet remedies' advocated by individuals who desired endorsement rather than suggestion or modification."[21] Coolidge's agricultural conference, assembled in late 1924 under recently appointed Secretary of Agriculture William Jardine, reiterated support for cooperative marketing, financing subsidies, and increased research. The Conference report also included a call for protective tariffs – a clear acknowledgment of at least one of the Farm Bloc's wishes. But relations were raw on both sides of McNary–Haugen, and progress proved difficult. As with previous debates over economic policy, reasoning had taken a backseat to sectarian suspicions. An exchange between Wisconsin economist B.N. Hibbard and Henry A. Wallace, editor of *Wallace's Farmer* (and son of Secretary of Agriculture Henry C. Wallace) captured the dynamic. Incredulous about a radio interview Hibbard gave in Madison, Wallace ran an editorial mocking the "classical economist" and his antiquarian thinking. Hibbard, clearly hurt by the attack, responded with a sharp letter likening the pro-McNary–Haugen crowd to those who supported Bryan's Free Silver campaign in 1896 and accusing the popular farmers' periodical of myopia.

Taylor's dismissal from the BAE in the summer of 1925 did little to soothe tensions. Although he had certainly assisted in the preparation of the McNary–Haugen Bill in his capacity as head of the Bureau, Taylor was far from an enthusiastic promoter – in fact, he had quite notably never endorsed the measure. Nevertheless, his work under Secretary Wallace placed him at odds with Coolidge and Hoover, both of whom viewed the Department of Agriculture as a source of strength for their political rivals. Wallace's passing in October 1924 presented an opportunity for the administration to strike a blow against the Farm Bloc, and Coolidge responded by appointing University of Kansas President William Jardine. Jardine and Taylor clashed until the latter's dismissal in August 1925. University of Wisconsin sociologist Edward A. Ross, still every bit the agitator, praised Taylor for his "stand against the powers that be" and likened it to his contested dismissal from Stanford 25 years prior.[22] Yet Taylor's actions were far from controversial. Whereas Ross had at least "earned" his dismissal through inflammatory speech and public criticism of his employer, Taylor was the victim of political maneuvering, plain and simple. His role in McNary–Haugen had been that of an expert advisor, and his public lobbying for the measure all but non-existent. The pro-McNary–Haugen crowd had not had much use for professional economists in the first place, as they largely refused to back the price-fixing plan. But the Coolidge administration's brash actions crushed what little remaining relevancy professional economists enjoyed in the debate over farm relief. Taylor's dismissal meant that, more so than ever, economic expertise was a matter of opinion.

The subsequent outpouring of support for Taylor revealed the absurdity of the situation. Jardine took a positive shine toward the cooperative marketing plans advanced since Taylor's dismissal – an odd development since, as Black noted in a letter, they were the same plans forwarded by Taylor the previous year.[23] That the move was political was clear to the Madison Plow Company's Charles W. Holman, who worried that the Bureau of Agricultural Economics was being transformed into a "political bureau."[24] Clarence Cannon, a Missouri Representative, echoed this concern while lamenting the "packing" of the Department of Agriculture.[25]

The back-and-forth sniping between supporters and opponents of McNary–Haugen raged on as farm prices continued to slump. Those who predicted the market would readjust itself, such as Roger Babson, founder of Babson's Statistical Organization, continued to predict an impending return to prosperity despite the lack of action in Washington.[26] But the assumption that farmers could adjust in a timely fashion to evolving market conditions through better planning and hard work proved wrong. According to the Department of Agriculture, farmers had indeed responded to the price-level crisis by raising productivity by 15 percent between 1922 and 1926, yet their purchasing power remained well-below pre-war levels and Secretary of Agriculture Jardine's optimistic annual report for 1926 was met with resentment and skepticism.

Economists continued to push for reform, their mantra largely unchanged from the end of the war: support cooperative marketing, avoid tariffs, provide financing, and reduce production on marginal lands. Alas, the discipline remained wholly dependent on outsiders to seize on their ideas and marshal them through the policymaking process. While pondering the life of what he called "kept researchers," meaning economists tasked with providing relevant research to the larger community, new economist Walton H. Hamilton encouraged his colleagues to pursue projects that would cut to the core of the agricultural problem.[27] What Hamilton's rallying cry failed to take into account was the fact that the problem was no longer a lack of information or compelling evidence. As with the money and labor questions, the professional economics community had provided a rough but reasonably clear solution to the problem in question at the beginning of the debate. Just as skepticism and entrenched partisans bogged down the process of reform in the past, the battle between the Farm Bloc and Hoover's Department of Commerce delayed and compromised agricultural reform.

Toward crisis

Hoover eventually broke the political logjam and won the battle over farm reform when he made the move from the Department of Commerce to the Oval Office in 1928. His campaigning against McNary–Haugen ensured that the bill stalled in Congress from 1924 to 1926. Hoover was also instrumental in persuading Coolidge to veto the measure when it passed Congress in 1927 and 1928. His triumph over McNary–Haugen further polished his credentials as the nation's economic czar. Throughout the 1920s, the press had referred to Hoover as an economist and continued to do so in the build-up to his 1928 presidential victory. Referred to as a "glutton for statistics," a "new kind of candidate," or just plain "an economist," the press touted Hoover's credentials as an economist without any recognition that the import of such a label was often ambiguous.[28] A widely publicized endorsement from Yale's Irving Fischer cemented the former engineer's image as the technocrat candidate in the 1928 Presidential election.[29] The endorsement was misleading, however. Fisher's support derived from Hoover's support for Prohibition rather than his economic prowess.

For the same reasons that the discipline struggled to act in a unified voice on policymaking issues, economists failed to point out that Hoover – although arguably more savvy about economic issues than many of his political colleagues – still fell short of qualifying as an economic expert. Perhaps association with the high-flying politician suited economists just fine. Or, in the case of Mitchell, Fisher, and other economists directly connected to Hoover, it is possible that a desire for a role in Washington muted criticism. Regardless, Hoover swept into office with the credentials of an economist and a reputation as a politician dedicated to the solicitation of expert advice.

In the wake of McNary–Haugen's defeat, Hoover managed to gather enough support for his vision of farm reform. The Agricultural Marketing Act was passed in 1929. The measure was a compromise of sorts, as it authorized the Federal Farm Board to provide competitive loans to farm organizations and "manage surpluses" through the use of a five hundred million dollar fund. Advocates of the Act argued that providing loans to farm groups, rather than to farmers themselves, would stimulate the growth of farmers' cooperatives. Beyond that, the plan was exceedingly vague, as commentators were quick to note in leading economics journals. The mechanism for controlling surpluses was left to the discretion of the Federal Farm Board and as such was unclear. The Act also hinted at the possibility of limiting acreage, but again provided no firm guidance to the chagrin of economists and farmers alike. As the farm crisis deepened, the concept of allotment (paying farmers not to grow crops that would contribute to overproduction) had gained traction in professional economics circles. Realists noted that it was difficult enough to secure subsidies for crops; the likelihood of convincing policymakers to pay farmers for not growing seemed impossible.

A brewing economic disaster soon tested the Agricultural Marketing Act and Hoover's ability to manage the economy in general. His response to the economic downturn that gave way to the Great Depression has been recognized as in-line with progressive economic theory at the time. Hoover shook off the advice of the Social Darwinists within the Republican Party and tried to reverse the downward spiral. His attempts to organize wage minimums and prevent layoffs on a voluntary basis, his encouragement of state public works projects, and his administration's cash infusions to key public institutions and the national banking system all reflected some of the wisdom that had spilled forth from economics departments and research bureaus in the preceding decades.

It is possible to oversell this version of events. Even after it became clear that the recession was quickly devolving into a depression, Hoover hesitated to wield the power of the state. The composition of his "economic general staff" – five businessmen, two government representatives, one labor representative, and only two economists – reflected his adherence to private sector solutions. Although he urged public works projects and the maintenance of wages to encourage consumer consumption, he and the conservative Congress remained wedded to the spirit of Associationalism and voluntary measures.

Panicked and frustrated, lawmakers turned to antiquated policy by promoting the Smoot–Hawley tariff bill in an effort to raise the cost of foreign goods and stimulate the consumption of domestic products. Despite Hoover's later attempts at downplaying the significance of the Smoot–Hawley bill, it was a shockingly poor decision with wide-ranging consequences.

After watching in silence as he delayed farm reform and co-opted the discipline's prestige, the professional economics community finally mobilized. More than 1,000 economists from 178 colleges publicly petitioned the passage of the Smoot–Hawley tariff bill on the grounds that it would raise the cost of living and further the hardships of American farmers.[30] One-time Hoover supporter Wesley C. Mitchell joined Fischer and others in signing the petition. The protest made front-page news. For the first time since the "Minnesota Memorial," professional economists had organized to issue a public statement expressing their consensus about a key economic issue of the day.

Equally unconvinced that the Smoot–Hawley Act would ameliorate the increasingly desperate economic conditions, Senator Robert Wagner pushed a bill designed to stem the loss of jobs. The Wagner Act, a precursor to the better-known Wagner Act of 1935, called for federal oversight of employment offices and large-scale public works projects. Frustrated with Hoover's lack in interest in the bill, Wagner publicly attacked the now-embattled president for refusing to apply the "public works principle," which had been "recommended as both sound and feasible by the united opinion of economists."[31] Furthermore, Wagner characterized Hoover's response to the growing depression, which had abided by his morally guided Associationalist philosophy, as nothing more than a series of "pep meetings" led by a number of Hoover-appointed "cheer leaders."

Economists, business leaders, and labor leaders soon followed with another public letter in support of the bill. Signatories included the prominent economists Frank Taussig, John B. Andrews, William Leiserson, Paul H. Douglas, and Fisher. In addition to submitting a copy of the letter to Congress, letter organizers made a point of sending a copy to Hoover. As with the Smoot–Hawley petition, the letter received front-page coverage. By late 1930, Hoover had lost his credentials as a practicing economist. Economists' criticism of the Smoot–Hawley Act was merely the beginning of their assault on Hoover's conduct as President.

The nation's professional economists temporarily established their role as a monitor of federal economic policymaking through their public criticism of Hoover. To be clear, the discipline lacked cohesion and continued to spurn the opportunity to turn professional organizations into lobbying groups. But the once-strong voice within the community of professional economics that had advocated a socially active role for economists reemerged. By the time voters began to consider their options in the 1932 presidential election, economists' criticisms of federal policy had gained more attention in the press. Not surprisingly, the Democratic candidate, Franklin Delano Roosevelt, joined in the attack of Hoover's capability as an economic policymaker and vowed to deliver the economic solutions Hoover feigned to possess.

Into depression

The severity of the Great Depression forced policymakers to accept agricultural economists' long-held understanding of the need to thoroughly research and coordinate the agricultural sector. It was a long time coming for the millions of rural Americans who suffered throughout the 1920s. The failure to wed economic expertise to policymakers' decisions resulted in a lost decade for the agricultural sector and surely contributed to the economic pre-conditions that fueled the Great Depression of the 1930s. As with the shortcomings of monetary and labor policy at the turn of the century, it is difficult to assign "blame" for the apparent disconnect. The nation's professional economists, for their part, failed to effectively organize and publicize their concerns about the state of the agricultural sector. Nor did the discipline demonstrate a willingness to challenge Hoover's credentials as an economist, leaving the public to believe in his Associationalist program as a *bona fide* theory. The nation's farmers – including their representatives in Washington – unflinchingly dismissed economists' skepticism toward price-fixing schemes as partisan sniping and backed the ill-fated McNary–Haugen for too long. The fight for unlimited price supports and protective tariffs undoubtedly delayed painful but necessary adjustments in acreage and marketing, as it encouraged the notion among farmers that market forces could be suspended by legislative decree.

The ascent of Roosevelt and his "brain trust" surely echoed the promise that accompanied Wilson's first term in office. His was a campaign that seemingly valued the input of professional economists and suggested a key role for economic experts in the Roosevelt administration. The adoption of an agricultural allotment program in 1933 finally began to impose some measure of order in the agriculture sector, but the Roosevelt years still proved frustrating to professional economists. Beholden to the same political, social, and cultural forces as the policymakers that had preceded them, New Deal policymakers often kept the nation's economic experts at arm's length as they sought compromise on economic policies that were not designed to work when adopted in part.

As the Great Depression of the 1930s developed into a full-blown political and economic crisis, the discipline that had grown in response to economic turmoil with the express goal of preventing such disasters remained just one voice among many. Rather than serving as an authoritative source of knowledge and policy recommendations for beleaguered representatives on Capitol Hill, professional economists continued to struggle with the challenge of applying economic theory to practice. The harsh realities of the 1930s economy did little to quell the layman's suspicion of trained economists. If anything, the sudden and dramatic collapse of the economy seemingly added credibility to the claim that economists' ideas were not only useless, but actually dangerous. Irving Fisher's infamous claim that "stock prices are not too high and Wall Street will not experience anything in the nature of a crash" one month prior to the market crash that came to be known as Black Tuesday reflected poorly on the discipline.[32] His later persistence that the slump was but a minor bump in an otherwise smooth road contributed to his image as an aloof academic and lent ammunition to those who were critical of professional economics in general.

Fisher was not the only widely quoted professional economist during the depression decade, and therein lay another problem. Competing voices lent credence to longstanding claims that economists simply lacked the consensus necessary to effectively advise policymakers. Such claims were, as discussed in the preceding chapters, not wholly without merit. Although consensus existed in certain matters, like the harm posed by a tariffs or the general need to manage the money supply, virtually every issue had its share of contrarians and problematic details. Politicians, lobbyists, and newspapermen eagerly seized on dissenting opinions within the discipline in an attempt to rally support to their cause, or at minimum to sell more newspapers. Throughout the depression decade, the same forces that had combined to sap professional economists' influence earlier in the century continued to stifle the connection between economic expertise and economic policy while millions of Americans struggled to understand why no one, including the nation's professional economists, seemed capable of ending the malaise.

This claim stands in sharp contrast to the widely held perception of 1930s Washington as a hotbed of economic experimentation that was led by economists infused with the pro-interventionists policies of England's John Maynard Keynes. Roosevelt, who had notably surrounded himself with a coterie of respected intellectuals during the 1932 presidential race, continued to call on the members of his Brain Trust and additional interlopers to provide bold solutions to the nation's problems. According to the popular narrative, the combination of desperation and the appeal Keynesian ideas overthrew any vestiges of the *laissez-faire* associationalist approach to economic management (albeit *sans* Keynes' direct involvement, as he reputedly rubbed FDR the wrong way). Instead, an emerging consensus among economists in favor of counter-cyclical government spending spurred policymakers to adopt large public works projects that could "prime the pump" and stimulate economic activity. This narrative also suggests that the consensus on the need to stimulate consumer spending helped drive through social welfare legislation such as the Social Security Act and protections for worker's collective bargaining rights – both of which were thought beneficial because they put money in the pockets of those most likely to spend. The fact of the matter is that federal policymakers continued to ignore, dismiss, or modify professional economists' recommendations just as they always had. Roosevelt in particular was notorious for his tendency to lure advisors into a false sense of sympathetic understanding only to ignore their recommendations.[33]

The few clear examples of economists' influence on economic policy stand as notable exceptions that prove the rule and highlight the discipline's failure to achieve the new economists' lofty ambitions to tightly bind economic analysis with government policy. Agricultural economists' success in persuading policymakers to thoroughly regulate farm production through an allotment plan serves as an illustrative example. The system of checks on production implemented by the Agricultural Adjustment Act of 1933 closely resembled the ideas articulated by a number of agricultural economists near the end of the 1920s. Unlike the problematic price guaranties of the McNary–Haugen plan, advocates of allotment contended that paying farmers not to grow certain crops would directly relieve economic pressure on rural Americans by raising prices without simultaneously encouraging overproduction. The success of the Agricultural Adjustment Administration (AAA) proved to have a lasting effect on agricultural policy in the US because the framework it established allowed for the coordination and management of agricultural production over subsequent decades (although arguably at great cost to efficiency and long-term prosperity).

Citing this momentous shift in agricultural policy as evidence of professional economists' influence proves problematic for several reasons, however. To begin, the measure's lengthy gestation period serves as a reminder that agricultural economists' expertise was challenged throughout the policymaking process. Professional economists had called for a reform of national agricultural policy in the immediate aftermath of the World War I. The concept of allotment, to be fair, had emerged later in the decade. But professional economists had been consistent in their call for reduced production and federal aid. Policymakers in the Farm Bloc nevertheless continued to support the untenable McNary–Haugen measure, thus soaking up the attention of Washington and agricultural economists for far too long.

Additionally, the agricultural interest groups that had effectively undercut professional economists' influence did not simply disappear during the Great Depression. The farmers' groups and businessmen who depended on the agricultural industry continued to lobby lawmakers and hold sway in Washington, as evidence by the appointment of George Peek as administrator of the AAA. The former Moline Plow Company executive, whose plan for a price-guaranty program had led to the proposed McNary–Haugen bill, continued to clash with those who insisted on reducing output. His attempts to wrest control of the AAA away from the Department of Agriculture and implement a price-guaranties program backed by cartel agreements proved unsuccessful, but nevertheless illustrates the persistent challenging of professional economists' expertise.

Roosevelt's mercurial pursuit of expert advisors raises even stronger challenges to the notion of the 1930s as the dawning of a golden era for professional economic. He does not appear to have engaged the discipline by sorting through salient arguments and making decisions based on the consensus of expert opinion. Rather, Roosevelt considered professional economists' recommendations alongside political considerations, always searching for the right combination of economic and political expediency.

Roosevelt's attitude toward the relationship between expertise and policymaking might help explain why the Treasury Department pursued such a problematic monetary policy during his first term. Following Cornell agricultural economist George F. Warren's advice, Roosevelt encouraged his Secretary of the Treasury and longtime political companion Henry Morgenthau, Jr., to combat deflation by purchasing large quantities of gold. Warren's influence is notable for its hints of nepotism and short-sightedness – neither of which are traits typically associated with the marriage of expertise and public policy.

The White House's interest in Warren as a monetary advisor was noted as peculiar from the beginning. As national newspapers illustrated, prior to 1933, Warren's background was almost exclusively in agricultural economics. To be sure, he was familiar with fields outside his specialty, but Fisher's claim that Warren was counted among the world's preeminent monetary theorists was a stretch. In fact, most leading American economists who specialized in monetary theory, including those with access to Roosevelt, disagreed with Warren's assertion that raising the price of gold would automatically raise commodity prices.[34] On the eve of the annual AEA meeting, Walter E. Spahr, chair of the Department of Economics at New York University, publicly noted that virtually none of the nation's leading monetary theorists endorsed Warren's plan. Warren's presentation of his plan alongside colleague Frank Parson led to something of a spectacle at the AEA meeting when economists packed the auditorium to poke holes in the commodity-dollar theory. O.M.W. Sprague, a widely respected monetary expert, resigned in protest from his position as economic advisor to the Treasury Department when Roosevelt refused to abandon an economic policy that was far afield from the discipline's consensus. Following his resignation, Sprague criticized Roosevelt's monetary policy in a series of nine articles written for *The Hartford Courant*, though he later returned to the Treasury Department as a consultant.[35]

The question of why Roosevelt ignored the professional economics community's consensus and placed so much faith in Warren begs answering. One obvious explanation is that Roosevelt and Morgenthau were familiar with Warren. Roosevelt previously had called on Warren to provide policy as a member of his Agriculture Advisory Commission, which Roosevelt had established shortly after his inauguration as governor of New York in 1929. Warren served on the panel alongside Morgenthau, a Roosevelt confidant and good friend since his their days in New York politics. An agriculturalist by trade, Morgenthau lacked any formal training in economics, but was certainly aware of the deflationary forces that had depressed agricultural commodity prices over the previous decade. Warren biographer Bernard Stanton notes that Warren's conduct as a member of the Agriculture Advisory Commission resulted in "a strong professional relationship" between the farm economist and future president.[36] During his first two years in the White House, lobbyists of all stripes assailed Roosevelt with a cacophony of monetary reform proposals. The question of whether or not to stay committed to the gold standard preoccupied not only the Roosevelt administration, but Washington at large. In the first half of 1933, at least twenty-four different bills designed to alter US monetary policy were introduced to Congress. Overwhelmed by the waves of economic advice that poured into the Oval Office, Roosevelt ultimately turned to Warren, who was a friendly and familiar face from his days as Governor of New York.

The simplicity of Warren's gold purchasing plan may also offer insight into why Roosevelt seized on the plan of one particular professional economist. Pressure to raise prices had mounted steadily since the early days of the Depression. The assumed connection between higher prices and economic recovery drove a growing number of lawmakers to promote inflationary policies, and the increasingly popular Thomas Amendment to the Farm Relief Bill proposed to fulfill the call through outright printing of money. Afraid of reckless inflation but in agreement that prices ought to raise, Roosevelt appears to have been attracted to Warren's plan as much for its political expediency as for his faith in its creator. The Gold Purchase Plan would in theory raise prices in proportion to the amount of gold purchased, thus maintaining the link between the nation's paper currency and its gold reserves while avoiding the temptation to print money outright.

But by early 1934 the plan was deemed a failure. The gold purchases did indeed devalue the dollar by 40 percent, but domestic commodity prices continued to decrease. Warren's argument that people still adjusted the value of goods and services based on fluctuations in the price of gold was quickly revealed as poorly conceived. The historical data that Warren and his colleague Frank Parson had used to justify their assumptions was exposed as problematic by their professional colleagues. The professional economics community's initial response to Roosevelt's decision regarding monetary policy was vindicated, but Roosevelt was hardly contrite. In the wake of the failed Gold Purchase Program, the president infamously dismissed the advice of British economist John Maynard Keynes, commenting that Keynes seemed to be more of a mathematician and political economist.

In typical fashion, the AEA remained above the fray, although its members continued to attempt to answer the call to end the economic malaise. Members were certainly sensitive to the issues at hand, but insisted on their long-held belief that academic freedom depended on organizational neutrality. Instead, the nation's professional economists sought to influence economic policy as individuals or members of intellectual camps. The results of such efforts were less than stellar. One of the more notable and ambitious efforts, the "Chicago Plan" for bank reform, fell well short of remaking the American banking system. The plan, first introduced in mimeographed form but soon elaborated in books and journal articles, called for 100 percent reserve banking at depository institutions as a means of stabilizing the American economy by preventing further bank runs and granting the federal government more direct control of the monetary system. The plan was the collaborative fruit of the University of Chicago's Department of Economics, which included Frank Knight, Henry C. Simon, Henry Schultz, and Paul H. Douglas. It found ready support among additional economists outside Chicago who appear to have arrived at similar conclusions independently of the Chicago crowd's influence. Simon, Douglas, Lauchlin Currie, and Irving Fisher all published books that promoted the plan in one form or another, and they did successfully attract attention in Congress. However, as historian Russell Phillips documents in his history of the proposal, the Chicago Plan failed to overcome political gamesmanship and a skeptical public.

A considerably less influential but no less interesting attempt to influence policy emerged from the economics departments of Harvard and Tufts, where seven young economists collaborated to publish *An Economic Program for American Democracy*, which strongly promoted government spending and the redoubling of New Deal efforts. Scholarly reviews of the book were critical. The young economists were chastised for failing to adequately defend their claim that the New Deal programs had considerably improved the economic situation, and they were similarly criticized for neglecting to include any real discussion of democracy in a book that purported to focus on the subject. The parallels between the upstart Keynesians of Harvard and the new economists of the late nineteenth century are intriguing to note. Both embraced new theories as a solution to pressing social problems and endured the criticism of their "elders" as a result. Similarly, both the new economists and the Keynesians appealed to the need for practical, real world solutions that would work within the inescapable rules of economics while also satisfying the demands of policymakers and their constituents. The book sold well in the Nation's capitol, but nowhere else.

Notes

1 Sections of this chapter appeared earlier in Franklin (2014).
2 It also, coincidentally, funded home economics programs in the Mid-West, thus helping to ensure the future vitality of home economics education. See Stage and Vincenti (1997).
3 Henry C. Taylor and Anne Dewees Taylor, *The Story of Agricultural Economics in the United States, 1840–1932: Men, Services, Ideas* (Westport, CT: Greenwood Press, 1974), 605.
4 Henry C. Taylor, "1907 Automobile Tour Transcript," N.D., 17, Henry C. Taylor Papers, 1896–1968 Box 32, Folder 7, Wisconsin Historical Society.
5 "The New Agrarianism," *The New Republic*, November 3, 1920. "Secretary Meredith on the Problem of the Farmers," *The Sun*, December 11, 1920. Popular press put the decline at $2.5 billion, but Meredith's report painted a slightly grimmer picture. Total receipts for the 1919 crop were estimated at $16 billion, whereas market price at the time of Meredith's report placed the 1920 crop's value at $13.3 billion.
6 Edwin G. Nourse, "The Place of Agriculture in Modern Industrial Society: II," *Journal of Political Economy* 27, no. 7 (July 1919): 577.
7 Ibid., 480–81.
8 These tariffs, also known as Corn Laws, had been a prominent trope in debates over free trade from their repeal in the mid-nineteenth century onward.
9 John D. Black, "The Role of Public Agencies in the Internal Readjustments of the Farm," *Journal of Farm Economics* 7, no. 2 (April 1925): 156–58. "Correspondence," 1919–1928, John D. Black Papers, 1915–1960, Wisconsin Historical Society.
10 The titles of the papers presented were: "National Policy for Land Utilization" (Ely); "The Financial Policy in Its Relation to the Price Level" (Mitchell); "The European Situation in Its Relation to American Agriculture" (Warren).
11 US House of Representatives, *Report of the National Agricultural Conference* (Washington, DC: Government Printing Office, 1922), 15.
12 Ibid., 186.
13 Theodore Tiller, "Farm Meeting Shows Signs of Insurgency," *The Sun*, January 25, 1922. "Gompers Scores Farm Conference," *The Washington Post*, February 26, 1922.
14 By 1922, Ely had begun his work with the Institute for Research in Land Economics and Public Utilities. The Merchants and Manufacturers Tax League's attack was two years in the future. See Chapter 5.
15 Winters' comments about Taylor's endorsement of the plan, such as it was, seems to be the most solid evidence of Taylor support, which has since been assumed by a number of secondary sources. Winters' claims stem from proceedings of the conference found in Taylor's personal papers – hardly a public clarion call. Fite and Shideler cite internal memoranda prepared by Taylor for Secretary Wallace in the aftermath of the National Agricultural Conference. Whereas Fite claims the memos reveal Taylor's reluctance to endorse the plan, Shideler claims Taylor offered the plan "sympathetic attention" without urging action. See Winters (1970); Fite (1954); Shideler (1957).
16 For examples of professional economists' resistance to McNary–Haugen and price-fixing, see Benner (1926); Boyle (1928).
17 Under Hoover, the Department of Commerce consolidated its control over a multi-tude of lesser agencies that, although technically under Department control, operated independently. In addition to streamlining these lesser "inbred bureaucracies," Hoover took control of the Bureau of Mines and the Patent Office from the Department of the Interior and pushed Congress to create the Housing Division (1922), Aeronautics Division (1926), and the Radio division (1927). Hoover biographers have noted the

numerous ways in which the reorganization of the Department of Commerce benefited the US economy, but his desire for control also revealed a contentious personality that did not bode well for agricultural reform (Hoover 1952).

18 As noted earlier in the chapter, the "sugar price control issue" was of particular interest to economists during the war because it served as a case study for determining the federal government's ability to control prices. In an August 1918 article in the *Quarterly Journal of Economics*, University of Minnesota economist Roy Blakey declared Hoover a "patriotic administrator" who demonstrated ample understanding of the economic issues surrounding the control of sugar prices. In addition to finding no fault in Hoover's strategy as food czar, Blakey defended Hoover against criticism that he had selected British sugar merchants (as opposed to sugar producers) by declaring such appointments a "favorable arrangement."

Blakey's article appeared before the end of the war and it is possible that pressure to produce "patriotic" scholarship limited Blakey's ability to criticize government officials associated with the war effort, such as Hoover. But Johns Hopkins University economist Joshua Bernhardt's similarly positive article, published a month after the signing of the Treaty of Versailles, indicates otherwise. Although Bernhardt's analysis of the sugar price control program noted the hardship Hoover's pricing plan placed on sugar beet farmers and consumers alike, Bernhardt emphatically concluded, "government control of sugar during the war was a success." See Blakey (1918); Bernhard (1919).

19 Herbert Hoover, *American Individualism* (Garden City, NY: Doubleday, Page & Co., 1922), 37.

20 Perhaps most surprising was Hoover's dismissal of Thorstein Veblen. Veblen, the noted institutional economist who had produced an impressive body of scholarship that was directly relevant to a bureaucrat in Hoover's position, did not seem to rate much attention in Hoover's world. Although biographer William Leucthenburg suggests Hoover's enthusiasm for a society managed by engineers stemmed from Veblen's similar enthusiasm as expressed in *The Theory of Leisure Class* and *The Instinct of Workmanship and the State of the Industrial Arts*, there is no evidence to indicate Hoover was even aware of Veblen's work. Hoover's lack of interest in the acclaimed economist is particularly telling, given both Veblen's popularity at the time and Hoover's intimate involvement with his alma mater Stanford University, which had at one time employed Veblen. See Leuchtenburg (2009).

21 Thomas P. Cooper, "Business Economics: An Opportunity for Agricultural Colleges," *Journal of Farm Economics* 6, no. 1 (January 1924): 8–19. The irony of Cooper's statement should be noted – his replacement of Taylor as head of the Bureau of Agricultural Economics meant that he effectively supported the "pet projects" of Secretary of Agriculture William Jardine, who in turn follow Hoover's advice (Cooper 1924).

22 Edward A. Ross, "E.A. Ross to H.C. Taylor," August 27, 1925, Henry C. Taylor Papers, 1896–1968 Box 53, Wisconsin Historical Society.

23 John D. Black, "John D. Black to H.C. Taylor," September 29, 1925, Henry C. Taylor Papers, 1896–1968 Box 53, Wisconsin Historical Society.

24 Charles W. Holman, "Charles W. Holman to H.C. Taylor," August 31, 1925, Henry C. Taylor Papers, 1896–1968 Box 53, Wisconsin Historical Society.

25 Clarence Cannon, "Clarence Canon to Henry C. Taylor," August 26, 1925, Henry C. Taylor Papers, 1896–1968 Box 53, Wisconsin Historical Society.

26 Roger W. Babson, "Effect of Business Upon Agriculture," *Journal of Farm Economics* 6, no. 1 (January 1924): 41–52. "People to Return to Thrift, Service and Unselfishness," *The Hartford Courant*, December 8, 1920. Roger W. Babson, "There Is Work to Be Done," *San Francisco Chronicle*, August 22, 1921. "Making Things Go!," *The Atlanta Constitution*, March 22, 1923. Howard C. Kegley, "Farm Needs Discussed," *Los Angeles Times*, March 27, 1926. "Babson Trade Review Advises Conservatism," *The Christian Science Monitor*, September 10, 1927.

27 Walton H. Hamilton, "Agricultural Research in a Changing Order," *Journal of Farm Economics* 8, no. 1 (January 1926): 56–62.
28 "Hoover's Candidacy Applauded in Nation's Press," *New York Times*, June 16, 1928. "Mr. Hoover's Economic Essay," *New York Times*, September 18, 1928. Charles Merrill, "Can Hoover Be Dramatized to the Electorate," *Boston Daily Globe*, June 17, 1928.
29 "Fisher Says Hoover Is 'A Genuine Dry'," *New York Times*, July 30, 1928.
30 "1,028 Economists Ask Hoover to Veto Pending Tariff Bill," *New York Times*, May 5, 1930.
31 "Hoover Job Policy Scored by Wagner," *New York Times*, October 29, 1930.
32 "Babson Predicts 'Crash' In Stocks," *New York Times*, September 6, 1929.
33 Norton similarly notes the tepid reception of economic advisors' ideas in Norton (1991).
34 Many prominent, non-economist "hard money" men also opposed the Gold Purchase Plan, including Treasury Undersecretary Dean Acheson, who was ultimately relieved of his post as a result of his dissent. See Wicker (1971); Bernstein (2001).
35 The series, which ran in the *The Hartford Courant*, began on November 29, 1933, and ended on December 20, 1933. According to the first article, a total of ten articles were planned, but only nine were ultimately published.
36 B.F. Stanton, *George F. Warren: Farm Economist* (Ithaca, NY: Cornell University Press, 2007), 329–30.

Bibliography

Allen, Robert Loring. *Irving Fisher: A Biography*. Cambridge, MA: Blackwell Publishers, 1993.

Alston, Lee J. "Farm Foreclosures in the United States During the Interwar Period." *The Journal of Economic History* 43, no. 4 (December 1983): 885–903.

Babson, Roger W. "Effect of Business Upon Agriculture." *Journal of Farm Economics* 6, no. 1 (January 1924): 41–52.

"Back Matter." *Journal of Farm Economics* 2, no. 1 (January 1920).

Baster, A.S.J. "An Economic Program for American Democracy." *Economica* 6, no. 24 (November 1939): 467–68.

Benner, Claude L. "Agricultural Research in a Changing Order: Discussion." *Journal of Farm Economics* 8, no. 1 (January 1926): 62–65.

——. "Discussion (Agricultural Research in a Changing Order)." *Journal of Farm Economics* 8, no. 1 (January 1926): 62–65.

Bernhard, Joshua. "Government Control of Sugar During the War." *The Quarterly Journal of Economics* 33, no. 4 (August 1919): 672–713.

Bernstein, Michael A. *A Perilous Progress: Economists and Public Purpose in Twentieth-Century America*. Princeton, NJ: Princeton University Press, 2001.

——. *The Great Depression: Delayed Recovery and Economic Change in America, 1929–1939*. Cambridge, UK; New York: Cambridge University Press, 1987.

Black, John D. *Agricultural Reform in the United States*. New York: McGraw-Hill, 1929.

——. "John D. Black to H.C. Taylor," September 29, 1925. Henry C. Taylor Papers, 1896–1968 Box 53. Wisconsin Historical Society.

——. "Social Implications of the Restriction of Agricultural Output." *The American Economic Review* 21, no. 1 (March 1931): 114–24.

——. "The Role of Public Agencies in the Internal Readjustments of the Farm." *Journal of Farm Economics* 7, no. 2 (April 1925): 153–75.

Blakey, Roy. "Sugar Prices and Distribution Under Price Control." *The Quarterly Journal of Economics* 32, no. 4 (August 1918): 567–96.

Boyle, J.E. *Farm Relief: A Brief on the McNary-Haugen Plan*. Garden City, NY: Doubleday, Doran and Company, 1928.

Brand, Charles J. "The Price Balance Between Agriculture and Industry." *Proceedings of the Academy of Political Science in the City of New York* 11, no. 2 (January 1925): 9–35.

Carver, Thomas N. "The Possibilities of Price Fixing in Time of Peace." *The American Economic Review* 9, no. 1 (March 1919): 246–51.

Chew, Arthur P. "The Agricultural Depression." *The New Republic*, June 6, 1928.

Christensen, Alice M. "Agricultural Pressure and Governmental Response in the United States, 1919–1929." *Agricultural History* 11, no. 1 (January 1937): 33–42.

Clarke, Sally H. *Regulation and the Revolution in United States Farm Productivity*. Cambridge; New York: Cambridge University Press, 1994.

Cooper, Thomas P. "Business Economics: An Opportunity for Agricultural Colleges." *Journal of Farm Economics* 6, no. 1 (January 1924): 8–19.

Culver, John C., and John Hyde. *American Dreamer: The Life and Times of Henry A. Wallace*. New York: W.W. Norton & Company, 2000.

Currie, Lauchlin B. *The Supply and Control of Money in the United States*. Cambridge, MA: Harvard University Press, 1934.

Davis, Joseph S. "The Case for the Agricultural Marketing Act." *Annals of the American Academy of Political and Social Science* 155, no. 1 (May 1931): 56–64.

Douglas, Paul H. *Controlling Depressions*. New York: W.W. Norton & Company, 1935.

Dummeier, E.F. "Some Possibilities and Problems of the Federal Farm Board: Discussion." *Journal of Farm Economics* 12, no. 1 (January 1930): 20–24.

Ely, Richard T. "American Association for Agricultural Legislation." *Journal of Farm Economics* 1, no. 3 (October 1919): 109–14.

Everest, Allan Seymour. *Morgenthau, the New Deal, and Silver: A Story of Pressure Politics*. New York: King's Crown Press, 1950.

Ferger, Wirth F. "An Economic Program for American Democracy." *Southern Economic Journal* 6, no. 1 (July 1939): 89–91.

Fisher, Irving. *100% Money*. New York: Adelphi, 1935.

——. "Reflation and Stabilization." *Annals of the American Academy of Political and Social Science* 171 (January 1934): 127–31.

Fite, Gilbert Courtland. *George N. Peek and the Fight for Farm Parity*. Norman, OK: University of Oklahoma Press, 1954.

Fogel, Robert William, Enid M. Fogel, Mark Guglielmo, and Nathaniel Grotte. *Political Arithmetic: Simon Kuznets and The Empirical Tradition in Economics*. Chicago, IL: University of Chicago Press, 2013.

Franklin, Jonathan S. "Truly Handmaidens to Policy? Evaluating Agricultural Economists' Claim to a Distinct Tradition of Applied Economics." *History of Political Economy* 46, no. 4 (Winter 2014): 545–71.

Gideonse, Harry D. "An Economic Program for American Democracy." *Political Science Quarterly* 54, no. 2 (June 1939): 266–68.

Gilbert, Richard V. *et al. An Economic Program for American Democracy*. New York: Vanguard Press, 1938.

Gleason, John Philip. "The Attitude of the Business Community Toward Agriculture During the McNary-Haugen Period." *Agricultural History* 32, no. 2 (April 1958): 127–38.

Grimes, W.E. "Some Possibilities and Problems of the Federal Farm Board: Discussion." *Journal of Farm Economics* 12, no. 1 (January 1930): 25–28.

Hamilton, Walton H. "Agricultural Research in a Changing Order." *Journal of Farm Economics* 8, no. 1 (January 1926): 56–62.

——. "Agricultural Research in a Changing Order." *Journal of Farm Economics* 8, no. 1 (January 1926): 56–62.

Hart, Albert G. "A Proposal of Making Monetary Management Effective in the United States." *The Review of Economic Studies* 2, no. 2 (February 1935): 104–16.

Holmes, C.L. "The Economic Future of Our Agriculture." *Journal of Political Economy* 32, no. 5 (October 1924): 505–25.

Hoover, Herbert. *American Individualism*. Garden City, NY: Doubleday, Page & Co., 1922.

——. *The Memoirs of Herbert Hoover: The Cabinet and the Presidency, 1920–1933*. New York: Macmillan, 1952.

——. *The Memoirs of Herbert Hoover: Years of Adventure, 1874–1920*. London: Hollis and Carter, 1952.

Ise, John. "Two Books on Agriculture." *The Quarterly Journal of Economics* 39, no. 4 (August 1925): 635–43.

Kemmerer, Edwin W. "Economic Advisory Work for Governments." *The American Economic Review* 17, no. 1 (March 1927): 1–12.

Kennedy, David M. *Freedom From Fear: The American People in Depression and War, 1929–1945*. New York: Oxford University Press, 1999.

King, Willford I., and Wesley C. Mitchell. *Income in the United States: Its Amount and Distribution 1909–1919*. New York: National Bureau of Economic Research Publications No. 1–2, 1922.

Leuchtenburg, William Edward. *Herbert Hoover*. New York: Times Books, 2009.

Norton, Hugh S. *The Quest for Economic Stability: Roosevelt to Bush*. Columbia: University of South Carolina Press, 1991.

Nourse, Edwin G. "The Place of Agriculture in Modern Industrial Society: I." *Journal of Political Economy* 27, no. 6 (June 1919): 466–97.

——. "The Place of Agriculture in Modern Industrial Society: II." *Journal of Political Economy* 27, no. 7 (July 1919): 561–77.

Nourse, Edwin G., and W.F. Gephart. "Price-Fixing Discussion." *The American Economic Review* 9, no. 1 (March 1919): 272–79.

Olsen, Nils Andreas. *Journal of a Tamed Bureaucrat: Nils A. Olsen and the BAE, 1925–1935*. Edited by Richard Lowitt. Ames, IA: Iowa State University Press, 1980.

Peck, Harvey W. "The Economic Status of Agriculture." *Journal of Political Economy* 34, no. 5 (October 1926): 624–41.

Peek, George N., and Hugh S. Johnson. *Equality For Agriculture*. Moline, IL: H.W. Harington, 1922.

Phillips, Ronnie J. *The Chicago Plan & New Deal Banking Reform*. Armonk, NY: M.E. Sharpe, 1995.

Porter, Kimberly K. "Embracing the Pluralist Perspective: The Iowa Farm Bureau Federation and the McNary-Haugen Movement." *Agricultural History* 74, no. 2 (Spring 2000): 381–92.

Rader, Benjamin G. *The Academic Mind and Reform: The Influence of Richard T. Ely in American Life*. Lexington, KY: University of Kentucky Press, 1966.

Shideler, James H. *Farm Crisis, 1919–1923*. Berkeley: University of California Press, 1957.

Simons, Henry Calvert. *A Positive Program for Laissez-Faire: Some Proposals for a Liberal Economic Policy*. Chicago: University of Chicago Press, 1934.

Smith, Gene. *The Shattered Dream: Herbert Hoover and the Great Depression*. New York: Morrow, 1970.

Sobel, Robert. *Herbert Hoover at the Onset of the Great Depression, 1929–1930*. New York: J.B. Lippincott Company, 1975.

Soth, Lauren. "Agricultural Economists and Public Policy." *American Journal of Agricultural Economics* 58, no. 5 (December 1976): 795–801.

Stage, Sarah, and Virginia Bramble Vincenti. *Rethinking Home Economics: Women and the History of a Profession*. Ithaca: Cornell University Press, 1997.

Stanton, B.F. *George F. Warren: Farm Economist*. Ithaca, NY: Cornell University Press, 2007.

Sturtevant, C.D. "Opposing the Agricultural Marketing Act." *Annals of the American Academy of Political and Social Science* 155, no. 1 (May 1931): 65–73.

Taussig, F.W. "Price-Fixing as Seen by a Price-Fixer." *The Quarterly Journal of Economics* 33, no. 2 (February 1919): 205–41.

Taylor, Henry C., and W.J. Spillman. "The Development of the American Farm Economic Association." *Journal of Farm Economics* 4, no. 2 (April 1922): 92–100.

Taylor, Henry C., and Anne Dewees Taylor. *The Story of Agricultural Economics in the United States, 1840–1932: Men, Services, Ideas*. Westport, CT: Greenwood Press, 1974.

"The Activities of the Federal Farm Board in the United States." *The Economic Journal* 40, no. 157 (March 1930): 69–78.

US House of Representatives. *Annual Reports of the Department of Agriculture For the Year Ended June 30 1920*. Washington, DC: Government Printing Office, 1921.

——. *Report of the National Agricultural Conference*. Washington, DC: Government Printing Office, 1922.

US Senate. *Preliminary Report of the Agricultural Conference*. Washington, DC: Government Printing Office, 1925.

Veblen, Thorstein. *The Theory of the Leisure Class: An Economic Study of Institutions*. New York: MacMillan, 1899.

——. *The Instinct of Workmanship and the State of the Industrial Arts*. New York: MacMillan, 1914.

Viner, Jacob. "The Tariff in Relation to Agriculture." *Journal of Farm Economics* 7, no. 1 (January 1925): 115–23.

Warren, George F. "Some After-the-War Problems in Agriculture." *Journal of Farm Economics* 1, no. 1 (June 1919): 12–23.

——. "Some Purposes and Results of Price Fixing." *The American Economic Review* 9, no. 1 (March 1919): 233–45.

Warren, George F., and Frank A. Pearson. *The Agricultural Situation: Economic Effects of Fluctuating Prices*. New York: Wiley, 1924.

Wicker, Elmus. "Roosevelt's 1933 Monetary Experiment." *The Journal of American History* 57, no. 4 (March 1971): 864–79.

Willard, John D., and H.C.M. Case. "Agriculture and Prices." *Journal of Farm Economics* 2, no. 2 (April 1920): 70–82.

Wilson, Joan Hoff. *Herbert Hoover: Forgotten Progressive*. Boston: Little & Brown, 1975.

Winters, Donald Lee. *Henry Cantwell Wallace: As Secretary of Agriculture, 1921–1924*. Urbana, IL: University of Illinois Press, 1970.

Wirth, Louis. "The Urban Society and Civilization." *American Journal of Sociology* 45, no. 5 (March 1940): 734–55.

——. "Urbanism as a Way of Life." *American Journal of Sociology* 44, no. 1 (July 1938): 1–24.

Conclusion
The legacy of the professional economist

A full account of professional economists' individual efforts to resolve the Great Depression would require a book of its own. But if the period leading up to the Depression and the examples discussed in the previous chapter are any indication, the recurrent themes noted throughout this study likely extended through the 1930s. Interdisciplinary strife, the prominence of folk economics, and the connection between political savvy and influence over economic policy have proven to be persistent barriers to the melding of economic expertise and policy. It should come as no surprise that these themes resonate in the twenty-first century, as they were embedded into the discipline early in the professionalization process.

The push to establish economic expertise in the United States was rapid and contentious, which left room for not only dueling methodologies, but also prominent folk economists like Henry George and William "Coin" Harvey. These untrained economists were just as influential, if not more so, than the academically trained professional economists whose social capital derived from the nation's growing colleges, universities, and later, federal agencies and bureaus. George's proselytizing failed to yield the land and tax reforms he argued would place productive resources in the hands of the working poor, but his work did directly challenge the legitimacy of those professionals who cautioned against such radical reform and led to the creation of single-tax political clubs. Likewise, Harvey's books and public debates with the University of Chicago's J. Laurence Laughlin did not result in a move off the gold standard, but his voice combined with others to establish an intellectual justification for changing the nation's monetary policy that rivaled the solutions brought forth by the academy.

The relative ease with which those untrained in economics were able to publicly confront and repudiate professional economists' ideas and policy recommendations dealt a severe blow to the new economists' early hopes for a more technocratic society. Eager for the public's participation, and perhaps a bit desperate for their annual membership dues, the American Economic Association embraced public participation in the first decades of the organization's existence. But by the 1910s, the gap between professional and amateur had grown and become increasingly problematic. As noted in Chapters 3 and 5, the widening gulf between trained and untrained economists exacerbated the public's skepticism regarding professional economists' intent and allegiances. There were exceptions, such as banker Paul Warburg, who successfully engaged with economists by participating in their conferences and engaging with their work on a regular basis. Yet economists who joined activist organizations, such as the Manufacturers and Merchants Federal Tax League that attacked Richard T. Ely for his opposition to a single-tax, were noticeably detached from the discipline. This gulf consistently undermined economists' efforts to apply economic theory and research to practice, as the constant stream of criticism folk economists directed toward the discipline mitigated some of the social capital that stemmed from establishing economics departments on every major college campus by the 1920s.

Of course, folk economists' critiques were not always unsubstantiated. The discipline did do a poor job of presenting a unified front, seemingly by design. As noted in Chapter 3, the discipline only gradually worked through disagreements over methodology. By the 1920s, a reasonable degree of consistency had been obtained when it became clear that the new economists' methodological revolution had in fact largely resulted in the modification of earlier classical theory. Disagreements persisted, however. Professional economists never reached the sort of compact that would allow for near unanimous agreement on economic policy. Realizing the potential danger of trying to force such agreement at an early stage, the AEA committed itself to strict neutrality on policy matters with mixed results. On the one hand, professional economics thrived as an open and democratic field of inquiry. On the other, economists slowly, and unfairly, gained a reputation as highly skilled technicians incapable of offering direct answers to questions about economic policy. In fact, a general consensus had emerged on at least some of the key issues of the day. As discussed in Chapter 2, professional economists overwhelmingly cautioned against free silver monetary policy. A study of labor economists and the struggle to reform labor relations strongly suggests that the discipline predicted New Deal labor reforms, though few policymakers paid close attention. Similarly, Chapter 6 illustrates how agricultural economists reached a reasonably clear consensus about the need for federal reform of the agricultural market that went unheeded until crisis forced the adoption of an allotment program.

It is tempting to say that economists "got it right" in all three instances, but were unfairly or unwisely ignored by policymakers and the general public. Of course, the case studies I examined were conducted with the benefit of hindsight. Professional economists in the US only rarely presented a unified front – as they did promoting taxation during World War I or opposing the Smoot–Hawley tariff at the beginning of the Great Depression. More often than not, the nation's community of professional economists appeared to be in such disagreement as to delegitimize their findings. Even after separating from sociology, the new economist-cum-institutionalists' push to incorporate sociology, history, and psychology into their work threatened to subvert economists' authority by destabilizing the discipline through the addition of an ever-expanding catalogue of methodological turns. The bulk of US economists, including many of those "young turks" who had initially challenged the maxims of classical thought with ideas from the German Historical School, gradually accepted the premise of a reasonably rational man. A century, and counting, of rough consensus followed, yet jokes about indecisive and inconsistent economists have persisted.

This is not to suggest that professional economists did not exert any influence on US economic policy in the early twentieth century. The ideas that emerged from the Wisconsin School clearly shaped Wisconsin state economic policy and served as a model for equally progressive communities. Likewise, the economists who attended the Indianapolis Monetary Commission, served on the War Industries Board during World War I, and advised FDR in the depths of the Great Depression surely played a role in crafting policy. Even so, the evidence makes clear that these minor triumphs fell well-short of the ideal relationship between economic expertise and economic policy pursued by the early professional economists.

As noted in the three case studies on monetary, labor, and agricultural policy, professional economists struggled to gain traction without the strong political backing that emanated from outside the discipline. Although the AEA's recommendations on monetary policy garnered scant attention, economists managed to assert some authority in the fight over monetary reform through the Indianapolis Monetary Commission. In the case of Commons and the Wisconsin School, the popularity of liberal governor Robert La Follette elevated the state's leading economists from intellectuals to key policy advisors. Likewise, George Warren's association with Henry Mogenthau, Jr., and FDR turned the otherwise unremarkable economist into one of the nation's leading experts in a field outside his expertise. In each instance, political expediency and networking played a large role in determining whose ideas were chosen by policymakers when trying to craft economic policy. It was a far cry from the marriage of knowledge and practice that the new economists had envisioned when they drafted the first constitution of the AEA.

Into the post-World War II period

This poorly defined but oft-discussed relationship between professional economists and policymaking has persisted throughout the twentieth century, which helps explain why economists draw praise for their intellectual prowess in one sentence and criticism for their failure to prevent economic catastrophe in the next. To be sure, in the approximately 25 years following the end of World War II it seemed there was praise more often than not. There is a fairly strong consensus regarding a golden age in the United States in which economic expertise was wed to public policy, starting with World War II and collapsing in the face of seemingly insurmountable challenges during the 1970s. Whether explaining the course of economic thought, the source of post-war economic prosperity, or the "state of the world" in the period preceding the rise of neo-liberalism, many seem to agree that the decades immediately following World War II were marked by careful collaboration between professional economists and economic policymakers. The move toward a more active, interventionist federal government is undeniable, and the Keynesian Revolution certainly seems to have been a real phenomenon. The emergency economic reforms of the 1930s were expanded through the 1960s.

The number of economists in general, and Washington in particular, increased. AEA membership grew nearly three-fold from 1935 to 1960, and professional economists continued to find employment in the expanded bureaucracy of the federal government. The creation of the Council of Economic Advisors by way of the Employment Act of 1946 established an official body of professional economists to advise the President and help craft the office's annual economic report, thus formalizing the advising process between the nation's leading professional economists and policymakers.

Newspapers and popular magazines such as *Time* and *Business Week* ran glowing profiles of the nation's leading economic experts, while public discussion of macroeconomic issues such as GDP, unemployment, and growth became commonplace. The most prominent economists of the era embraced the role of public advocate and furthered the image of the discipline as conquerors of the economic uncertainty that had plagued previous generations. Walter Heller spoke positively of his relationship as an advisor to Presidents Kennedy and Johnson; Herbert Stein concurred that a general cooperation between professional economists and government defined the immediate post-war period, as did Arthur Burns. John Kenneth Galbraith stepped away from his duties at Harvard to embark on a wildly successful career as a public intellectual, diplomat, and government advisor. His books on the nature of capitalism and the American economy were best-sellers – further evidence of the mounting influence of and respect commanded by professional economists. This trend toward a stronger relationship between economists and policymakers deepened the already prevalent misconception that professional economists were inherently well-suited – and indeed required – to play a role as direct participants in the policymaking game.

If anecdotes and personal recollections are not enough, proponents of the narrative that connects economic expertise and economic policy can point to the overwhelming success of the American economy as evidence of an apparent link that blossomed soon after the discipline's awkward adolescence. The American economy did, after all, grow steadily from 1945 to 1973. Furthermore, unemployment remained well-below 1930s levels and the percentage of Americans living in poverty was gradually reduced during the 1950s and 1960s. The American middle-class became the envy of the world. Success on such a large scale does not just happen, the argument goes, but was rather the result of coherent and well-thought-out economic policies designed to build a class of prosperous consumers. Professional economists must have played a large role in developing and implementing policies that kept energy prices low, raised paychecks, and educated a record number of Americans. The goal for policymakers and the American public in general, it would seem, is to recreate this era of symbiosis between expertise and policy in order to recapture the economic magic of the post-War period.

The notion that Keynesian economists introduced a fundamentally new concept when they advocated counter-cyclical government spending should strike students of nineteenth century labor and reform movements as questionable. The idea that government ought to spend in order to employ the out-of-work until the economy recovered may have been novel to professional economists but it certainly was not unheard of among laborers in the nineteenth and early twentieth centuries. Voters and policymakers in the 1930s likely did not wait for professional economists to validate their impulse toward government relief – rather they called for such reform based on desperate need and then cited the relevant experts as justification. It is worth exploring whether this relationship between political need and justification persisted post-World War II. In particular, did economic policymakers in 1945 pursue policies based on the arguments presented by professional economists, or did they pursue policies based on the need to sustain political coalitions and gather support at the polls? Were Keynesian policies the "right" policies because they derived from a consensus among professional economists and delivered economic prosperity, or were they the "right" policies because they satisfied voters' demands and happened to succeed because global economic conditions promised American prosperity, barring all but the most ludicrous economic policies?

Further complicating matters is the dramatic rise of the business economist in the post-war decades. Connections between academic economists and private business were fairly common in the early twentieth century, but the formation of the National Business Economists Association in 1959 seems to suggest a new dynamic. Private businesses increasingly employed professional economists and used their in-house research to lobby Washington. Should privately employed, trained economists be included in discussions of professional economists' influence over public policy, given their presumed allegiance to the firms or industries they are paid to represent?

Given the degree to which the pre-World War II policymakers managed to include professional economists without necessarily incorporating their advice, perhaps it is time to question the connection between expertise and policy in the post-World War period. It is clear that presence does not equal influence and that political expediency more often than not overrules the type of systematic thinking toward which professional economists are inclined. Given the nature of the discipline and the structure of its leading organizations, it is unlikely that professional economists offered policymakers clear, actionable, and non-contradictory advice from 1945 to 1973. A case in point: future AEA president William Baumol's conclusion, presented to the FCC, regarding reasonable rates for AT&T services in a pivotal case, was ignored. Economist William Melody had offered a competing analysis of AT&T's rate structure and the regulators accepted it as the more politically attractive of the two expert conclusions. It is admittedly a relatively small incident in the grand scheme of things, but how many such examples might be discovered if we begin to look closely?

The decades following the collapse of the Keynesian consensus prove no less problematic to our understanding of the connection between economic expertise and economic policy in the US. As most would agree, by the 1970s the political viability of Keynesian policies began to fade quite rapidly. The combination of growing unemployment and stubborn inflation led many to question the wisdom of counter-cyclical spending and the maintenance of social safety nets. As more and more Americans grew to fear rising taxes and decreasing benefits, the

University of Chicago's neoclassical guru Milton Friedman appeared to siphon Galbraith's public prestige. With each passing year it seems more appropriate to characterize the Keynesian years from 1941 to 1973 as a transient period of relatively high cooperation between professional economists and public policy-makers – albeit a qualified cooperation with many exceptions.

Faced with declining real incomes and confused by the intellectual battle between Keynesian and more conservative neoclassical economists, many Americans questioned the discipline's usefulness. The public skepticism noted throughout earlier chapters proved resilient, as many wondered whether economists were still capable of offering competent advice to policymakers. A 1979 study published in the *American Economic Review* in response to mounting criticism that the discipline lacked either coherency or relevancy offered a more complicated picture. The professional economists who responded to the survey showed a fairly high degree of consensus on 20 of the 30 issues addressed, such as the tendency of tariffs to reduce economic welfare, rent controls' negative effect on the availability of housing, and the tendency of a minimum wage to increase unskilled unemployment. The survey also revealed a lack of consensus on ten pressing issues, however. These included the efficacy of wage-price controls in fighting inflation, the connection between monopolistic practices and oil prices, and the Federal Reserve's monetary policy. In sum, the survey found strong evidence of consensus among US professional economists on theoretical issues, but notable disagreement around the hot-button issues of the day that most required expert advice. A similar dynamic was revealed in a survey 16 years later, although as the study's authors noted, opinions regarding monetary issues had shifted. Sociologist Andrew Abbott suggests this perpetual state of change within disciplines is entirely predictable, as the changing fortune of intellectual paradigms mimic the rise and decline of new generations of scholars. Such a proposition seemingly deals a sharp blow to the visions of a rigorous, consistent, and scientific discipline expressed by the US's earliest professional economists.

The ascent of Ronald Reagan to the White House ushered in a new era in American economic policy. "Reaganomics," as it was colloquially known, emphasized tax cuts and reductions in social spending as a means to reducing the national deficit and restoring economic prosperity. Many professional economists in the US strongly disagreed with the basic assumptions of Reagan's economic policies, including Nobel Laureates Robert Solow and James Tobin.[1] The two invoked the consensus of the discipline in their condemnation of Reaganomics, prominently published in a Sunday edition of *The Washington Post*, where they declared "After only a year of Reaganomics, the country senses what the economics profession knew all along; the wilder claims of 'supply-side economics' are a joke. Massive tax reductions do not pay for themselves. No instant productivity miracle can be had."[2] Reagan's image as an economic maverick has since stuck, and with good reason. The former governor of California had campaigned on the image of being a gunslinger in the world of public policy. As economist and Reagan advisor Martin Anderson noted in his sympathetic account of Reagan's rise to national prominence, "The most important player on Ronald Reagan's economic team [was]

Ronald Reagan."[3] This apparent flouting of economic expertise, combined with the subsequent radical departure from the economic policies of the immediate post-war period, opened Reagan to accusations of being an economic Luddite – a modern day folk economist.[4]

Reaganomics did find substantial support among professional economists, however. The turn toward supply-side policies therefore raises the impossible-to-resolve matter regarding the relationship between consensus, advising, and policy. Reagan's word may have been final, but he counted among his advisors Milton Friedman, Arthur Burns, and Hendrik Houtakker, all three former presidents of the AEA. Additional advisors included George Schultz, Alan Greenspan, and Paul McCracken, all assuredly worthy of the title "professional economist." Despite Reagan's independent streak, Anderson counted no fewer than 74 economic advisors on Reagan's campaign team in the build-up to the 1980 presidential election. Reagan may have ignored or selectively implemented his economic advisors' advice, but the same could be said of any administration in the twentieth century. The composition of the Council of Economic Advisors and the President's Economic Policy Advisory Board can be scrutinized, but a connection between economic expertise and economic policy nevertheless remained.[5]

Solow claimed that the discipline stood in defiance of Reagan's economic policies, yet the survey published in the AEA's own journal offered a more complicated explanation that suggested growing numbers of economists were turning away from the Keynesian policies of the 1950s and '60s. This raises an interesting question regarding the development of economic theory in the US. Did the relatively brief supremacy of Keynesian theory spur the young economists of the 1960s and '70s toward new intellectual pastures as a means of distinguishing themselves in an increasingly competitive discipline? Perhaps it is possible that professional economists were attracted by the political opportunities offered by a switch to classic liberal thought, just as new economists may have consciously or sub-consciously seen opportunity in abandoning classicism in the early twentieth century. In his account of economists' role in government, William J. Barber speaks of a "two-way street" relationship in which public service has an unspecified effect on the views of professional economists. His comments note that the realities of governance undoubtedly shape the economist's understanding of what can and cannot work in terms of policy, but they implicitly raise the question of professional integrity. If professional economists are prone to adapt their conclusions in an attempt to secure better positions then one must seriously reconsider the role they play in the policymaking process.

It is an important issue that echoes historian Mary Furner's argument that the new economists of the late nineteenth century abandoned their radicalism in exchange for lengthy careers in academia. In the wake of the recent sub-prime mortgage financial collapse critics assailed not only the discipline's alleged incompetence, but also its apparent lack of ethical standards. In response, the AEA moved to establish a committee to draft a code of ethics that included Reagan critic Robert Solow. The Committee found itself more limited than some would have preferred. When asked whether the Committee would address issues such as whether or not an economist should advise an oppressive government, Solow responded "I doubt this committee wants to go there, one man's despot is another man's hero."[6] Solow's comment highlights the dilemmas inherent in accounting for economists' earnestness. One man's opportunistic charlatan is another man's intellectual champion, and we must be careful when distinguishing between the two lest we write off significant portions of the discipline because they do not mesh with ideal narratives or personal beliefs regarding what constitutes sound economics.

A need for nuance

Continuing to chart the connection between economic expertise and economic policy is crucial, as it may fundamentally alter the way we interpret our economic past and understand economic policy options in the present. Consider the dilemma of Reagan in his first term of office – inflation was out of control, unemployment increasing, and the rate of growth declining. Reagan openly flouted Keynesian professional economists' opinions, and it is perhaps easy to understand why, given perceptions at the time. Over the course of the 1970s, federal economic policy had appeared unable to deal with the challenges that accompanied changes in the global economy. But Reagan's dismissal of Keynesian economists rested on the assumption that those experts were responsible for guiding economic policy in decades past. We know, in certain cases, that professional economists' advice during the assumed era of Keynesian influence was wholly ignored at crucial junctures. Johnson refused to believe that the US would struggle to afford both a major war and expansion of social welfare programs and rejected his economic advisors' suggestion to raise taxes. Similarly, Nixon ignored his economic advisors' strong reservations against price-fixing and implemented controls in a vain attempt to stem inflation.

Furthermore, a growing body of research suggests that support for neoclassical economic policy not only survived during the years of alleged Keynesian dominance, but actually thrived. Correspondence between Chicago School economists Milton Friedman and George Stigler reveals that the two prominent thinkers perhaps felt embattled, but were never marginalized by their Keynesian rivals. Noted pro-free market public intellectuals like Friedrich Hayek and Ayn Rand were popular throughout the 1940s and '50s. The astounding circulation numbers of Hayek's *Road to Serfdom* or Rand's *Fountainhead* and *Atlas Shrugged* strongly suggest that the pressure of public skepticism consistently countered whatever influence Keynesian American professional economists possessed.[7]

How we characterize the connection between economic expertise and economic policy therefore carries significant implications for how we identify cause and effect in economic history. If we are to conclude that the Keynesian consensus was genuine, then deeper study is needed to adequately explain how professional economists managed to overcome internal dissent and deliver coherent economic policies on which policymakers could act. Why did the public temporarily suspend its skepticism of economic experts and accept their recommendations? And how did policymakers manage to integrate professional economists' advice alongside that of the many other lobbyists constantly demanding attention?

If, on the other hand, it seems more likely that the Keynesian consensus has been misunderstood, then it becomes difficult to talk about the historical efficacy of particular economic theories and practices. The past suddenly becomes less of a guide for future policy than a reminder of continued failure to extract maximum value from what should be a prized source of policy insight. To repeat an oft-used maxim of the past 50 years, ideas matter. Ideas do matter – including the idea that ideas matter. Overselling the significance of economic policies *as prescribed* while deemphasizing factors that typically nullify economic advisors' timely advice can lead to a poor understanding of cause and effect.

Given all the roadblocks to applying economic theory to economic practice in the US, it seems unrealistic to ever expect economic policy to match the general consensus of professional economists. As historian Gabriel Kolko notes in his analysis of American capitalism, the failure to apply technical ability to public problems seems strong evidence of American capitalism's inherent instability. Such a critique suggests a fundamental resistance to the absorption of the lessons derived from the study of economics. Although much of this study finds evidence for this claim, such a conclusion seems a bit hasty. Kolko is correct in pointing out the US's poor track record of applying theory to practice, but he is incorrect to suggest that this has been a fatal flaw, or that there has not been tremendous progress along the way. Economic advisors in the Great Depression may not have been able to solve the economic crisis that unraveled before them, but at least they were in the room and equipped to offer solutions. That is more than can be said of the 1877 or 1893 economic depressions.

It is perhaps misguided to look at the situation in terms of success or failure in applying the "right" policies, as determined by economic experts. After all, as those of the German Historical School at the turn of the twentieth century might remind us, desired outcomes are often dependent on cultural and social conditions. Much of the struggle over economic policy has revolved around disputes regarding optimal outcomes – issues that require the input of philosophers and political scientists just as much as economists. One of the discipline's alleged shortcomings is its inability to offer a one-shot solution to society's economic problems. But economists cannot possibly be expected to offer such panaceas given the myriad of interest groups engaged in lobbying for special considerations from government. Simply put, the common-sense solutions that the new economists briefly thought would emerge once the data was laid before lawmakers and the voting public failed to materialize, although the public's expectations of such miracles persists.

The enthusiasm of the new economists, powerful though it was, did not wholly fit with the realities of American politics and its fractious nature. Still, early professional economists recognized the importance of freedom in general and academic freedom in particular. Historian Mary Furner's suggestion that the social sciences had attempted to abandon subjective morality by the early twentieth century was largely correct, save this one notable exception. Early economists may have pursued a common language, but they strongly resisted the temptation to codify economic theory and its study. Rather than adopting an identity based on exclusion, economists insisted on an "open-tent" philosophy – albeit a philosophy undercut by the *de facto* gender and race segregation. Home economics remained a respected and recognized discipline in American colleges and universities until the 1950s, at which point cultural change began to chip away at the gender divide. Home economics gradually became a source of jokes and derision in American culture, and schools across the country responded by changing the name of their home economics departments in an attempt to avoid criticism. Perhaps not coincidentally, opportunities emerged for women in professional economics over the same stretch of time. The number of women who received degrees and employment in economics increased during the second half of the twentieth century, albeit at a slow rate. From 1956 to 1970 the proportion of women among Ph.D. recipients averaged around 4 percent, and then showed signs of substantial change by rising to 11 percent between 1971 and 1976. The upward trend continued until recently, when the proportion of women among Ph. D. recipients reached 34 percent in 1999 and has remained at that level since.[8] Not surprisingly, women remain underrepresented at all levels of academic employment. The discipline continues to be a predominantly male endeavor, which begs questions regarding the relationship between social identity and economic expertise in American society.

The cost of this qualified intellectual freedom has been high, for it has continually undermined disciplinary consensus and fueled suspicion and animosity among voters and their political representatives. Widespread willingness to accept the persistent presence of lay dissenters and trust the American public and its policymakers to seek out the proper economic policy has resulted in a messy process. Surveying the second half of the twentieth century, it is difficult to identify individual amateur economists whose influence matches that of either William "Coin" Harvey or Henry George at the turn of the century. Yet the persistence of calls to return to the gold standard or the brief popularity of Herman Cain's "9-9-9" tax reform plan in the 2012 Republican Presidential primary race, neither of which would have garnered support from members of the AEA, clearly indicate a sustained audience for folk economics. American economic thought and policy continues to be shaped not just by advances within academia but also the less formalized thinking of the American public.

It is difficult to fault either the discipline or policymakers for this apparent failure to link economists' expertise to economic policy in a more reliable fashion. Economists have operated in a democratic society with many competing interests and an underlying commitment not only to economic efficiency, but also to shifting notions of personal liberty. Balancing efficiency and liberty was as much a challenge then as it is today. Understanding this consistent challenge is crucial to understanding the oft-expressed existential angst of economists who acknowledge the proliferation of contradictory ideas within the discipline without offering a viable plan to resolve the conflict.[9]

Furthermore, although professional economists appear to have rarely delivered precise, detailed recommendations, they did presage necessary policy adjustments with some regularity. In regard to the "money question," professional economists were near universal in their call for a centrally controlled, gold-backed, flexible currency. The nation adopted a rigid gold-backed standard until the panic of 1907 finally drove lawmakers to pursue the type of central banking system that economists in the 1890s had envisioned. A similar dynamic was repeated in the case of collective bargaining and an allotment-based relief plan in agriculture. In both instances, professional economic advisors and commentators struggled in vain to steer lawmakers away from ultimately untenable reform plans. John R. Commons recognized the futility of Walsh's show-hearings but had to wait until the 1930s before his solution – collective bargaining – became tenable. Henry C. Taylor, John D. Black, and additional leading agricultural economists similarly criticized the McNary–Haugen Plan as strong in sentiment but weak in practice. Black's call for an allotment-based system that could raise prices while avoiding ruinous overproduction stalled for a decade before it finally gained traction.

In the wake of the 2008 financial meltdown, a group of economists met to specifically discuss why the discipline still seems to fail in the face of economic crisis. The conference participants offered three lines of argument that were quite different from those presented in this study: the uncertainty of markets; the unpredictable impact of global forces; and the role of economic models that failed to take into account intangible factors, like morality.[10] While these three points are certainly true, they ignore how the very ambiguity of professional economists' role in society might have contributed to the crisis. It is clear that the failure to predict crises reflects poorly on the discipline, although it is not necessarily the indication of incompetence some frustrated lay persons would claim. To begin, critics who focus on the discipline's failure to predict and warn of the impending financial crisis tend to overestimate the degree of coordination within professional economics. The atomization of the discipline is part of the legacy of the professionalization process through which the discipline underwent from 1885 to 1929. Economists generally cooperate, hence the codified terminology and robust institutions like the AEA. But just like any other profession, practitioners of the dismal science pursue their chosen research topics in relative isolation. Professional economists' attentions are divided among a myriad of pressing micro- and macroeconomic issues, which makes it difficult to arrive at accurate and confidently supported conclusions about the likelihood of sudden shocks.

More importantly, narratives of the 2008 Financial Crisis that blame professional economists assume that economists exercise some degree of control on governments' economic policy – either directly through their bureaucratic posts or indirectly through a vaguely defined role as watchmen on the wall. The level of influence exerted by lobbyists for the financial industry alone challenges such assumptions, and professional economists in the US have consistently insisted that theirs is the role of a passive advisor, however. In fact, some economists of high repute did express concerns about investment trends in the housing market and the potential for economic disaster fueled by loose credit and risky speculation, though it is fair to note that very few economists seem to have consistently and accurately identified the systemic risk that became apparent in 2008. Prominent economists Henry Kaufman and Nouriel Roubini did accurately warn of the danger, but their reputations as doomsayers ensured that their opinions were marginalized by investors and lawmakers when times were good.[11]

The lessons of the past are not directly transferable, but if we consider the genesis of professional economists in the US alongside the role they have come to play as economic experts in the twenty-first century, it becomes clearer why crises continue to confound policymakers. Neither the AEA nor any of its sister organizations are any closer to regulating economic thought than they were in the early twentieth century. Such a goal continues to be both unthinkable and impractical. As a result, the voting public and their elected representatives are forced to wade through a sea of conflicting ideas generated by those who are at liberty to describe themselves as economic experts. Meanwhile, the struggle to balance voter preference and economic imperatives continues to drive policymakers toward politically expedient, but not necessarily economically savvy, decisions.

Notes

1 Tobin received his prize in 1981, one year prior to publicly condemning Reaganomics, while Solow's came five years later in 1987.
2 Robert Solow and James Tobin, "Liberals Have to Do More Than Laugh," *The Washington Post*, January 10, 1982, sec. D.
3 Martin Anderson, *Revolution* (San Diego: Harcourt Brace Jovanovich, 1988), 164.
4 British economist Nicholas Kaldor offered particularly biting criticism, suggesting that Reagan and British Prime Minister Margaret Thatcher's near simultaneous turn toward monetarism would be linked by later generations to the witch trials of the Middle Ages owing to both movements' sudden and complete adoption of previously rejected false notions.
5 Porter cited the growing demands placed on the US presidency as cause for reform in his discussion of the matter at the 1981 meeting of the AEA, but not Reagan's actions in particular. He similarly chose not to criticize the Reagan administration in a later article on the history of the CEA. See Porter (1982, 1997).
6 John J. Siegfried, "Minutes of the Meeting of the Executive Committee," *American Economic Review* 102, no. 3 (May 2012): 645–52. The Committee eventually recommended disclosure policies for articles published in any one of the AEA's journals and also provided guidelines for studies that included human participants.
7 Thanks to reprint requests from business organizations and reading clubs, over one million copies of *Road to Serfdom* were circulated in 1945 alone. Rand's *The Fountainhead* also enjoyed strong sales of over 100,000 in 1945 and was followed by the highly anticipated and commercially successful *Atlas Shrugged* in 1957. See Burgin (2012); Burns (2009).
8 Marjorie B. McElroy, "2012 Report of the Committee on the Status of Women in the Economics Profession," *Newsletter of the Committee on the Status of Women in the Economics Profession American Economic Association* (Winter 2013): 1.
9 Walter W. Heller, "What's Right with Economics?," *The American Economic Review* 65, no. 1 (March 1975): 1–26. Soul searching has taken many forms, but none perhaps as consistent and revealing as that of the Presidential Address. For a great example and summary, see Walter Heller's 1975 speech, which included a retrospective of past economists' laments regarding the shortcomings of the discipline (Heller 1975). See the following for additional examples of reflection on the discipline: McCloskey (1990); Stigler (1982); Calkins (1966); Worswick (1972); Reder (1999); Weintraub (2002).
10 Robert Skidelsky and Christian Westerlind Wigström, eds., *The Economic Crisis and the State of Economics* (New York: Palgrave Macmillan, 2010).
11 Roubini's warnings were largely issued through his blog and online articles throughout the early 2000s. He, more than any other economist, was credited with having accurately predicted the crisis in the immediate aftermath of bubble's bursting.

Bibliography

Abbott, Andrew. *Chaos of Disciplines*. Chicago: University of Chicago Press, 2001.

Alston, Richard M., J.R. Kearl, and Michael B. Vaughan. "Is There a Consensus Among Economists in the 1990's?" *The American Economic Review* 82, no. 2 (May 1992): 203–9.

Anderson, Martin. *Revolution*. San Diego: Harcourt Brace Jovanovich, 1988.

Backhouse, Roger E. *Economists and the Economy: The Evolution of Economic Ideas*. New Brunswick, NJ: Transaction Publishers, 1994.

Barber, William J. "The Spread of Economics Ideas Between Academia and Government: A Two-Way Street." In *The Spread of Economic Ideas*, edited by David C. Colander and A.W. Coats, 119–26. Cambridge, UK; New York: Cambridge University Press, 1989.

Bernstein, Michael A. *A Perilous Progress: Economists and Public Purpose in Twentieth-Century America*. Princeton, NJ: Princeton University Press, 2001.

Burgin, Angus. *The Great Persuasion: Reinventing Free Markets Since the Depression*. Cambridge, MA: Harvard University Press, 2012.

Burns, Arthur F. *The Management of Prosperity*. New York: Columbia University Press, 1966.

Burns, Arthur F., and Robert H. Ferrell. *Inside the Nixon Administration: The Secret Diary of Arthur Burns, 1969–1974*. Lawrence: University Press of Kansas, 2010.

Burns, Jennifer. *Goddess of the Market: Ayn Rand and the American Right*. Oxford; New York: Oxford University Press, 2009.

Calkins, Robert D. "The Production and Use of Economic Knowledge." *The American Economic Review* 56, no. 1/2 (March 1966): 530–37.

Commons, John R. *Myself: The Autobiography of John R. Commons*. New York: The Macmillan Company, 1934.

Congleton, Roger D. "On the Political Economy of the Financial Crisis and Bailout of 2008–2009." *Public Choice* 140, no. 3/4 (September 2009): 287–317.

DeMartino, George. *The Economist's Oath: On the Need for and Content of Professional Economic Ethics*. Oxford; New York: Oxford University Press, 2011.

Elias, Megan J. *Stir It Up: Home Economics in American Culture*. Philadelphia: University of Pennsylvania Press, 2008.

Furner, Mary O. *Advocacy & Objectivity: A Crisis in the Professionalization of American Social Science, 1865–1905*. Lexington, KY: The University Press of Kentucky, 1975.

Hammond, J. Daniel, and Claire H Hammond, eds. *Making Chicago Price Theory: Friedman-Stigler Correspondence 1945–1957*. New York: Routledge, 2006.

Hargrove, Erwin C., and Samuel A Morley, eds. *The President and the Council of Economic Advisers: Interviews with CEA Chairmen*. Boulder, CO: Westview Press, 1984.

Hayek, Friedrich A. Von. *The Road to Serfdom*. Chicago: University of Chicago Press, 1944.

Heller, Walter W. *New Dimensions of Political Economy*. Cambridge, MA: Harvard University Press, 1966.

———. "What's Right with Economics?" *The American Economic Review* 65, no. 1 (March 1975): 1–26.

Jones, Daniel Stedman. *Masters of the Universe: Hayek, Friedman, and the Birth of Neoliberal Politics*. Princeton, NJ: Princeton University Press, 2012.

Kaldor, Nicholas. "How Monetarism Failed." *Challenge* 28, no. 2 (June 1985): 4–13.

Kaufman, Henry. *On Money and Markets: A Wall Street Memoir*. New York: McGraw-Hill, 2000.

Kearl, J.R., Clayne L. Pope, Gordon C. Whiting, and Larry T. Wimmer. "A Confusion of Economists?" *The American Economic Review* 69, no. 2 (May 1979): 28–37.

Kolko, Gabriel. "Intelligence and the Myth of Capitalist Rationality in the United States." *Science & Society* 44, no. 2 (Summer 1980): 130–54.

McCloskey, Deirdre N. *If You're So Smart: The Narrative of Economic Expertise.* Chicago: University of Chicago Press, 1990.

McElroy, Marjorie B. "2012 Report of the Committee on the Status of Women in the Economics Profession." *Newsletter of the Committee on the Status of Women in the Economics Profession American Economic Association,* Winter 2013, 1.

Milonakis, Dimitris, and Ben Fine. *From Political Economy to Economics: Method, the Social and the Historical in the Evolution of Economic Theory.* London; New York: Routledge, 2009.

Nasar, Sylvia. *Grand Pursuit: The Story of Economic Genius.* New York: Simon & Schuster, 2011.

Norton, Hugh S. *The Professional Economist: His Role in Business and Industry.* Columbia, SC: University of South Carolina Press, 1969.

——. *The Quest for Economic Stability: Roosevelt to Bush.* Columbia: University of South Carolina Press, 1991.

Porter, Roger B. "Organizing Economic Advice to the President: A Modest Proposal." *The American Economic Review* 72, no. 2 (May 1982): 356–60.

——. "Presidents and Economists: The Council of Economic Advisors." *The American Economic Review* 87, no. 2 (May 1997): 103–6.

Prindle, David F. *The Paradox of Democratic Capitalism: Politics and Economics in American Thought.* Baltimore: Johns Hopkins University Press, 2006.

Rand, Ayn. *The Fountainhead.* Indianapolis: Bobbs-Merrill, 1943.

——. *Atlas Shrugged.* New York: Random House, 1957.

Reagan, Barbara B. "Stocks and Flows of Academic Economists." *The American Economic Review* 69, no. 2 (May 1979): 143–47.

Reay, Michael J. "The Flexible Unity of Economics." *American Journal of Sociology* 118, no. 1 (July 2012): 45–87.

Reder, Melvin Warren. *Economics: The Culture of a Controversial Science.* Chicago, IL: University of Chicago Press, 1999.

Siegfried, John J. "Minutes of the Meeting of the Executive Committee." *American Economic Review* 101, no. 3 (May 2011): 677–83.

——. "Minutes of the Meeting of the Executive Committee." *American Economic Review* 102, no. 3 (May 2012): 645–52.

Silk, Leonard Solomon. *The Economists.* New York: Basic Books, 1976.

Skidelsky, Robert, and Christian Westerlind Wigström, eds. *The Economic Crisis and the State of Economics.* New York: Palgrave Macmillan, 2010.

Stein, Herbert. *Presidential Economics: The Making of Economic Policy from Roosevelt to Reagan and Beyond.* New York: Simon and Schuster, 1984.

Stigler, George J. *The Economist as Preacher and Other Essays.* Chicago: University of Chicago Press, 1982.

Temin, Peter, and Louis Galambos. *The Fall of the Bell System: A Study in Prices and Politics.* Cambridge, UK; New York: Cambridge University Press, 1987.

Viner, Jacob. "The Short View and the Long in Economic Policy." *The American Economic Review* 30, no. 1 (March 1940): 1–15.

Weintraub, E. Roy, ed. *The Future of the History of Economics.* Durham, NC: Duke University Press, 2002.

Worswick, George David Norman. *Uses of Economics.* Oxford: Basil Blackwell, 1972.

Index

Abbott, Andrew 107, 156
academic freedom 9, 25–7, 60, 66, 74, 109, 159: AEA 9, 60, 77, 108, 109, 144; committee on 108; Laughlin 67; new economics 72; Wisconsin School 95
Acheson, Dean 147n34
Adams, Henry C. 22, 35n27, 65
Agricultural Adjustment Act (1933) 13, 141
Agricultural Adjustment Administration (AAA) 141, 142
Agricultural Marketing Act (1929) 138
Agricultural Research Service 5
agriculture 125–45, 152, 161: agrarian ideals 18; aid 6, 13; farmers' associations 4; folk economists 30–1
Agriculture Advisory Commission 143
Aldrich, Morton Arnold 26
Aldrich, Nelson 55
Aldrich Plan 55
Aldrich–Vreeland Act (1908) 54
allotment plan 138, 140, 141–2, 152, 161
Altemeyer, Arthur 98n11
American Academy of Political and Social Sciences 61
American Academy of Social Sciences 33
American Association for Agricultural Legislation (AAAL) 127, 134
American Association for Labor Legislation 89
American Association for the Advance of Science 23
American Association of Agricultural Economists 126
American Association of University Professors (AAUP) 108, 109
American Bimetallic Union (ABU) 45
American Bureau of Industrial Research (ABIR) 90, 91
American Economic Association (AEA) 22–4, 161, 162: 1909 meeting 67–8; academic freedom 9, 60, 77, 108, 109, 144; agriculture 31, 134; amateur economists and businessmen 113, 114, 117; annual meetings 24; code of ethics 157–8; Committee on Economic Theory 24; Committee on Foreign Trade 106–7; Committee on Practical Training 92; Committee on Price-Fixing 105; Committee on the Economic Problems of the War 105; Committee on the Purchasing Power of Money 105; Committee on War Finance 105, 107; committees 24, 105; conflicts 13; constitution 22–3, 102, 153; Currency Committee 51–3; divisions 34; economic definitions committee, rejected proposal for a 111; economic theory roundtable 112; eugenics 64; folk economics 160; founding 4, 22–3, 84; functions 118; George 33; goals 22–3, 67; growth of AEA 112, 154; growth of economics 60–3, 65; influence 89; Institute for Research in Land Economics and Public Utilities 115; Institutionalism 112; Laughlin 47, 67; Membership Committee 112; membership numbers 6, 22, 60, 103, 112, 154; methodological struggle 66, 67–8; Meyer 131; money question 40, 48, 51–3, 153; neutrality 152; organizational overlap 112–13; propaganda avoidance 84; prospectus 23; public image of professional economics 75–6; public participation 151; publications 24, 61–2; Reaganomics 157; records 11; religion 72; Roosevelt (FDR) administration 143, 144; single-tax movement 114, 115; sociology 21; support from

For Product Safety Concerns and Information please contact our EU representative GPSR@taylorandfrancis.com Taylor & Francis Verlag GmbH, Kaufingerstraße 24, 80331 München, Germany

Printed and bound by CPI Group (UK) Ltd, Croydon, CR0 4YY

01/05/2025

01858459-0006